INDUSTRIAL INTERNAL AUDITING

MCGRAW-HILL ACCOUNTING SERIES

Blocker and Weltmer, Cost Accounting
Foulke, Practical Financial Statement Analysis
Henrici, Standard Costs for Manufacturing
Keller, Management Accounting for Profit Control
MacFarland, Ayars, and Stone, Accounting Fundamentals
March, Cost Accounting
Smith and Ashburne, Financial and Administrative Accounting
Taylor and Miller, C.P.A. Problems and Questions in Theory and
Auditing
Taylor and Miller, Solutions to C.P.A. Problems
Taylor and Miller, Intermediate Accounting
Walker and Davies, Industrial Internal Auditing

Dean F. H. Elwell of the University of Wisconsin was Consulting
Editor of the McGraw-Hill Accounting Series from its inception until
his retirement in 1955.

Industrial Internal Auditing

by W. A. WALKER, *Vice President, Accounting, United States Steel Company; Certified Public Accountant, Pennsylvania*

and W. R. DAVIES, *Director, Audit Division, United States Steel Company; Certified Public Accountant, Pennsylvania; Member, Institute of Internal Auditors*

McGRAW–HILL BOOK COMPANY, INC. · 1951

New York   Toronto   London

IV

The purpose of this book is to fill a present need for the discussion of internal auditing principles with special reference to the requirements of industrial companies. In an effort to stimulate a current discussion of the modern concept of industrial internal auditing, the material has been compiled for use in a course on this subject given at the University of Pittsburgh.

The chapters are intended to provide a general basis for internal auditing in industry. This comprises a discussion of the objectives, scope, authority, and history of internal auditing. Basic and auxiliary internal controls are pointed out in their relation to the auditor's program. In addition to a general discussion as to planning and making an audit, specific functional audits are outlined in considerable detail. The text then naturally leads into a discussion of types of internal audits, internal audit reports, fraud, special assignments, organization of internal audit staffs, and an appraisal of the standards of internal auditing as a profession.

The problems presented in the Appendix have been taken from various actual experiences of the authors. The cases were selected to illustrate internal auditing in action and to give practical expression to the principles discussed in the text.

Grateful acknowledgment is made to certain members and headquarters personnel of the Internal Audit Staff of United States Steel Company for their valuable assistance in the preparation of material and the manuscript.

W. A. WALKER
W. R. DAVIES

PITTSBURGH, PENNSYLVANIA,
June, 1951

CONTENTS

vii

CHAPTER 1

INTRODUCTION

The words "internal auditing" are not new in business circles, but the present concept of the internal auditor's scope and objectives is very new. Few colleges and business schools have recognized the fact that a new and different branch of accounting is firmly entrenching itself, through its deeds, in the accounting divisions of our forward-looking business organizations, many of which, even yet, do not fully understand or appreciate the present concept and either do not have the internal audit function or confuse it with routine checking.

The Institute of Internal Auditors

A great part of the literature on the modern trend in internal auditing and the education as to the changing approach thereto have been fostered by the Institute of Internal Auditors, a membership corporation whose Members are men in the auditing profession associated with companies in diversified lines of business and industry. Associate Members include representatives of the leading public accounting firms, and Junior Members include students pursuing the study of internal auditing and others engaged in internal audit work.

The Institute is the outgrowth of the belief on the part of internal auditors that an organization was needed to develop the true professional status of internal auditing and that a medium should be provided for interchange of ideas and information among those engaged in its practice.

Crystallizing this belief, a group of internal auditors met in September 1941 to form the Institute of Internal Auditors. This association was incorporated formally in November 1941 under the laws of the State of New York as the Institute of Internal Auditors, Inc.

Since then its growth has been steady, and today it is the recognized professional organization in the field of internal auditing, with a membership rapidly approaching two thousand in about thirty chapters located in most of our principal cities.

The objectives of the Institute are:

1. *Educational.* To create, disseminate, and promote an interest in information concerning internal auditing and related subjects. To cause the publication of articles on practices and methods pertinent to the subject of internal auditing.
2. *Ethical.* To establish and maintain high standards of professional conduct, honor, and character among internal auditors.
3. *Social.* To maintain a library and reading, meeting, and social rooms for the use of its Members, Associate Members, and Junior Members for the purpose of facilitating and promoting social activities.
4. *General.* To do any and all things which shall be lawful and appropriate in furtherance of any of the foregoing purposes.

Since the Institute was organized, its accomplishments have been substantial evidence of the energy and vision of its members, directors, and officers and the integrity of the belief that such an organization was needed in the structure of American business. These accomplishments include:

1. The organization of men from outstanding companies into a body representing the interests of the internal auditing profession.
2. The establishment of a forum for discussion of internal auditing problems. Features of this are the chapter meetings and the annual conferences.
3. The publication of books covering the subject matter of such forums.
4. The publication of books covering various aspects of modern internal auditing and demonstrating its value to management.
5. The introduction of lectures and courses on internal auditing into the curriculums of a number of schools and universities, thus making education in internal auditing accessible to many thousands.
6. The establishment of a quarterly publication, *The Internal Auditor.*

7. The establishment of a committee to function jointly with those of other professional organizations on subjects of mutual interest.

8. The development of a research program with the objectives of establishing the fundamental philosophy and concepts of internal auditing, promoting the study of internal auditing practice in general and as applied to specific industries, and developing the literature of internal auditing.

The Institute defines modern internal auditing as follows:

Modern internal auditing is more than mere mathematical checking or routine examination of accounts. It comprises a complete intra-company financial and operation review.

Specifically:

It is an essential part of management. Regardless of formal systems of managerial control, there is no satisfactory substitute for first-hand observation of conditions and for personal contact with people on the job. Internal auditing is a practical medium for supplying reliable data upon the analysis of which remedial measures depend for the elimination of waste, the institution of economies, and the determination of standards of performance.

It perfects and completes the system of internal control. No matter how perfect the design of an accounting system, it must be reviewed constantly to assure its proper functioning and to guard against collusion, since collusion can by-pass the best of accounting controls. In addition, internal auditing provides a check of those transactions which cannot be controlled practicably by other means.

It is essential in the verification of financial statements. The work of the internal auditor and public accountant dovetails. The responsibilities and liabilities of the public accountant have increased materially during the last few years, with the result that the work of the internal auditor has been expanded substantially. This has made it possible for the public accountant to eliminate a considerable part of his detail checking and has enabled him to focus his attention on major principles and policies of the type with which he can and must deal to discharge his responsibility to directors and stockholders.

The early years of the Institute coincided with the war period, and the wartime expansion of industry increased the demands upon internal auditors. The close of the war and the conversion of business to a peacetime basis brought new problems to corporate management.

After removal of wartime controls, the expansion of the nation's economic structure set the stage for increasingly competitive operations and the development of new methods of manufacture and distribution. A prime necessity of management is prompt, unbiased, and well-balanced factual reporting of the effectiveness of management policies in actual operation.

In all areas of corporate activity, appraisal and revaluations of policy, standards, and accomplishments need to be made. The internal auditor operates as a reviewer and critical analyst for management. His reviews in these years of economic change must evidence a broader technique and give the foundation for new management decisions of sound policy.

On July 15, 1947, the Research Committee of the Institute presented its Statement of the Responsibilities of the Internal Auditor. It was not intended, however, that the treatment of the various matters in the Statement be considered in any sense as final or fixed. Rather it was recognized that the principles and concepts relating to internal auditing are evolving constantly. The Statement, therefore, represents essentially an endorsement of what the Institute believes to be a fair and considered analysis of the responsibilities of the internal auditor at their present stage of development and is subject to such further modification in the future as may appear to be warranted in the light of new conditions and needs, and as may be required by further development of the professional stature of the internal auditor. The Statement follows:

RESPONSIBILITIES OF THE INTERNAL AUDITOR

Nature of Internal Auditing

Internal auditing is the independent appraisal activity within an organization for the review of the accounting, financial, and other operations as a basis for protective and constructive service to management. It is a type of control which functions by measuring and evaluating the effectiveness of other types of control. It deals primarily with accounting and financial matters but it may also properly deal with matters of an operating nature.

Objectives and Related Activities

The over-all objective of internal auditing is to assist management in achieving the most efficient administration of the operations of the organization. This total objective has two major phases, as follows:

1. The protection of the interests of the organization, including the pointing out of existing deficiencies to provide a basis for appropriate corrective action.

The attainment of this objective involves such activities of the internal auditor as:

   a. Ascertaining the degree of reliability of accounting and statistical data developed within the organization.
   b. Ascertaining the extent to which company assets are properly accounted for and safeguarded from losses of all kinds.
   c. Ascertaining the extent of compliance with established policies, plans, and procedures.

2. The furtherance of the interests of the organization, including the recommendation of changes for the improvement of the various phases of the operations.

The attainment of this objective involves such activities of the internal auditor as:

   a. Reviewing and appraising the policies and plans of the organization in the light of the related data and other evidence.
   b. Reviewing and appraising the internal records and procedures of the organization in terms of their adequacy and effectiveness.
   c. Reviewing and appraising performance under the policies, plans, and procedures.

Scope of Authority and Responsibility

Internal auditing is a staff or advisory function rather than a line or operating function. Therefore the internal auditor does not exercise direct authority over other persons in the organization.

The internal auditor should be free to review and appraise policies, plans, and procedures, but his review and appraisal do not in any way relieve other persons in the organization of the primary responsibilities assigned to them.

Independence

Independence is basic to the effectiveness of the internal auditing program. This independence has two major aspects, as follows:

1. The head of the internal auditing department should be made responsible to an officer of sufficient rank in the organization as will assure adequate consideration and action on the findings or recommendations. The organizational status of the internal auditor and the support accorded to him by management are major determinants of the range and value of the services which management will obtain from the internal auditing function.

2. Internal auditing should not include responsibilities for procedures which are essentially a part of the regular operations of a complete and adequate accounting system or of a properly organized operating department. In some instances management may assign current operating responsibilities to the internal auditing department, but in such cases the execution of the current operating responsibilities should be performed by separate personnel and be subjected to the same review and appraisal as is accorded other operations.

These general statements can be condensed into a very short and practical set of objectives which may well be adopted by any company as its guiding policy for the operation of its internal audit staff:

1. Determination that all procedures involved in the recording and physical handling of all or any of a company's business are such that a minimum possibility of loss exists, considering also the cost of providing protection.

2. Determination that all of a company's assets, liabilities, income, and expense have been properly accounted for; that value was received for expenditures; and that collectible income to which the company is entitled has been or will be received.

3. Determination of the extent of compliance with established rules and policies of the company relative to matters properly subject to audit.

Relation of Internal Auditing to Management

Since internal auditing is basically the auditing of internal affairs or the policies and procedures adopted by management, the auditing approach must be harmonious with the viewpoint of management.

One of the first services that internal auditors can perform for management is to teach management what to expect of internal auditing. Since this particular field of accounting and financial management is relatively new in its present form, a great many of the members of top management do not fully appreciate how they can use the service to the best advantage. Of course, one of the best ways of accomplishing this is by "doing," so that management can see the results of a good audit program. In the majority of medium size companies which do not have a well-organized Internal Audit Division, such a group has a great opportunity to advance to an important place in the organization, and the individuals who head such Audit Divisions have an unusually promising personal opportunity to perform a worthwhile job and to attract the attention of management to a function to which, in many cases, they have heretofore given very little consideration.

Medium size organizations are specifically mentioned because it is probable that most of the large companies now have internal auditing organized in an intelligent manner and that most of the very small companies do not need internal auditing. This refers to companies in which top management can, by virtue of the size of the business, keep a full knowledge of all the phases of the operation at their finger tips at all times. It is only when management sits for the most part in the "ivory tower" and lays down policies and observes results from pieces of paper that "management by exception" becomes a necessity, since the details are so voluminous that they cannot all be viewed by management. It is then that management needs a group which can sift the chaff from the wheat and let them know where the points of special interest are in their companies. When speaking of "management by exception" it is meant those departures which are exceptionally good and deserve the commendation of top management, as well as those which are departures from management's policies and procedures or good sound business practices. These latter need to be called to management's attention for correction.

Probably the most widely accepted reason in the minds of top management in the majority of companies for the existence of an Internal Audit Division is for verification, the assurance that the figures presented to them on financial and operating statements are reasonably correct and that there are no material irregularities in the accounts. However, while verification is necessary and is a primary reason for the existence of an Audit Division, organizations which limit their audit staffs to this function alone are certainly not deriving the full benefits which may be had from their staffs. It is the suggestions for improvement developed by the auditors while engaged in their verification work which permit us to sell management the principle that an Audit Division can be a definite and positive factor in the search for improvement, rather than merely of negative benefit by attesting to the correctness of figures. To illustrate this point: Practically every audit made will entail a review of how employes are doing their job in order to determine that existing procedures are being followed. This part of the job is verification, and it has served an important purpose in assuring management that their instructions are being followed. However, that is only one part of the job. The auditor should also review those procedures from the viewpoint of necessity and economy to determine whether all the steps being followed are necessary, or whether changing conditions have made the procedures cumbersome and expensive. It is not, of course, the auditor's job to install procedures, but it is his job to point out the need for revision.   No one in the organization is in a better position to determine this need than the auditor. He is one of the few individuals who has the opportunity to observe the many phases of the operations and appraise them objectively.

Management should have the definite knowledge and feeling that the work of the internal auditors is being done for their benefit and that it is their right arm sorting out for them those points which need their administrative action.   By management, in this connection, it is meant management at all levels, including the Board of Directors, the President, Vice Presidents, Plant Superintendents, Plant Accountants, Foremen, Department Heads, etc.   All these people should feel that the job is being done for them, not that they are being audited. This is a "must" in order to create a successful internal auditing organization.   For it is only by utilization of the auditor's findings in order to correct or improve conditions that the work of the internal auditor is justified.   Without the utilization of these findings, he has wasted his time.   Because a great majority of these findings for improvement will be of a character which will not warrant action by the President or Board of Directors, but should be handled at lower levels, this utilization will come about through the acceptance by management at these lower levels of the recommendations of the auditors.   Accordingly, it behooves the auditor to gain this acceptance in order that his work may be utilized and may be profitable.

Acceptance must not be gained by merely overlooking those matters which may engender controversy or by creating a cordial feeling toward the auditor by reason of the fact that the auditor never causes any trouble since all the audit reports are written with a whitewash brush.   To reiterate, acceptance must not be gained in that way; a mutual feeling must be created by which both the auditor and the person being audited feel that they are working together to enhance the company's profits to the greatest possible extent.   The person being audited must have a heartfelt feeling that the auditor is trying to help him disclose those conditions within his jurisdiction which he wants to know, so that he can get his work in the shape he would like to see it.   He must not feel that the auditor is out to "get him."   It is up to the auditor to see that every person gets that understanding of his attitude.   Accordingly, his attitude must be just that.   The auditor cannot expect the other fellow to get that sort of feeling toward him if, in his mind, he gloats over "getting" someone, rather than feeling merely a justifiable satisfaction in having helped the supervisor. The auditor's innermost feelings will be reflected in his attitude. His attitude will be reflected in the acceptance. The acceptance will be reflected in the utilization of the findings and, accordingly, govern the success or failure of the audit program.

The auditor's viewpoint, then, must be helpful, not critical. There are several definite things which the auditor must do to maintain this viewpoint. In the first place, it is very essential that the auditor keep the faith with local and lower levels of management. In other words, each item of an audit must be frankly discussed with the immediate supervisor of that function before it is discussed in any way with his superiors. He should be given the opportunity to make such comments as he may wish, either in support of the present practice, or to straighten out the auditor on certain phases which may be pertinent, or to agree with the auditor and outline the general principles which he will employ to improve the situation. This is very important in order that no level of management will feel that the auditor is going over his head. Auditors in general, by their very name, set up a certain barrier against themselves, but anyone is willing to make an individual exception of a particular auditor and will consider him as being a good fellow and one with whom he is anxious to cooperate. It is a sales job, and it is therefore necessary that the auditor's constructive remarks be presented in such a fashion that they will be accepted as helpful suggestions. It is necessary that all supervisory personnel know in so many words that the audit staff is not a "gestapo" and, subsequently, that they can see for themselves, day in and day out, that the members of the audit staff do not consider themselves as a "gestapo."

In order to accomplish the objectives set forth above, it is essential that top management establish a clear understanding throughout the company that the audit staff has full and free access to all departments and records of the company and that there are no restrictions on its audit activities. It is essential to providing proper service to management that auditing be operated as a staff function as distinguished from a line function. By this is meant:

1. Auditing is not a substitute for management. The auditors have no authority to set up procedures, make policies, or direct or

instruct anyone as to how he should conduct his activities. Auditing is a purely staff function of coordinating, investigating, and advising. It is the auditor's function to determine whether the company procedures and good accounting practices are in effect and whether the practices in effect are adequate to provide proper internal control for the company.

2. The audit staff should not be used for special line assignments not connected with the auditing function. To do this sets a precedent which sometimes leads to the use of auditors as fill-ins for line absentees and results in inadequate audit coverage.

3. The auditor should not be used as a glorified line clerk. In other words, routine checking which is performed on a day by day, week by week, or any other periodic basis in connection with the checking of accounts payable vouchers, etc., is a part of the line function, and it is the responsibility of the line supervisor to provide adequate assurance that the work turned out is accurate. This type of work does not deserve the name of auditing. It is merely checking and should not be a part of an internal audit staff function. This much abused concept of auditing is one which tends to weaken the function of internal auditing staffs in many companies. Some routine auditing is necessary, such as the ordinary verification of time reporting and payroll calculation, but this should be confined to the same type of test audit made by public accountants. The audit staff should not make the type of routine checking of payrolls which is required as an integral part of the preparation of each and every payroll.

Relative to the technique of internal auditing, there are various methods of approach and types of coverage which should be made in order that the Internal Audit Division can be of the greatest possible service to management, consistent with maintaining the staff at a reasonable cost.

In the first place, it is imperative that top management understand that the Audit Division cannot possibly cover any great percentage of the matters subject to audit scrutiny in any given year, assuming, of course, that the Internal Audit Division works, as it must, with an intensive, comprehensive, searching coverage. The viewpoint, that the analysis of a particular subject, to be beneficial to management, must be complete, should be emphasized. That is one of the main differences between an audit of a function performed by the Internal

Audit Division and the coverage given by the public accounting firm to any particular function in the course of a balance sheet audit.

An internal audit done for the benefit of management cannot be a check list type of audit, but must be one in which the auditor goes in with a general program for a known purpose and uses all the ingenuity, imagination, and ability that he can command to develop improvements which he would want to see in effect if it were the money out of his own pocket with which he was dealing. Because of the need for exhaustive investigation, it has been found that, in general, a more productive survey is gained by narrowing the scope of the review and performing what is called a functional audit, as compared with a responsibility audit. A responsibility audit is one which covers, in a general way, all the matters within the jurisdiction of a particular department. Because of the breadth of functions usually embraced in such an audit, it is virtually impossible to do more than to touch upon various points; whereas, in a functional audit, the auditors concentrate on particular points within a responsibility and dig into them, leaving no stone unturned. However, in the performance of a functional audit, intensive investigation does not comprehend coverage of all the details of clerical accuracy. Clerical accuracy is, as previously stated, the responsibility of line management. However, the audit must ascertain in detail whether or not the policies of the company and sound business practices are being adhered to, that the procedures adequately furnish complete internal control and protection, that revenue is fully protected, and that costs are consistent with proper control and are at a minimum. In the audit of any function, a certain amount of test checking of details must be done. If, in doing that, an exorbitant number of clerical errors are encountered, these errors are not important in themselves but merely point to another principle, which is that adequate control over accuracy is not present.

In order that the Audit Supervisor may perform the most helpful service to management, it is necessary that he have a rather broad and thorough acquaintanceship with all phases of the company's business, so that in the selection of the functions which the Audit Division will have the manpower to audit, the most productive and most vital matters will be done first. Therefore, he should attempt to cover those matters where lack of control can, and will, result in an actual loss of money as compared with those audits which pertain merely to distribution accounting. Notwithstanding this general viewpoint, the Audit Supervisor must still concern himself with the fundamentals that an audit staff is expected to cover. For example, certain coverages of cash, time reporting, payroll calculation, etc., are always required, but these only to a minimum degree, in order that the auditor can be satisfied that these functions are adequately performed and controlled.

The Auditor

With all his effort to perform a constructive service and to sell it, the auditor must maintain his own independence of thinking and exploration. He cannot permit his boss to dictate to him what his thoughts should be. This is another selling job. He should try to arrive at the facts and, after careful consideration, present these facts in such a manner that, even though they may be in conflict with present company policies or thinking, they will be accepted and given the proper consideration due them; since, by the method of presentation, they are obviously the sincere and considered viewpoint of the auditor, presented for what he believes is for the best interest of the company. There is no set rule as to how this independence should be accomplished organizationally, but regardless of the auditor's position on the organization chart, there is only one way of achieving independence, and that is by being independent.

It is unfortunate that no one has yet been able to think of a better title than "auditor" because of the stigma that has become attached to him as a fellow with a long nose and a sharp pencil who can add figures faster than the other fellow. The most important requirement of an auditor is that he use good common sense. Possessing this characteristic, an auditor can examine and analyze conditions and offer constructive suggestions to line supervision, even though they have been daily concerned for years with their functions and admittedly know more about them.

The Audit Division does not confine itself solely to the Accounting Department, or Treasury Department, but makes itself available to any department for examination of any function in which the protection of assets, revenue, or costs is involved. This includes, therefore, virtually everything which the company does, including the work of the Sales Department, Operating Department, Purchasing Department, Treasury Department, Production Planning Department, etc. This being the case, the auditor must not forget, however, that he is not an industrial engineer, a management engineer, a metallurgist, an industrial relations expert, or the president of the company. Few practices have gotten the auditor into more hot water, and justifiably so, than that of pretending to know more about the technical phase of a subject than the technician himself. The auditor must try to arrive at a delicate balance which permits him to examine and render help in any department having a bearing on the financial status of the corporation while, at the same time, confining himself to those matters on which he can render sound opinions. An auditor is essentially a fact-finding examiner, and the judgment is up to the appropriate management group.

Effectiveness of the Audit Division

The value of an internal audit staff cannot be measured in dollars and cents alone; for it is not possible to set down a column of figures which represents the savings made by the Audit Division and balance them against another group of figures which represents the cost of the Audit Division.

Management will judge the effectiveness of the Audit Division on the quality of the report rendered and the effect of the action taken. It is necessary, therefore, that these reports be well-written in concise business English. They should set forth to top management the conditions surrounding a particular situation, the auditor's recommendations for improvement, and the favorable or unfavorable comments of the one or more levels of management directly responsible for the function. Accordingly, top management has all sides of the picture as they read the report. The report must indicate the action that has been taken or planned, and it should be a part of the Audit Division's function to follow up, within a reasonable time, to see that line management has made the corrections indicated.

Another service that the Audit Division should perform is the training and supplying of men qualified to accept responsibilities and, with the background of management's viewpoint, to assume executive positions in the various functions throughout the corporation. Men in the Audit Division will get a complete education as to the company's policies and how these policies tie together for a smoothly operating business. It should be the ambition of the Audit Supervisor to be constantly losing his best men to other de-

partments of the business, where training of this type is needed to
fill executive positions. Not only will this tend to create an organization of men with broad vision, but it will enable the Audit Division to maintain a staff of men of the caliber needed to do the job
at hand because they know what opportunity exists for a job well
done.

Relation to Public Accountants

Normally, the audits performed by the public accountant take the
form of a balance sheet audit requiring, principally, the verification
of the assets and liabilities as of a certain date and such analysis of
the income statement as will enable the auditor to certify that they
have been stated properly. In brief, the audit approach of the independent public accountant is to establish accuracy of accounts,
account by account, while the internal auditor's approach is department by department, or function by function, and to establish that
good business practices are in effect in each. Thus, it is apparent
that the work of the two need not conflict, because basic approach
and emphasis are different.

Much has been written and said about coordination and cooperation between the external and internal auditor, but it boils down
principally to this:

1. Each must stay out of the other's road, for although the emphasis varies, use of the same records is sometimes necessary.
   Accordingly, their audit time schedules should be so correlated as not to interfere with each other's programs and not
   to burden the line personnel who prepare and use the records.
2. The coverage of the internal auditor may reduce the detail
   work necessary to satisfy the external auditor of the existence
   of adequate internal control.

CHAPTER 2

INTERNAL AUDITING AS A PROFESSION— STANDARDS

As a Profession

Like many other groups, internal auditors aspire to see their vocation recognized as a "profession." Engineers, teachers, public accountants, and many others so term their occupations. Accordingly, it seems that the internal auditor is justified in attempting to qualify his function as a profession.

There are, however, in common with tax accountants, controllers, systems and procedure accountants, etc., several points to which the internal auditor must give consideration before full professional status can be achieved, for example:

1. The staff or advisory character of the work must be accepted as the auditor's function to the complete exclusion of participation in or supervision over the routine work connected with the various phases of the company's activities. As previously stated, in the compilation and disbursement of a payroll, for example, the entire operation is carried on without any participation by the internal auditor who enters into the picture only occasionally for a test review. This same detachment from the "line" operations should exist in all phases. In other words, the internal auditor is truly the "dispensable" man, insofar as the conduct of the day-to-day affairs is concerned, being purely investigatory and advisory.

2. The character and value of the auditor's knowledge and advice must be developed to a professional plane, and his work and conduct must be such that top management, by observation and contact, comes to appreciate the professional approach and talent of the internal auditor. Growth of stature in this direction will develop as higher standards of education and training for internal audit work are adopted by internal auditors and so recognized by management.

Public accountants have given consideration to these matters and are continuing to improve such phases of their relationship to the business world; likewise, internal auditors, through their Institute, increasingly are achieving a similar acceptance by management.

3. There must be a growing understanding among public accountants, internal auditors, and management in general that the internal auditor and the public accountant work in collaborating fields and not competing fields.

4. The internal auditor must educate management that his unbiased views are worthy of consideration regardless of the fact that they may be opposed to the views of management. In other words, he must sell management that he has a right to a degree of independence of expression comparable to the company's public accountants. Accordingly, the internal auditor, if he is to earn a professional rating, will be so accepted to the extent that managements desire an unbiased view of the adequacy and operation of various company policies in effect.

Standards for Internal Auditing

For years the preponderance of accounting literature has set forth auditing "procedures" for various activities. Recently, however, the public accounting profession has attempted to distinguish between "auditing procedures" and "auditing standards" and has outlined certain standards particularly applicable to their work.

In any endeavor, such as auditing, in which no objective measurements are possible, such standards are necessarily of a very abstract character. Nevertheless, there are some standards of performance against which the activities of an internal auditing staff can be compared in a general way, as follows:

1. The staff must have a "professional approach" to the task—with a spirit of complete helpfulness—without a thought of destructive criticism—and, above all, with the attitude that they are professional auditors and not detectives.

2. All thinking members of management, at every level, must wholeheartedly accept the audit staff as their right arm. Only adherence to all internal auditing standards by all members of the staff will win and hold such acceptance.

3. The auditor's factual data must be meticulously correct. Almost superhuman accuracy is expected and demanded of the auditor.

He cannot be too careful. He must check his facts and have them carefully rechecked. The natural tendency of the groups under audit is to concentrate to such an extent on discussion of any error committed by the auditor that often the constructive effect of the balance of the audit findings is nullified.

4. The auditor must be qualified by education, training, experience, and tact to deal with the company executives in a manner which will engender their respect and assure proper consideration of his recommendations.

5. The auditor must not be a theorist. He must know good theory, but, primarily, he must view matters as a practical businessman. His recommendations must be workable and always reflect good business judgment.

6. The staff must have the degree of independence of thought and action previously commented upon.

7. His reports must be interesting, constructive, easily understandable, generally well prepared, and, most important of all, must be unobtrusively forceful and convincing, with the effect that they get action.

8. The programming and planning of audits must be timely; show evidence of careful selection of most important and productive subject matter; result in no duplication with other staffs, other audits, or the public accountants; and must not waste staff and company time on nonessential matters.

9. The auditors should review all the significant control points and be thoroughly familiar with the internal control procedures covering all important functions. They must persistently work for the ultimate in controls that can be achieved at a cost consistent with the risks involved.

10. The auditor must be thoroughly discreet. No loose talk, gossip, or taletelling can be a part of any auditor's make-up. Further, his reporting must be complete and unbiased, with no attempts to glorify the auditor whether at another's expense or not.

Measurement of Audit Staff Effectiveness

Our experience indicates that the value and effectiveness of an internal audit staff is not subject to expression concretely in dollars, but rather it is something that you feel. It may be summarized as follows:

1. The cash savings disclosed in overbillings from vendors and contractors in audits of construction appropriations and other disbursements.
2. The improper cash disbursements prevented because control weaknesses are discovered and remedied before loss.
3. The care taken by the line organization in order that the audit will be "clean."
4. The frauds that are not committed because of the psychological effect of the fear of discovery through audit.
5. The losses that are prevented through closer adherence to company procedure and policies in all divisions of the company —Purchasing, Traffic, Production Planning, Shipping, etc.
6. The increased revenue from disclosures of improper billings to customers and improper estimating or price establishment.
7. The favorable adherence of the audit staff to the 10 standards for auditing established in the preceding paragraph.

Any attempt to measure the size of the audit staff suitable for various operations will, of course, evoke considerable controversy, since the size will vary considerably with the organizational structure, size, and complexity of a company.

However, purely as a guide, and at the risk of incurring considerable criticism from our colleagues in this profession, we suggest the following for any company or plant location with all the normal functions subject to audit:

1. For large operations (plants having a total employment of 1,000 or more employes) , .5 to .75 of 1% as many internal auditors for the normal audit coverage as there are accounting and clerical employes.
2. For smaller integrated locations, a somewhat higher percentage of audit time as compared to accounting and clerical employes.

Training and Education

The so-called "learned" professions and others are predicated upon formal education and some sort of provision for actual training. Thus, the trend of educational prerequisites for certified public accountants is toward college education or the equivalent, and the awarding of certificates is also predicated on actual public accounting experience or its equivalent.   Similarly, definite educational and training prerequisites should be required in order to preserve the professional aspects of internal auditing. The following background is accordingly recommended.

1. College education or equivalent, majoring in general accounting, including a special course in internal auditing. Moreover, since internal auditors must be good businessmen rather than theoretical accountants, it is recommended that their elective studies cover allied business subjects such as industrial management, marketing, statistics, and finance.

2. A program of diversified training on the job of junior auditors should be instituted by all companies having Internal Audit Divisions. Senior auditors should be expected to supervise this training. Audit Supervisors should arrange that the junior auditors be assigned a variety of audit work so that all will receive a well-rounded experience. Where there are a number of plants involved, new junior auditors should be conducted on a tour to familiarize them with operations and related basic records and plant accounting.

The training of senior auditors to prepare them for duty as district supervisors is also an important part of the professional training program. It should cover such subjects as (a) corporate organization, (b) technique of handling men, (c) technical auditing subjects, (d) technical accounting subjects, (e) standard costs, and (f) incentive wage payments.

3. A professionally written audit manual should be provided as a reference book. To the extent that it is intelligently, but not slavishly, used by an audit staff, it can be a great aid in obtaining a high standard of professional auditing.

Appraisal of Personnel

In other professions, state examinations are provided to appraise those aspiring to professional careers. However, because of the private nature of internal auditing, appraisal of personnel will probably be accomplished largely at the time of hiring, on the basis of educational qualifications, experience, and any psychological characteristics which may be evident to an experienced interviewer. An examination in accounting and auditing such as is used by some public accounting firms is desirable to give some indication as to knowledge, aptitude, and accuracy.

Periodic progress reports as to the development of personnel after a period of education, training, and experience in the Audit Division should be submitted by supervisors. These should be reviewed, and, where individual analysis may be helpful, recommendations for improvement should be made to the individual.

The appraisal procedure should lead to definite conclusions in respect to each individual which will answer such questions as (1) What are his strong points? (2) What are his weak points? (3) Can he develop?

CHAPTER 3

INTERNAL CHECK, CONTROL, ADMINISTRATION, AND DELEGATION OF FUNCTIONS WITHIN A BUSINESS

INTERNAL CHECK AND CONTROL

Foreword

Briefly stated, the objectives of a system of internal check and control are to protect a company's assets against irregularities, to ensure the accuracy of recorded transactions, and to assure management that the information on which it must base decisions is authentic and reliable.

Attention is periodically directed toward internal controls by newspaper reviews of certain cases of fraud. These cases prove that "it really can happen" and that concern over adequate internal controls is not just talk and theory. In all such cases, however, many practices will be noted which create an appearance of control but actually are not controls.

One purpose of this chapter is to point out the weaknesses and dangers in certain control practices and to set forth the fundamental principles underlying a sound system of internal control.

Allocation of Duties and Responsibilities

In one fraud case reviewed in the news, several procedures usually thought to constitute controls over accounts payable were present, such as:

1. Approved purchase requisitions supported all purchases.
2. Purchase orders were issued by the Purchasing Department.
3. Purchase invoices were approved as to terms and prices by the Purchasing Department.
4. Receiving reports were issued by a Receiving Department.

5. Invoices were checked to receiving slips, and extensions were checked.
6. A separate group entered the invoices in a voucher record.
7. Checks were presented for signature and countersignature with all supporting documents attached.

However, in spite of the presence of these procedures which have been accepted as axioms of internal control, they actually did not produce control because it was possible for one man, in whom related duties were concentrated, to introduce forged documents into the procedures.

The danger of such a concentration and of relying on personal integrity for protection is illustrated by the statement of a surety company that, in 90% of fraud cases, deficiencies in internal procedures permitted an individual to embezzle large amounts without aid from either within or without the organization.

Equally important is the proper division of duties between departments in order that no single department assumes complete responsibility for all or a majority of the phases of a function. An example of improper concentration of responsibility can be drawn from the accounts payable procedures cited above in that, if receiving and stocking were under the Purchasing Department, issuing of purchase orders, approval of invoices, and handling of materials are all performed by the one department.

The preparation and analysis of organization charts and clerical procedure flow charts, in such detail as may be necessary, not only will reveal the existence of improper allocations of duties and responsibilities, overlapping responsibilities and duplications of effort, as well as other weaknesses, but also will serve as a guide in the development of an effective internal control program.

Safeguarding Assets Other than Cash

Unquestionably, in any internal control system particular care would be taken to ensure the protection of cash. However, the fact that many defalcations occur in functions that do not involve the handling of money requires that there be no weaknesses in the controls established over such functions.

The tendency to emphasize the control over cash and to slight the control over other assets may be illustrated by the conditions noted in a company having an imprest fund of several thousand dollars, the responsibility for which was invested in bonded cashiers who worked in a cage to which only they had keys. All other employes were excluded from the cage except when the cashiers were present. Control was exercised through unannounced audits by an Accounting Department representative. In contrast to this tight control, inventories worth several million dollars, consisting of easily pilfered and readily disposed-of goods, were accessible to anyone and were accounted for by stock records having no value from a control standpoint.

Application of Control Procedures

Control procedures based on sound principles may be weakened by conditions attending their application or by lack of knowledge or understanding on the part of those exercising the controls. A control program must, therefore, provide for educating this personnel as to duties and responsibilities, the importance of the procedure, and the dangers of faulty application. For example, the value of approvals on various documents is lost unless those authorized to approve are qualified to do so by their knowledge of the particular transactions and those who process the approved documents know who has the authority to approve and that the approval is authentic.

Management's Responsibility

Many of the weaknesses in a system of internal control exist because of management's reluctance, while recognizing these weaknesses, to institute changes in duties, responsibilities, and authorities for policy or other reasons. Nevertheless, regardless of the difficulties involved, it is management's responsibility not only to safeguard the company's interests, but also to protect its employes from the temptation to commit irregularities.

Fundamentals of Internal Control

As previously indicated, usage has created many concepts of internal controls which are not real controls, as they are only helpful and make fraud less convenient. Accordingly, those responsible for instituting controls must not become panicked into going control-crazy, but should analyze their situations to see that they have all the basic controls and all the other "trimmings," the cost of which will be consistent with the risk involved.

It will take careful analysis to determine just what the basic controls in a given function are. Basic controls are those steps in a procedure which make it practically impossible for significant losses to go undetected for an extended period without collusion. When a set of basic controls has been developed for a situation, no step in this chain of controls can be omitted—they must be considered as a unit. However, there may be other steps in a procedure which can be added in order to:

1. Restrict still further the amount of any defalcation.
2. Shorten the period during which it might go undetected.
3. Widen the circle of people who must be in collusion.

These may be termed internal control trimmings, and control procedures should encompass as many detail checks as possible, but only those for which, in the best judgment of management, the cost of maintaining the control will be justified. It is necessary to be practical and to recognize that small activities cannot spread responsibility over as many individuals, so as to obtain maximum internal control benefits, as is possible in larger organizations. In such cases the internal audit tests must be done in greater volume and, accordingly, the audit staff becomes closer to being an integral part of the internal check system.

Normally, of course, the internal auditors, in coordination with external auditors, will periodically review the theory and practice of the controls, although neither of these groups is an integral part of a routine checking system. It is also important to impress on management, at all levels, that they must be alert to recognize signals of irregularities or improper handling. There is hardly a case of fraud in which most of the clues which finally led to discovery were not substantially available far in advance of actual recognition.

The three functions which are most vulnerable to loss through lack of adequate control are Accounts Payable, Payrolls, and Billing. Two of these are selected for illustration:

Consider, first, the control over Accounts Payable by the Accounting Department. It is essential that the Accounts Payable procedure have as its basic concept the following principles:

1. After review and approval by the Purchasing Department for price and terms, bills go to Group A which handles the debit (dis-

tribution) side of the transaction. Group A may be the Cost Department, for example, and it may compare invoices with purchase orders and freight documents; after which invoices will be entered into the proper accounts and sufficient data extracted to prepare the distribution of the Accounts Payable.

2. Group A then submits the original bills to Group B which compares them to independently prepared receiving reports and approves for payment. Both Groups A and B submit the summary of their side of the transaction directly to a General Ledger Group, which investigates any differences and authorizes correction of the records of Group A or B, as the case may be.

3. Then Group C records the bills, prepares checks, and submits monthly balances to the General Ledger Group.

4. The Treasurer signs the checks and furnishes the debit to the Accounts Payable to the General Ledger Group, making periodic tests of supporting documents.

5. Checks are returned to another independent group which makes regular and complete bank reconcilements.

Actually, without collusion, no one supervisor is in a position to introduce forged invoices or make improper payments over any extended period without detection. These basic controls do not require complicated or expensive procedures. In fact, the procedures for Accounts Payable at some locations will be found to contain steps aimed at control which would fall into the classification of trimmings, for which the cost is not commensurate with the possible risk and the loss involved.

Secondly, a similar situation will be found to exist in many spots with regard to control of payrolls. For example, in some plants great expense is encountered in order to ensure against any employe punching-in more than one time card. With a sound approach to the matter of basic internal controls, it is not of utmost importance how many time cards a man punches "in" or "out," because he cannot do anything with them anyhow. Accordingly, this would be one of the trimmings which it is well to have in addition to basic controls, provided it can be achieved at a reasonable cost. What then is the heart of the control? What must be accomplished by a timekeeping system? It is necessary to know how many hours each man worked and what he did. Who can tell this? Timekeepers, time-takers, clerks, etc., can be as thick as flies throughout the plant, but actually the one man who is in a position really to know, without prohibitive timekeeping expense, is the Operating Department foreman. This does not mean the mill superintendents, general foremen, or other higher level supervisors, but the actual foremen themselves who may supervise, on the average, 25 to 30 men each. They know who is working for them and what they are doing. The story about making clerks out of foremen is an old one. This must not be done, but the recording of the time worked by such a few men is not time consuming and is an integral part of the supervision job. The system should make this job as painless as possible, but it cannot eliminate this function. The basic problem of control then, in a plant of say 6,000 men, is to determine that approximately 200 foremen are properly reporting the men working, the hours worked, and the positions filled or the work done. This should be accomplished along the following lines:

1. The payroll recording system should be set up in such a fashion that for jobs paid for on an incentive basis, and for construction and maintenance, the reports prepared by production recorders, etc., will be regularly reconciled to the time worked by individuals as a matter of routine.

2. Jobs on which regular crews are essential for the operation, or are normally used, are readily controlled, but reports of deviations from normal crews should be submitted daily by the Payroll Department to the two supervisory levels immediately above the foremen.

3. Daily force reports of the number of men on each occupation in each responsibility will be prepared for the remainder of the working force (15% to 20%), constituting labor crews not requiring a consistent size. This daily force report would also be submitted daily directly to the two supervisory levels above the foremen who compare actual number of men to normal and sign these reports as an integral part of the payroll control system. Without collusion between these various levels of operating supervision, it is inconceivable that any appreciable number of employes could be padded to individual payroll groups for any extended period.

It will be recognized that the risk is spread over scores of foremen, most of whom are honest and will report accurately. It cannot be disputed that a foreman here and there can favor an employe by marking him working when he is not, or other such dishonest acts, but the cost of a system which will forestall such minor acts will be many times the probable loss with the type of basic control outlined.

The time reports thus prepared will be accumulated by men of one section of the Payroll Department, and a separate control section of the Payroll Department will maintain such detail as is deemed feasible for control of the total hours worked. The Payroll Department will submit completed payrolls to a paymaster or cashier, who will prepare the payroll checks, or supervise the preparation of the cash to be paid, and will pay the men who submit suitable identification, by using employes other than those involved in the preparation of the payrolls and other than foremen or other operating supervisors. If payment is made by check, bank reconcilements will be performed by another separate group responsible to neither the Payroll Department nor the paymaster.

It would be impossible to outline all the items which should be considered in reviewing the adequacy of internal controls. However, the accompanying check list presents a sufficient number of thoughts on the subject to enable the student to gain a practical concept of specific control requirements.

Specimen Check List of Internal Control Requirements

1. *General*

   a. Employes in positions of trust should be bonded for amounts that are adequate in relation to their control of company assets.

   b. Where employes in positions of trust take regular annual vacations, it is desirable that their duties be then assumed by other employes.

   c. Subsidiaries, plants, or branches of a company should be visited periodically by internal auditors, with written reports being submitted to the general office.

   d. Procedures for approving various documents should be so designed that the individuals authorized to approve are qualified to do so by their knowledge of the particular transactions and those who process the approved documents know who has the authority to approve and that the approval is authentic.

   e. Organization charts and such responsibility charts and clerical procedure flow charts as may be required to supplement the organization charts should be prepared and kept current.

   f. Provision should be made for periodic analysis of the charts cited above to determine that the division of duties to executive officers conforms with the provisions of the by-laws and that changes in allocations of duties at lower organizational levels do not lessen the effectiveness of established controls.

g. New policies or practices should be reviewed to determine their effect on the internal control system.

2. *Cash*

a. An employe who keeps cash records should not have other duties which permit him directly or indirectly to influence entries in ledgers or any other books of original entry.

b. Officers and employes having authority to sign or countersign checks should not have other duties related to cash which provide them with opportunity directly or indirectly to influence entries in any of the ledgers.

c. Vouchers and supporting documents should accompany checks presented to officials for signature and should be subsequently marked to prevent resubmission to the check signer for duplicate payment.

d. Where circumstances require that officials sign blank checks for emergency use in their absence, a practice to be avoided if possible, it is the responsibility of the signer to determine, subsequently, that such checks have been used properly.

e. To the greatest degree possible the issuance of checks payable to currency should be avoided.

f. Spoiled or voided checks should be preserved to facilitate the accounting for serial check numbers.

g. Employes preparing or approving checks should not effect or have supervision over bank reconciliations.

h. Bank reconciliations should be made regularly and in such detail as may be required for an effective reconciliation that is consistent with the degree of completeness of the internal control over the transactions that prompted the issuance of the checks.

i. An independent record of incoming remittances should be prepared at mail opening for comparison later with the collections recorded and deposited by the cashier. The other duties of the respective employes preparing the record and making the comparison should not be such as to reduce the effectiveness of this procedure.

j. Cash receipts should not be diverted to the petty cash fund or other uses but should be deposited intact in the bank daily.

k. The handling of petty cash preferably should be on an imprest fund basis. Reimbursement checks should be made payable to the custodian of the fund and should be processed in conformance with the control requirements set forth in the foregoing items relating to checks and their supporting documents. The fund should be subjected to internal audit at frequent but irregular intervals.

l. The procedures surrounding the handling of and accounting for cash sales should be such as to assure that the cash received from cash sales will be recorded properly on the books and will be deposited promptly in the company's bank account.

3. *Payroll*

a. Employment and payroll procedures must be so designed and correlated that names do not appear on the payroll unless they rightfully belong there.

b. The authorization of changes in salaries, hourly rates, piece rates, or performance standards, etc., should be vested in personnel other than those engaged in the actual work of payroll preparation.

c. The respective phases of payroll work, such as the accumulation of time and attendance records, including production records for incentive paid employes; calculation of earnings; preparation of the payroll lists; preparation of pay checks or envelopes; checking the payroll; approving the payroll; and distributing the checks or envelopes should be delegated to separate employes or groups of employes. The danger of influence being exerted over related functions is thus minimized, and unless there is collusion, each individual or group acts as a check on the individual or group performing the preceding function. Obviously, where control through such a division of duties may not be practicable, as in a small organization, payroll audits must be made more frequently.

d. Pay checks or envelopes should be distributed to employes only upon presentation of suitable identification. Where payment is in cash, a bona fide receipt should be obtained. An added protection against irregularities is afforded where payment is by check, through inspection in connection with the reconciliation of the payroll bank account.

e. Safeguards should be provided to prevent the diversion of unclaimed wages to improper uses.

4. *Purchases*

a. Purchase orders should be executed in writing and should be based on properly authorized requisitions.

b. The duty of placing orders with suppliers should be vested in personnel other than those initiating the purchases.

c. The prices at which materials and supplies are purchased should be reviewed periodically by an official or responsible employe not connected with the Purchasing Department to ascertain that such prices are the most advantageous to the company.

d. The approval of invoices should be the dual responsibility of the Purchasing and Accounting Departments, with the Purchasing Department making a comparison of the unit prices, description of merchandise, terms, etc., shown on the vendor's invoice with the corresponding items on the purchase order, and the Accounting Department making a similar comparison and check and, in addition, checking extensions and amounts.

e. It is desirable that merchandise received be counted, weighed or measured, and reported by employes who are not connected with the receipt of the merchandise and who have no advance knowledge of the quantities to be received.   If practical considerations preclude this, frequent physical inventories, followed by rigid investigation of any irregularities, should be made by personnel outside the Purchasing and Receiving Departments.

f. Procedures should be instituted to ensure the filing of claims against carriers for shortages and damaged materials.

g. The matching of receiving reports with invoices should be performed by employes having no part in the functions of ordering or receiving material.

h. Where merchandise is purchased for direct shipment to customers, procedures must be instituted to ensure that the customers are charged properly.

i. The procedures covering returned purchases must ensure the recording of a charge to the vendor and provide for proper handling of all phases of the transaction.

5. *Stores and materials*

a. Stocks of stores and materials should be under the control of a storekeeper, with access to the storeroom being denied, to the greatest degree possible, to persons other than the storekeeper and his assistants.

b. Deliveries should be made only on written requisitions approved by authorized employes qualified to do so by knowledge of the circumstances prompting the requisition.

c. Materials withdrawn from the storeroom and not used should be returned to the storeroom, placed in stock, and properly recorded in the stock records.

d. Where stock ledgers are kept in quantities and money, adequate control must be established to ensure correct pricing of the material requisitions by the ledger-keepers.

e. Differences between recorded quantities and physical counts should be investigated by personnel other than those responsible for inventory discrepancies and should be adjusted only on proper authority.

f. The duty of determining when stocks are obsolete or slow-moving and the approval of the adjusted value and disposition of such stocks should not be delegated to an employe responsible for purchases. The employe should, of course, be familiar with the company's stocks and required quantities thereof, as well as with conditions in the market in which such merchandise is to be disposed.

g. Where consigned stocks are received or shipped, periodic confirmation should be made of the quantities shown on the records of such stocks.

6. *Outgoing and incoming freight*

a. Where freight is prepaid for customers, adequate procedures must be instituted to ensure recovery of the amount prepaid.

b. In-transit privileges for storing or processing materials en route are available for certain types of commodities. These privileges are known as "fabrication-in-transit," "milling-in-transit," "barreling-in-transit," etc. When advantage is taken of these privileges, a "through" or reduced rate applies. Control must be exercised to ensure proper arrangements with the carrier to avoid the payment of two rates.

c. Credits to or deductions by customers for freight paid by them should be approved for propriety by the department authorized to make arrangements with customers regarding settlement of transportation charges and approved for amount by employes familiar with freight rates and tariffs.

d. Adequate procedures must be instituted to ensure recovery of freight paid on purchases shipped "freight allowed."

e. To preclude the payment of excessive freight charges, all freight bills should be checked by an employe familiar with rates and tariffs or by an outside agency that is qualified to perform this service.

ADMINISTRATION AND DELEGATION OF FUNCTIONS WITHIN A BUSINESS

The delegation of powers, authorities, and duties by the Board of Directors to the executive officers of a company is usually set forth in the by-laws. For example, in a typical case, the Controller will be designated as the chief accounting officer of the company, with powers, authorities, and duties such as the following:

1. He shall establish and maintain, or cause to be established and maintained, all accounting, including cost accounting, policies, and the methods and procedures of carrying out such policies.

2. He shall be responsible for the design, installation, custody, and operation of all accounting, including cost accounting, books, records, and forms of the company.

3. He shall prepare, or cause to be prepared, all checks, drafts, and other orders for the payment of money for authorized disbursements, or for the transfer of funds of the company, except as may be otherwise provided in respect of any special or limited bank account. He shall not prepare or countersign, or permit the countersigning of, any such checks, drafts, or other orders for the payment of money of the company if such payment is in excess of an amount properly authorized by any rule or regulation established by the Board of Directors or by any officer having authority to establish such rule or regulation.

4. He shall examine and/or audit, or cause to be examined and/or audited, all financial and business records and all receipts and disbursements of the company, including all books and accounts of all officers and agents of the company who are charged with the receipt and disbursements of money or material or who have jurisdiction over labor. He shall make, or cause to be made, such examination and/or audit with established regularity and as often as dictated by good business methods and practices.

5. He shall audit or investigate, or cause to be audited or investigated, any matter the audit or investigation of which may be requested of him by or at the instance of the Board of Directors or the President.

6. He shall analyze and check, or cause to be analyzed and

checked, and assist other officers of the company in analyzing and checking, the policies and activities of the company, as revealed by the records. He shall also assist other officers in determining future policies and plans by developing and interpreting facts and applying good business judgment to the conclusions to be deduced from such facts.

7. He shall prepare and interpret, or cause to be prepared and interpreted, all statistical records and reports and all financial statements and reports of the company whether for internal or external use.

8. He shall establish and maintain, or cause to be established and maintained, budget control and the consolidation and coordination of budgets.

9. He shall take and evaluate, or cause to be taken and evaluated, all physical inventories and all matters relating thereto.

10. He shall be responsible for all matters relating to taxes and shall prepare and file, or cause to be prepared and filed, all tax returns and other papers relating to taxes.

11. He shall place and effect, or cause to be placed and effected, all insurance, including employes' indemnity bonds, in order adequately and properly to safeguard the properties and business of the company and in accordance with policies established by the Board of Directors or by officers whose function it is to establish the same.

12. He shall determine, or cause to be determined, that all expenditures against appropriations are made pursuant to and in accordance with proper authorization and are properly accounted for and shall have authority over the establishment and maintenance of proper and adequate records of authorized appropriations.

13. He shall be responsible for the approval of the auditing and accounting provisions of all contracts, leases, and agreements of the company and the maintenance of adequate records thereof.

14. He shall coordinate, or cause to be coordinated, the clerical and office systems and facilities throughout the company.

15. He may delegate actual performance of any of his work to other departments in the interest of efficiency and economy. Such delegation will not, however, affect his responsibility

for and/or authority over policies, methods, or procedures or the accuracy and results of any work so delegated.

16. He shall render to the Board of Directors, whenever requested by it, an account of his transactions as Controller.

17. Whenever requested by the President or the Board of Directors or independent auditors designated by or under authority of the stockholders he shall exhibit his books and accounts to them or to any of them during business hours.

18. He shall give a bond, in such form and in such amount and with such sureties as the Board of Directors may require and approve.

Given the above powers, authorities, and duties, the Controller will proceed to delegate the actual work to his subordinates.

From the above it is evident that the internal auditor is concerned with the delegation of duties on two planes:

1. Those conferred by the Board of Directors upon the several executive officers.

2. Those delegated by each executive officer to his subordinates.

In the first category, covering the broad delegation of functions within a business, a discussion of proper internal controls at the departmental level is necessary.

As previously stated, it is important that a proper segregation of duties between departments and a review and approval of the activities of one department by another be practiced to assure proper internal control at the departmental level. It is a duty of the internal auditor to determine that such control exists and, if they do not, to be able to suggest the required changes in alignment with the various functions.

The internal auditor should analyze the organization in his company. As a sample of such analysis, an outline of a typical company is set forth on the following pages. Some of the functions are enumerated, and it is indicated under the several departments whether that department is in primary control (P) of the function, or whether it "approves" or "assists" (A), and thus constitutes internal control at the executive officer level. It is understood, of course, that all matters of the company's business are subject to final approval by the top executives (President, Chairman of the Board, Directors, Executive Committee, or other similar titles).

	ACCOUNTING	TREASURY	SALES	OPERATING	PURCHASING	LAW-SECRETARY	TRAFFIC	LABOR RELATIONS
A. FUNCTIONS WHICH ARE PRIMARILY UNDER THE CONTROL OF THE ACCOUNTING DEPARTMENT								
1. All accounting operations	P							
2. Prepare and interpret all accounting and statistical reports	P							
3. Take and evaluate inventories	P			A	A			
4. Coordinate budgets	P	A	A	A	A		A	A
5. Establish cost accounting methods	P		A	A				
6. Establish accounting and clerical procedures	P							
7. Tax returns	P					A		
8. Control expenditures on operating, capital, maintenance and other budgets	P		A	A	A			
9. Weigh, count and report production and time worked	P			A				
10. Audit all matters concerning the business of the company	P							
11. Weigh, count or otherwise measure and report materials received	P			A				
12. Measure operating performance against standards	P			A				
B. FUNCTIONS WHICH ARE PRIMARILY UNDER THE CONTROL OF THE TREASURER								
1. Custody of all funds and securities	A	P						
2. Recommend depositories used	A	P						
3. Collect money due company	A	P	A			A		
4. Determine and apply credit policies		P	A					
5. Make all payments based on vouchers properly prepared and audited by the Accounting Department	A	P						
6. Maintain records of all cash received and paid	A	P						
C. FUNCTIONS WHICH ARE PRIMARILY UNDER THE CONTROL OF THE SALES DEPARTMENT								
1. Determine donations	A		P					
2. Compile data on market trends and competitors and forecast sales	A		P	A				
3. Determine types and quantities of product to be sold			P	A				
4. Determine sales prices and terms (other than credit)	A		P					
5. Plan distribution of products by area, industry, company, etc.		A	P	A				
6. Determine quantity of stocks to be maintained	A		P	A				
7. Sell company products			P					
8. Maintain satisfied customers		A	P	A				
9. Plan trade relations programs			P		A			

Fig. 1. Sample of auditor's analysis of the organization of a typical company.

	ACCOUNTING	TREASURY	SALES	OPERATING	PURCHASING	LAW-SECRETARY	TRAFFIC	LABOR RELATIONS
D. FUNCTIONS WHICH ARE PRIMARILY UNDER THE CONTROL OF THE OPERATING DEPARTMENT								
1. Develop old and new products			A	P				
2. Service customers in matters of a technical nature regarding the use of products			A	P				
3. Determine inventory requirements of raw materials and operating supplies	A			P	A			
4. Develop specifications for materials purchased				P	A			
5. Perform all operations and inspections regarding manufacture of company's product				P				
6. Package, load and ship products				P				
7. Maintain facilities				P				
8. Establish manufacturing practices				P				
9. Develop and improve operating facilities, methods and products				P				
10. Design and construction of all operating facilities				P	A			
11. Determine amount and type of requests for capital and maintenance expenditures	A			A	P			
12. Establish operating standards	A				P			
13. Establish production schedules					P			
E. FUNCTIONS WHICH ARE PRIMARILY UNDER THE CONTROL OF THE PURCHASING DEPARTMENT								
1. Purchase all raw materials, supplies, equipment and services throughout the company				A	P			
2. Procure sources of supply and quotations					P			
3. Develop trends in markets of products purchased					P			
4. Test quality of material purchased				A	P			
5. Dispose of surplus materials or supplies				A	P			
6. Settle claims regarding purchased materials	A			A	P			

Fig. 1. (Continued.)

	ACCOUNTING	TREASURY	SALES	OPERATING	PURCHASING	LAW-SECRETARY	TRAFFIC	LABOR RELATIONS
F. FUNCTIONS WHICH ARE PRIMARILY UNDER THE CONTROL OF THE TRAFFIC DEPARTMENT								
1. Develop all information relative to traffic matters involved in company business							P	
2. Represent company in Government agencies in formulation of policies regarding traffic problems							P	
3. Represent company in freight rate and I.C.C. hearings, etc.							P	
4. Seek modification of adverse rates and regulations							P	
5. Review propriety of all transportation charges	A				A		P	
6. Secure all needed transportation					A		P	
7. Outline most advantageous routes for shipments and receipts			A	A			P	
8. Prepare and file all traffic claims	A						P	
G. FUNCTIONS WHICH ARE PRIMARILY UNDER THE CONTROL OF THE LAW DEPARTMENT								
1. Purchase, sale, lease property, patent rights, etc.	A		A	A		P		
2. Place insurance	A					P		
3. Custody of corporate matters such as stock books, corporate seal, minute books, etc.						P		
4. Legal advice and guidance to all departments						P		
5. Handle all litigation						P		
6. Review and approve all contracts and agreements	A	A	A	A	A	P	A	A
7. Contact all outside or Governmental investigators	A					P		
H. FUNCTIONS WHICH ARE PRIMARILY UNDER THE CONTROL OF THE LABOR RELATIONS DEPARTMENT								
1. Determine policies regarding personnel administration	A	A	A	A	A	A	A	P
2. Recruit personnel requirements								P
3. Determine policies regarding wages and salaries and evaluation of jobs	A				A	A		P
4. Prepare and negotiate labor agreements and grievances					A	A		P
5. Develop training programs	A	A	A	A	A	A	A	P
6. Organize medical and safety programs								P
7. Develop pension and other benefit plans	A							P

Fig. 1. (Continued.)

The delegation of duties by an executive officer to his department heads, from the point of view of internal control, has already been touched upon under the heading of Allocation of Duties and Responsibilities. Continuing with the Controller's Department as an example, a review of the Specimen Check List of Internal Control (page 27) will demonstrate the necessity for careful assignment of duties among the rank and file of employes. Two undesirable conditions to be avoided are (1) the combining in one person of duties which permit that person to embezzle funds or appropriate property belonging to his employer without collusion, and (2) the encouraging of collusion by not properly separating employes having supplementary duties.

CHAPTER 4

FRAUD CASES

Introduction

In our previous discussion of basic and auxiliary internal controls we have touched upon the problem of fraud and its relation to the adequacy of the system of internal check. While it must be borne in mind that the discovery and prevention of fraud is not the prime duty of internal auditing, the subject is of professional interest to the auditor and is worthy of specific treatment.

Despite the existence of good accounting proceedures and a satisfactory system of internal check, the auditor must not be lulled into a false feeling of security, because it must be acknowledged that no system exists which cannot be circumvented if eternal vigilance is relaxed. Therefore, from time to time, as perfection is not quite achieved and as the element of collusion may creep in, fraud cases will arise. Then too, although less than 1% of employes are basically dishonest, it is nevertheless impossible to predict just when the individuals comprising this small group will stray from the path of rectitude.

In order that the internal auditor may prepare himself for the prompt discovery of fraud when it does occur, it is desirable that he become familiar with the many types of obscure weaknesses which have made fraud possible and with the methods followed by embezzlers in the past.

Methods Used by Defrauders

A number of bonding companies have made comprehensive studies of the causes of actual fidelity losses. In making these studies they were particularly concerned with the accounting and physical controls over assets, income, and expenditures. Moreover, in making the studies of particular cases they made it a point to ascertain how a loss occurred, how it was concealed, and what brought about its exposure. Means could then be devised to prevent recurrences by making such recommendations for improving existing procedures which permitted the loss to remain undetected. This is the proper procedure for the internal auditor to follow, and the following discussion, based upon actual fraud cases, should serve to illustrate such procedure.

Overstating Production under Incentive Wage Payment Plan

An incentive plan covered two positions normally employing a group of layers-out and another group of plate burners. Incentive payments were made to plate burners based on total lineal inches flame-cut, with allowances for machine set-ups for plates and machine cleaning. A layer-out would prepare the production reports for his crew of burners and was paid an incentive on the average performance of his crew. Cursory examination of incentive records indicated that production was not being properly reported. Accordingly, a detailed review was made of the production reports for two months. It was found that the rough length of hot rolled and recut plates was overstated by the layers-out as evidenced by a comparison of flame-cutting production reports with rolling records, based on the marker's estimated rough length for hot rolled plates. The preceding operation produced steel plate, and it was a simple matter to obtain the quantity and measurements of plate produced, which had to be laid out and flame-cut. These data, reduced to terms of lineal inches to be cut, was compared to the cutting reported by the layers-out.

The over-reporting of inches cut was substantial, and set-ups were considerably over-reported. It was found that the corrected percentage of performance for the two months averaged much less than the average reported performance. Bonus payments were substantially excessive for the two months and quite large for the total period involved.

Defalcation in Payments for Trucking

In this case it was determined that a very large sum had been paid to outside interests during an extended period for which records were available. An equally large sum was estimated to have been paid in excess of competitive rates during the period audited. There was reason to believe that such losses occurred continuously for a much longer period than that audited.

The loss capable of determination was the result of fictitious entries made by shipping personnel in the company's warehouse. The chief shipper made entries and directed other employes under his supervision to make entries on a trucking report in such a manner as to indicate that shipments and deliveries had been made on the trucks of a contract trucker, although they had been made on other trucks or by rail. These employes also wrote the names of drivers working for the contract trucker on the "shipping ticket," indicating that the drivers had hauled the material to the loading platform or terminal of other truckers or railroads, although they knew the material had been loaded on other trucks or cars in the warehouse.

The trucking report was prepared in duplicate, and after totaling the weights for each class of shipment, summaries were prepared. One copy of the summary, together with a copy of the trucking report, was sent to the contract trucker, and the other copy was sent to the Accounting Department. The contract trucker then prepared an invoice to the company, in exact agreement with the summary, and delivered it to the company. The executive in charge of operations, or his assistant, compared the invoice with the summary and approved it. The Accounting Department also compared the invoice with the summary and approved it for payment, after which it was paid.

The loss was discovered by an employe of the Sales Accounting Division of the company. He had received instructions from the Sales Department to issue credit to a customer in settlement of a complaint. He examined the Sales Department file and secured the trucking report to determine that shipments had been made as stated. Not finding the shipments listed in the proper place on this report, he searched further and found them listed as being made on the contract trucker's trucks. He could not understand why the material would have been hauled on the contract trucker's trucks to the loading platform of another trucker. He therefore examined the bills of lading, which indicated that the outside trucker had called at the warehouse for the material.

He then referred the matter to the Controller, who asked the executive in charge to explain this discrepancy. The latter and the shipper advised the Controller and the Sales Accounting Division employe that the material had been hauled on the contract trucker's trucks. Since this did not conform to the bills of lading, the Controller instructed the Audit Supervisor and the Sales Accounting Division employe to investigate completely the one day's shipments. This investigation included visits to outside truckers, who confirmed that they had loaded the material in the company's warehouse and that it had not been hauled to their loading platforms. The same procedure was followed for rail shipments, with the same results. A detailed investigation was then initiated.

The investigation revealed the following procedures and defects in procedures which made this loss possible:

1. Drivers of the trucking contractor did not sign a receipt for material; therefore, there was no proof that material was loaded on his trucks.

2. There was no watchman at the gate to check out-going shipments.

3. Names of truck drivers were written on shipment tickets by shipping clerks, rather than by loading foremen who actually saw the material loaded.

4. The trucking record was checked with shipment tickets in such a manner that fraud was not detected. Instead of checking the shipment tickets directly to the shipment report, the executive in charge instructed a clerk to list the shipments on a piece of paper and release them at once and then, later, to compare the list with the shipment report and see that each item was listed. As a result of this small detail in the procedure, the fact that shipments were improperly entered on the trucking report was not discovered.

5. The trucker prepared his invoice from the company's records rather than from his own records.

6. The Traffic Department never saw the contract trucker's invoice of the shipment report.

7. The contract trucker's invoices were approved by an executive rather than through the regular channels.

8. All persons approving invoices assumed that they had been previously checked and were not familiar with procedures observed by others. The fact that an invoice was approved

by an executive was considered as satisfactory evidence of its
authenticity.

9. The accounting procedure did not provide for any analysis
   of trucking expense which would distinguish between that
   which should be charged to expense and that which should
   be shown as a deduction from sales. As a result, all trucking
   expense was deducted from sales, and the reports did not disclose that portion which represented operating expense. If
   this had been done, some officer should have noticed the
   high cost of unabsorbed trucking expense.

10. Customers' invoices did not indicate the exact routing of
    shipments when material was hauled from the warehouse
    to the loading platform or terminal of another trucker or
    railroad.

11. Checks were signed by the Treasury Department without
    reference to supporting papers.

12. Reports showing operating results of the business apparently
    had not been studied by department heads and executives.
    If this had been done, someone familiar with operations
    should have observed the failure to disclose the true cost of
    trucking.

13. Certain officers of the company insisted that the Controller
    should not have control over certain procedures and, although
    he was suspicious of the executive in charge of operations,
    and had been warned by his predecessor to insist on sound
    practices, the Controller did not insist upon taking such steps
    as are required in the effective discharge of his responsibilities.
    Until recently, the Controller had no Audit Division, and
    even then, the Audit Supervisor was denied access to certain
    records. Accounting personnel in branch offices was not
    directly responsible to the Controller, but rather reported
    to the branch manager. The Controller did not provide an
    accounting organization that was capable of carrying out his
    objectives.

The following additional facts were determined:

1. There was a very close contact between the executive in charge
   of operations, the shipper, and the owner of the trucking
   company.

2. The shipper received favors from the trucking company and had substantial amounts of cash in his possession.

3. Previously, when the company had owned its own trucks, it used trucks owned by the trucking company and permitted its own trucks to remain idle.

4. The company sold its own trucks to the contract trucker, which, it would appear, was part of a plan to force the company to favor the trucking contractor. Soon after this, most of the trucks were repurchased for use at another warehouse.

5. The shipper stated that the fictitious entries were made upon instructions of the executive in charge of operations, who later approved the invoice of the contract trucker. He further stated that lists of all fictitious entries were prepared in triplicate, that one was given to the executive and the other two were destroyed.

6. The executive admitted having received a large sum from the contract trucker during recent years but claimed this represented commissions for securing trucking business other than from his own company for the trucker. The owner of the trucking company admitted having made such payments as commissions but said they included payment for the trucking business of the subject company.

Payment of Fictitious Invoices

This embezzlement amounted to a huge sum, and it took place during a period of about a year. The culprit was cashier of the company and had been employed for many years. He had also been chief clerk of the voucher section of the Accounts Payable Department.

The mechanics of defalcation were as follows:

1. The cashier prepared checks payable to bona fide, well-known suppliers.

2. The checks would be supported by forged invoices and other forged documentary evidence for materials which were never received. Purchase requisitions and purchase orders were prepared with forged approval signatures. The stamp used by the Receiving Department was duplicated and imprinted on the purchase order.

3. The checks were entered in the voucher distribution record, from which postings were made to inventory accounts.
4. Upon presentation of the checks with the forged documents attached, two officers would sign and return the checks with the supporting documents to the cashier for mailing. The cashier then tore up the checks and the supporting documents.
5. The cashier then would make out other checks with supporting documents to several fictitious companies. These checks were also signed by two officers and returned to the cashier. The checks were for different amounts than those destroyed but aggregated the same.
6. The checks payable to the fictitious companies were not entered in the voucher distribution record, probably because the cashier feared that the posting clerks might question the names.
7. The names of the fictitious companies were registered by the cashier to do business in an Eastern state. These names resembled those of well-known suppliers.
8. The cashier also had letterheads and stationery prepared for the fictitious companies, as well as invoices, purchase requisitions, purchase orders, and Receiving Department approval stamp.
9. The cashier opened bank accounts for the fictitious companies, deposited the checks, and drew the funds out from time to time.

An inquiry made by another employe of the company in respect to one of the fictitious invoices led to the disclosure.

The company's procedure in preparing and signing checks was as follows:

1. All checks were prepared by the cashier.
2. Checks were signed by the Controller and countersigned by the Treasurer, Vice President, or President.
3. Supporting documents were attached to the checks when submitted for signature.
4. After the signatures were obtained, checks were returned to the cashier for mailing.
5. The cashier reconciled the bank accounts.

The above indicates glaring weaknesses in internal control. The cashier was in a position to introduce vouchers into the accounting routine, although he was responsible for preparing checks. The checks should never have been returned to the cashier for mailing. The reconciliation of bank accounts should have been delegated to some other employe not concerned with the preparation of checks.

The illegitimate disbursements were hidden in the inventory account, and although monthly reports were submitted showing a steady excessive increase in inventory, management was not sufficiently alert to observe this and initiate an investigation. Moreover, the taking of a physical inventory at least once a year would have disclosed an excess of book over physical inventory.

An interim cash examination either by internal auditors or public accountants would have uncovered this shortage, possibly in time to prevent it from reaching such proportions.

Defalcation Arising from Collusion between
Engineering Personnel and Outside Contractors

During World War II a large company subcontracted some of its war work. These subcontractors were furnished material and were reimbursed for their cost of labor, overhead, and profit based on hours spent on the work, which was of an experimental nature, the cost of which was not comparable with previous experience. However, the contracts required the certification of time spent by the company's engineers.

Some of the engineers, in collusion with some of the subcontractors, approved excessive hours spent on various contracts and received a "kickback." It also later developed that some contractors had padded their payrolls, supported by forged time tickets. In other cases, some contractors had relatives, not actually working, on their payrolls. It was also disclosed that some contractors were concerns organized by the company's own employes, who were also involved in the "split-ups" with the engineers.

The excessive payments could not have been discovered by normal auditing procedures. The bills were supported by contracts and apparently were properly approved by the company's engineers. Although the contracts provided for audit, there was no time during the war to conduct audits. Therefore, it was not until sometime later that it became evident from cost analysis by cost accountants that the company had been paying an exorbitant man hour cost on these contracts. Some of the subcontractors were approached, and one of them admitted what had transpired.

This case is a good example of collusion which sometimes occurs between company employes and outside contractors and suppliers. A similar scheme could be followed by technical personnel in respect to property additions. It illustrates the importance to management of carefully watching all costs.

Conclusion

The discovery of many fraudulent acts is accidental and often made by persons other than auditors. There is no doubt that many an embezzler is never caught. It is appropriate, therefore, to inquire as to why auditors do not discover more of these cases than they do. We have seen that the presence of an apparently good system of internal check does not always prevent fraudulent acts where management is not alert to recognize danger signals. It is also true that an audit program can never take the place of an alert and capable auditor. The auditor who goes through the audit motions mechanically and is guilty of lethargic checking will never discover fraud.

The study of fraud cases can be of practical value to the auditor as well as provide interesting reading of a professional character. The practical approach recommended is that the auditor give careful consideration to the weaknesses present in the cases reviewed, the methods used by the culprits, and danger signals available which permitted detection in order to be alert to recognize the same or similar conditions as he goes about his daily work. Where nothing has yet happened, he can make recommendations for correction of weaknesses, thus forestalling future trouble.

Not only must the auditor be alert and on his toes, but he must also have an inquiring mind and active imagination in order to recognize the possibilities of fraud in a given situation, and once given a clue, he must intelligently, diligently, and relentlessly build up his case.

CHAPTER 5

TYPES OF INTERNAL AUDITS

The greater portion of written matter devoted to auditing has been directed to the procedures for Balance Sheet audits, the purpose of which is to assure the auditor that (1) accepted accounting principles have been consistently applied, (2) all material facts are disclosed, and (3) an adequate basis exists for his opinion that financial statements are fairly presented.

In other words, contemporary literature on auditing has been concentrated largely from the viewpoint of the independent public accountant. Indeed, many of the articles, etc., purporting to address themselves to the subject of internal auditing have been actually more applicable to the work of the public accountants. This has been true because many persons, whose experience has been in public accounting, found themselves commissioned by their companies to establish and maintain internal audit programs, and in the absence of data on the most recent concepts of internal auditing as compared with public accounting, have not, in all cases, eliminated the duties of the public accountants from their programs.

In fact, we have heard internal auditors in some companies cite as an accomplishment the fact that the work performed by their staff during the past year reduced the fee of the company's public accountants by a significant sum. In our opinion, this admission, or assertion, is a definite indication of a lack of appreciation of the scope and responsibilities of the internal auditor. As outlined in other chapters of this volume, the activities of the internal auditor are, in the main, so divorced from the usual procedures of the public accountant that, if the internal auditor takes the time for such work, either (1) he is omitting the performance of audits which fall within his peculiar province and which would be of considerable benefit to the company, or (2) he is overstaffed.

As in the field of public accounting, several attempts have been made to classify audits into various types, such as test audits, complete audits, periodic audits, continuous audits, general audits, responsibility audits, departmental audits, feature audits, or functional audits. However, application of any definite terms on an absolute basis is difficult and probably unnecessary. It is more important to understand certain concepts of the type of audits the internal auditor performs.

1. In the first place, it should be recognized that two of the "types" of audits referred to above, namely, test audits and complete audits, are not really types but rather methods of conducting audits of any type. Any class of audit either can be performed by a complete check of all detail or may be confined solely to test checks. In our opinion, an audit requiring a complete check of detail should be indeed a rarity. Since the company's regular "line" organization should be directly and solely responsible for clerical accuracy, the auditor test checks to the extent necessary to satisfy himself that all the established procedures are adequate and are being adhered to and to ascertain that no significant degree of clerical inaccuracies are present. Since clerical accuracy, so controlled and test audited, will not normally be significant, and major discrepancies will usually result from misunderstanding or misapplication of principles, a test check will result in as good an audit as a complete coverage, and in many cases, better, since the auditor does not get so immersed in detail that he cannot "see the forest for the trees."

Such an approach, however, presupposes that an auditor knows when to be satisfied. If he is too easily satisfied, the test check may not be comprehensive enough to disclose all pertinent matters. On the other hand, if the auditor is too hard to satisfy he may waste time.

What, then, is a criterion for an appropriate degree of test checking? This is a subject which has received a considerable amount of treatment in public accounting articles and which is equally applicable to internal auditing. Unfortunately, however, no one has yet formulated any satisfactory substitute for the judgment of an experienced auditor, who through years of experience has gradually developed a "sense of touch" in this respect.

Any attempt to set up hard and fast rules on this subject would therefore be presumptuous on our part and subject to so many exceptions as to almost make them the rule. Purely as a flexible guide, and for whatever worth it may have for the reader, we set forth the following test checking criteria which may be considered reasonable as applied to one of the steps in an audit of an industrial payroll:

Step	% of Test Audit Coverage of One Selected Two-week Pay Period	Estimated Audit Hours Spent
Determine adequacy of control over reporting of time worked on an annual audit in a plant of 4,000 employes. Compare force reports, schedules, production reports, clock cards, maintenance job records, etc., to time reported. *Assume* employes are controlled under one of the following types of occupations:		
1. 50% of men on production incentive paid positions	5–10	10–20
2. 15% of men on maintenance job orders	5–10	7–10
3. 15% of men on other fixed crew jobs ..	5–10	6– 8
4. 20% of men on jobs not controlled through separate incentive production reports, maintenance job orders, or fixed crews	20–30	30–40

2. In the second place, it should be noted that two other so-called types of audits listed above, namely, periodic audits and continuous audits, are also not really types, but refer to the timing of the work rather than to its scope or content.   Audits of certain types of functions, payroll for example, are more adaptable to being audited periodically, that is, yearly, semi-annually, etc.   Certain functions, however, may be subject to audit at such frequent intervals that it is virtually a continuous audit.   As an illustration, audits of contractors' charges for large construction and maintenance jobs may require almost continuous coverage by the Audit Division in order that weaknesses in control which may develop during the various stages of the job are currently disclosed and corrective action is taken immediately.   On such large and relatively nonrecurring activities, audit after the work is fully completed is usually equivalent to locking the stable door after the horse is gone.

3. With those four designations (test, complete, periodic, and continuous) being eliminated in our attempt at classification of audits,

we come to general audits or responsibility audits. These two names we believe to be synonymous, but we prefer to use the term "responsibility audit." We have briefly referred to this type elsewhere in this volume. In such an audit an entire location, for which one man has the responsibility for its management, is subjected to a general review of the operation of all the activities under his jurisdiction. In other words, all the functions under that man's responsibility are being audited and appraised for the benefit of that man and his superiors.

An example of such an examination would be an audit of all the activities of the Accounting Department at a plant location of a company. The line work may be under the direct supervision of a man with a title such as Plant Controller, Plant Accountant, or Chief Accountant. The auditor would perform audits, such as outlined in the chapters in this volume, of all the functions under this supervisor's jurisdiction such as payroll, billing, cost accounting, or inventory control. Or the audit may cover all functions at the plant location which affect the financial affairs, together with such additional matters as production planning and incentive control, which may be under the direct jurisdiction of the Superintendent of the plant. In that case, the plant's Accountant and Superintendent would jointly confer in connection with the audit of their combined responsibility.

It can be readily seen that unless the plant is small the auditor would not be able to make a "responsibility" audit which would delve into all the functions on the most satisfactorily intensive basis in a reasonable time. When an audit covers too long a span of time, in our opinion, it loses some of its effect. Therefore, we recommend that responsibility audits be confined to those locations which, because of their small size or lack of complexity, enable such a comprehensive audit to be made in a reasonable time, or to those locations which, because of their distance from the audit headquarters, make it too expensive to visit often.

4. Therefore, we recommend that the greater part of the internal auditor's activities should be devoted to what we prefer to term "functional audits." These audits might also be called feature audits or even departmental audits, except that a function usually spans or affects several departments. We believe that the greatest benefit from the audit is achieved if the auditor follows all the processes

connected with a function of a business straight through from beginning to end without limitation as to the crossing of departmental
lines.   It is only in this way that a complete conception of the
internal control over the subject as a whole can be observed and
weaknesses or duplication detected.

Accordingly, the greater portion of this volume has been devoted
to a general description of the internal auditor's approach to various
functions of the business.   Just as certain locations are too large to
lend themselves to responsibility audits in which all functions are
reviewed in one audit; other locations may be so extensive that a
function contained in them may be too large to cover in one audit.
The field of the audit should then be broken down into segments.
For example, in audits of wage earners' incentive payments in a
steel mill, the function can first be broken down into departments:

Coke Works	Rolling Mills
Blast Furnace	Finishing Mills
Open Hearth	Shipping, etc.

The work in each department can then be broken down into
various phases of such an audit, such as:

1. Adequacy of control over reporting of production.
2. Compliance with terms of incentive plans.
3. Propriety of standards in use.
4. Study of profitability of plans, etc.

Attempting to establish a criterion for the proper degree of segregation of a function into separate audits is as subject to disagreement
as the degree of test checking and many other matters.   But again,
as a general guide, we shall commit ourselves and say that, in our
opinion, any single audit should not comprehend more than a team
of two auditors can satisfactorily examine in two months.

CHAPTER 6

ORGANIZATION OF INTERNAL AUDIT STAFFS

Scope and Authorities

In the formation of an audit staff it is important that its scope and authorities should be definitely determined and then specifically explained to all members of the organization by the company's President or its ranking administrative officer or body. In this connection, however, it must be realized that, to the extent that limitations are placed on the scope of the audit staff, management must recognize that audit coverage will be incomplete. As representative of the type of authorization necessary to eliminate confusion and misunderstanding and to assure cooperation with the program, we quote from a letter by the President of a large industrial firm addressed to all his chief executives.

> The Audit Division has full and free access to all departments and records, and there are no restrictions on their audit activities. I am sure this program will have the complete support of yourself and your entire organization.

His letter further states that the objectives of the audit program are, in part, as follows:

1. Determination that all procedures involved in the recording and physical handling of all or any of a company's business are such that a minimum possibility of loss exists, considering also the cost of providing protection.
2. Determination that all of a company's assets, liabilities, income, and expense have been accounted for, that value was received for expenditures, and that collectible income to which the company is entitled has been or will be received.
3. Determination of the extent of compliance with established rules and policies of the company.

With such a commission from the chief administrative officer, the scope of the Audit Division is clear.

Position of the Audit Staff in the Company Organization

A great deal of discussion has transpired, and more will ensue on this subject, and we predict that no firm answer acceptable to all will be determined. In our opinion, as long as the program has the support of the chief administrative officer or body along the lines set forth in the preceding paragraphs, the internal audit function can report to any member of management under whom the audit program can work smoothly and efficiently with support from all segments of management. In certain companies, depending upon the personalities involved or the over-all organizational structure, this may be the President, a Vice President, the Controller, the Treasurer, or (as stated in the Institute of Internal Auditors' Statement of Responsibilities of the Internal Auditor) "to any officer of sufficient rank as will assure adequate consideration and action on the findings and recommendations."

Some writers have advocated that the internal auditors should report directly to the board of directors. Although this may be feasible in some organizations, in our opinion it is not practical in most cases because we believe internal auditing can be most effective as a tool in the hands of active management.

Types of Audit Division Organizational Patterns

As might be expected, the organizational pattern of internal auditing varies considerably. We have terms, such as centralized, decentralized, resident auditors, and traveling auditors, which are found to have different meanings in various organizations. For example, one firm whose auditors formerly reported to a home office out of which they traveled recently established geographical groups under district supervisors who report to the home office supervisor. They say they are now "decentralized." Another firm who has exactly the same set-up currently says they have "centralized" auditing since all audit districts report to the home office, whereas, until recently, each subsidiary of the company had its own separate staff. Accordingly, we shall attempt to outline certain principles rather than discuss general terms.

First, in our opinion, all the audit activities of an organization should be controlled from one point regardless of whether the organization structure consists of plants and divisions or various separate subsidiary companies. After careful study and various experiences in that connection, we have concluded that the most beneficial auditing will result from such a centralization of responsibility for the following reasons:

1. Independent and unbiased reporting of all the facts is an essential requirement if top management expects to use internal auditing to the fullest advantage. The auditor is not independent if his salary and future depend on the actions of persons responsible for the functions being audited.

2. Few persons with extensive specialized knowledge of certain functions can be retained on any one plant, division, or subsidiary company staff since no one unit normally has enough auditing requiring such specialization to make it economical to retain such qualified men. With a broader scope of activities, the value of the audit staff to management is greatly enhanced by the extension of the use of experienced specialists. Our experience indicates this can be one of the outstanding advantages of that type of organization.

3. It is helpful to the various units of the company by providing an additional medium for an exchange of ideas and the making of comparisons.

4. It will reduce traveling expense and time, if properly set up, where geographical coverage of separate company divisions or subsidiaries overlaps.

5. Duplication of supervision and office space is also eliminated.

6. Such a centrally controlled audit staff in a diversified corporation provides opportunities to develop auditors with a broad experience normally obtainable only through public accounting experience. A central source of trained man power is provided, and the combined audit staff may be large enough to justify more adequate training programs.

7. Certain large public accounting firms, whose opportunity for observation of various methods in use have rendered them particularly well qualified to advance opinions, favor having all internal audit work done by a department attached to the central office.

8. In such a staff, the supervision of the audit function devotes its entire time and interests to auditing, while the primary

duties of divisional or subsidiary executives (having separate audit staffs reporting directly to them) are elsewhere and their interests are spread over many functions.

9. Centralized planning of audit programs will aid in performance of corporation-wide reviews of specific functions with uniformity of coverage.

10. Greater flexibility of the audit staffs is provided so that:
    a. Better distribution of qualified men throughout the various divisions can be secured.
    b. Rush or volume jobs can be better organized.
    c. Divisions top-heavy with experienced men can be equalized with those having a less satisfactory condition.

11. Because of the specialized experience necessary, it is often impossible to secure an adequately trained man for promotion to audit supervisory positions among the small group of auditors within a particular division or subsidiary. The result is that the general level of quality of the supervisory organization is lowered since the best person available in one unit is utilized rather than the best in the entire corporation.

12. More aggressive corrective action is normally noted where the Audit Division is a central office function.

Within such a general framework, the organization will vary as follows:

1. Where there is a concentration of the corporation's activities in a certain area, it will be most economical to establish a district headquarters. The auditors and their district supervisor will reside in that area, and traveling time and expenses will be reduced.

2. As the degree of concentration in certain areas is less, so will the advantage of district headquarters be reduced.

Some authorities have termed auditors permanently stationed in districts, as noted in paragraph 1 above, as resident auditors. This is probably a good term where the number of locations in the district is small; but where there are a considerable number of locations to be audited in a district and the auditors rotate among them and do not become too much of an integral part of any of the groups under audit, we do not feel that the disadvantages of a resident auditor set-up are encountered. In fact, if there are not a considerable number of locations and thus a lack of diversity of types of audits in a district, we question the establishment of a district since the auditors will truly be "resident" auditors, and consequently:

1. Tend to stagnate and accept existing conditions as proper.
2. Tend to become so close to the local management that they refrain from reporting violations of policy and procedure.
3. Tend to get their roots in the ground in a locality in which the choice of promotional opportunity is restricted and, therefore, foster too close relationship with those groups under audit.
4. Get a more restricted experience and development.

Organization within the Staff

Each staff must have, of course, at least one man with a broad accounting background and a good knowledge of the company's policies and operations who shall be designated as the supervisor. Such a supervisor will not normally become engaged in performing auditing work, but will confine his activities to planning, personnel, training, executive contacts, review of work done, and all purely supervisory duties. In our experience, the maximum number of auditors under such a supervisor, for best coverage, should be 30 to 35. Then for each 15 to 20 men a "working supervisor," who supervises several audits at all times while actually working on each, is recommended. This sub-supervisor corresponds to the rank of supervising senior, often used in the public accounting field.

We recommend the classification of auditors into three groups:

1. *Junior.* For less complicated phases under direct supervision, and assisting seniors.
2. *Semi-senior.* To handle complete audits of a limited variety, or to assist in complete audits of a wide variety.
3. *Senior.* To handle any and all phases of auditing; to be in complete charge of individual audits, involving supervision of others; to contact department supervisors audited; to discuss reports with responsible officials; and to train juniors and semi-seniors.

Considerable diversity of opinion can exist with regard to the number of each grade of auditor which should be found on a well-balanced staff.   Our experience indicates that approximately a third of the staff in each of the three grades yields the most satisfactory result as to actual performance of the work, economy, and development of man power in a steady flow.

Elsewhere in this chapter we briefly referred to specialists who can be utilized in larger staffs.   In our opinion, qualified men in various specialized fields will improve the quality and the quantity of audits performed by giving the auditor with only general experience guidance and concentrated education during the conduct of such audits. As examples:

Type of Specialist	*Type of Audit*
Industrial engineer	Incentive plans
Traffic specialist	Traffic audits
Cost accountant	Cost audits
Engineer	Construction costs
Operating man	Costs, sales pricing, incentives

Selection of Auditors

Many firms have set patterns, to which they attempt to adhere, for procuring auditors.   In our experience, no one pattern completely fills the needs.   Consequently, we are in favor of having the staff employ a mixture of varied backgrounds, as follows:

1. Young college or good business school graduates with little or no previous experience.
2. Young college or good business school graduates with several years of business experience, preferably with 2 to 4 years of public accounting.
3. Young college or good business school graduates who have had 2 to 5 years' experience in the company's own works' accounting department.
4. A few older, more experienced men who have had considerable experience in the company's own works' accounting department and are being given audit work for a specified period to assist in rounding out their experience.
5. A very few specialists, as previously commented upon.

Apart from the experience and educational backgrounds, as indicated above, it is even more important that the man has the ability to make a good impression in his contacts with the company personnel and his fellow staff members. Common sense in his dealing with people and his handling of auditing matters is the auditor's greatest asset.

Training and Placement of Auditors

"Doing the work" under intelligent and sympathetic supervision is after all the best training. A planned follow-up to see that each man gets the opportunity to work on each phase of the activities subject to audit over a reasonable period of time should be instituted. We believe it is a mistake to permit any of the auditors (with the exception of the few specialists) to concentrate virtually all their time on certain phases to the exclusion of others. All-round, executive-type men cannot be fully developed with that approach.

Other, less effective, training methods which can be employed with reasonable results are:

1. Training courses and meetings conducted by company employes or staff supervisors and specialists.
2. Evening courses at colleges and business schools.
3. Home study of audit manual or specified texts.

The audit staff supervisor should consider it an honor to be losing his best men, in a reasonable and steady flow, by promotion into the executive ranks of the company. He should make it his business to sell those men on his staff who are qualified into any opening which is developing. It is only by such a policy that the Audit Division will remain attractive to men of the caliber required for audit work.

Audit Manuals

An audit manual can assist in the performance of audits of specific functions, or it can stifle initiative to the extent that effective audits will not result. Accordingly, it is either beneficial or dangerous.

Audit manuals are dangerous if they are written in such detail that they constitute virtually a check list from which the auditor works like a robot. They can be used as a substitute for thinking, observation, imagination, initiative, and analysis and, as such, are dangerous.

However, if they are written as a guide to general approaches, as a kind of textbook from which the senior auditor can develop ideas and which will direct his thinking into all the channels of the problem, then they are beneficial.   In our opinion, the approach to specific functions contained in this volume, with slightly more specific adaptation to the individual company, would be a suitable style for an audit manual.

Relationship to Other Staff Activities

The field of the Audit Division is so broad that care must be exercised to give assurance that its activities are not encroaching on the functions of other staffs.   For example:

1. If a centralized tax staff reviews the work of company, division, or subsidiary personnel in the preparation of tax returns, any activity of the Audit Division in that connection would be an unnecessary duplication of the work of that trained, technical group.

2. Although the auditor must recommend certain principles and general methods to remedy conditions involving weaknesses in control, he should not, in our opinion, lay down specific procedures and methods, since:

    a. He would then be performing the duties and exercising the prerogatives of the procedure or methods staff, a specialized and technical field in itself.

    b. He cannot be completely unbiased in his future examination of the effectiveness of the procedures if he has instituted them himself.

CHAPTER 7

INTERNAL AUDIT REPORTS

Introduction

The internal audit report is the means by which the results of an audit are presented to management, and it is the latter's principal basis for judging the effectiveness of the audit, the Audit Division, and the individual auditor. Consequently, good form is a necessity. However, this form may vary somewhat with auditing subjects and their purpose. Thus, if the internal auditor reports direct to the controller, volume and style will differ from that of one who may report to stockholders, board of directors, or an executive committee. This is because top management will not be interested in details to the same extent as a line executive.

Although the recent trend of internal auditing has been toward a broader field, it is still necessary to recognize the place the internal auditor occupies in his respective company, his authority, and to whom he reports. As these and similar conditions vary, the form of reporting will vary.

If we consider physical form alone, it has been observed that reports may be oral, in memorandum, letter, or questionnaire form, or may be various types of technical reports.

Oral reports are used chiefly in small companies and are not satisfactory since they do not provide a record of the auditor's findings.

Memorandum reports are usually found where there is a close relationship between the internal auditor and his reporting authority, who is responsible for general policing and for satisfactory clerical and accounting standards. Inter-organization stationery is often used.

The letter report is usually rendered in multiple copies, with the original going to the reporting authority and the other copies to all other interested persons. It is used for functional audits or where an interim report is necessary to cover matters requiring prompt consideration by management.

The questionnaire type provides for "yes" and "no" answers to specific questions. This form is used where policing is wanted or where certain specific coverage is required. It does provide for uniformity of coverage and permits the use of less skilled personnel. Its disadvantage is that it encourages cut and dried auditing and does not encourage initiative.

Technical reports may be informal or professional. The style tends toward the conversational, and the order follows some fixed pattern, such as the balance sheet or income account classification. The form tends to be poor and invites a low valuation where the report is cheaply and poorly prepared.

For our present purposes we shall confine ourselves to a discussion of reports to be issued by an Internal Audit Division which is functioning as a true representative of management. This will require that sufficient time be taken to do a good job of report writing, as it is important that the audit reports reflect an attitude of constructive service to management with a clearly worded presentation of well-founded facts and carefully considered recommendations.

Preparation of the Report

Avoid complicated numbering and lettering systems in setting forth the comments. It is preferable to set the entire report up in paragraphs of consistent width, numbered consecutively in Arabic numerals throughout the report. Long schedules should be used only where it is impracticable to present necessary information in written or graphic form. Average readers will skip over long columns of detailed figures. Where it is unavoidably necessary to insert such details, an attempt should be made to condense the information in a graphic presentation if possible.

A brief definition of the scope of the audit should be covered in each report so that the reader will not get an exaggerated idea of the work done.

In the selection of audit comments it will be found that many of the findings in the average audit are of relatively minor importance. Generally, it is not difficult to determine what is a major finding which should be reported in all cases. Borderline cases should be carefully considered as to whether they are major or minor. Minor errors may be classified as follows:

1. Those which result from nonrecurring clerical inaccuracies or procedure failures should be excluded from the report. It is sufficient to bring such matters to the attention of local management during the course of the audit, with proper notation in the work papers.
2. Minor errors which indicate a weakness in control or a continuing procedure violation should be reported even though of only nominal importance. Care should be exercised to convey, in the handling of the report, that it is realized that the point is a minor one, but that it is being reported to emphasize a general condition in need of corrective action.

With regard to the important findings, all audit comments should include any necessary background to present adequately the facts so that they can be readily comprehended by executives not dealing with the problem in their daily activities. Fundamental causes of unsatisfactory conditions should be determined and clearly set forth since a complete understanding of such causes is necessary before corrective action can take place.

The comments should present the facts disclosed by the audit by reference to specific cases, rather than to generalities. Also, if possible, the estimated amount involved should be stated in order to stress the financial significance of important matters and to enable the auditor and reader better to judge those matters which are insignificant. This is not intended as an attempt to value auditing in dollars, but rather to center attention on the important findings. Estimates of the effect of the disclosure on future operating results should be properly earmarked as estimates only and should be presented on an annual basis.

Comments should reflect an understanding of major problems in connection with the conditions disclosed, and recognition should be given to the steps taken by management to correct or alleviate the conditions commented upon.

Comments should not be confined to those matters which are unsatisfactory. Situations which are handled extremely well should be briefly noted, and if the situation is generally well controlled, or if there are no major findings, we should say so.

The sequence of report items should follow the general rule of presenting the most important items first. However, all comments applying to a particular topic, or a subdivision of a topic, must be grouped together.

The importance of correct grammatical construction and careful selection of words as to meaning cannot be overemphasized.

The audit report is usually the only point of contact between the auditor and various levels of management for whom the work is intended. Good writing is characterized by grammatical correctness, clarity, conciseness, and force.

1. *Grammar.* Generally, ungrammatical reports are the result of carelessness, rather than ignorance. It hardly needs saying that nothing but a poor impression can result from an ungrammatical report; for it would be illogical to expect the reader to attach a greater importance to the report than that manifested by the writer, and sloppy grammar implies that the latter ascribed small importance to the matter communicated.

2. *Clarity.* A complete grasp of the subject to be conveyed is the foremost essential of clear writing. Therefore, the auditor should assure himself that he is thoroughly familiar with all the facts before he starts to write. The auditor should strive for words that express his exact meaning without, however, losing the simplicity obtained from the use of plain business English.

3. *Conciseness.* Conciseness in reports is desirable so that the reader may be brought face to face with the facts at a minimum expenditure of the reader's time and effort. A comment of a few words is not necessarily a concise one. It is far better to convey something useful than, by too stringent skimping, convey nothing at all.

4. *Force.* Usually, if the other elements of good construction, namely, good grammar, clarity, and conciseness, are observed, the auditor will have gone a long way toward making his writing forceful.

Simplicity and sincerity are the greatest allies of forceful expression. The thought is the important thing, and efforts to embellish the thought with extravagance more often weakens than strengthens. There is strength in understatement. For example, the statement "very inadequate control" is not so forceful as "inadequate control." We should specifically refrain from any wording which conveys any impression of having a double meaning or being barbed comments.

In addition to good composition, the auditor should choose diplomatic language which will be calculated not to arouse unnecessary animosities. Tactful and considerate choice of words will accomplish more than blunt and harsh language. Misinterpretations may be avoided by a very careful selection of words. An inoffensive approach can be accomplished without omitting important facts. Thus, careful wording will go a long way toward nullifying the intrinsically critical nature of audit work.

All reports should be written on the job so that any missing information and obscure points may be cleared up without delay.

Audit Recommendations

The audit report should attempt to set forth recommendations for the general practices necessary to improve the controls. These recommendations must be practical. Although the auditor does not need to work out the detail procedures or even to work out, in all cases, the individual steps in a corrective procedure, he should have well formulated in his own mind just how the corrective action can be secured. If the auditor can see no practical solution to the problem which will improve on the present method of handling, then no change should be recommended. There may be times when the auditor observes situations which he feels will be of interest to management, but does not feel qualified to make recommendations. On such subjects he should merely present a statement of facts for management's consideration and indicate that it is a point of information only.

Review and Clearance of Reports

Supervisors should not review reports too hurriedly. They should be considered from the point of view of the busy executive whom you want to read the report. He should be able to understand it without previously having close contact with the matter and without having anybody at his elbow to explain it. It must be practical and interesting so that he will take time to read it and then act upon it. It must be definite and complete so that he will not have to seek further information on the subject.

The audit report should then be discussed with the supervisors directly responsible for the function or department examined. For best effect, in our opinion, the comments should be made a part of the audit report itself and should be placed throughout the report following the audit recommendations on each point. Accordingly, when top management reads an item in the internal audit report, they have the facts, the audit recommendations, and the comments of the local supervision.

Cooperation of top management is therefore necessary to assure forthright, complete comments from local management. These comments should (1) tell what steps are to be taken to correct the condition or to conform to the recommendations, or (2) state any disagreement with the auditor's recommendations or opinions, and the reasons therefor. However, there should be no disagreement as to the facts. If in the discussion in connection with securing the comments such a disagreement occurs, both parties should examine the matter carefully and agree on the facts before the management comments are written.

If more than one division of local management is affected by the audit recommendations, comments should be received from each. However, local management should not be requested to comment on matters which are outside their jurisdiction or responsibility. Local clearance being completed, clearance in a similar fashion should be made in sequence through any intermediate management levels before the report is considered cleared for submission to top management. This is a very important principle since the various management levels will recognize that the Audit Division is performing its function "on top of the table" and is not spying or "going over their heads."

Summary Letters

From each report a summary letter should be prepared and submitted together with the report.

Summary letters should present all the significant matters in such a manner that top management can secure a thorough understanding of all the important topics covered in the audit report itself. This is undoubtedly the most difficult phase of the preparation of the report. There are very few audit reports which cannot be summarized adequately in a few pages at the most, and it is certain that the best way to get action from top management is to give them well-prepared "nutshell" summaries. Although the summary letter should convey to the reader a comprehension of the adequacy of control of the function audited, great care must be exercised that nothing is included in the summary which does not appear in the body of the audit report itself and which various levels of management have not had the opportunity to review and comment upon.

An extra copy of all summary letters should be submitted to the Audit Supervisor for reference to the public accountants.

Issuance and Follow-up

The report should be attractive and easy to read. A duplicating process should be used which will make clear copies. A clear, black impression on good paper is preferred, with a neat but not gaudy binding, and a minimum of title and index sheets.

Audit reports should be distributed to such top officials in a company as requested by the controller. Sufficient copies should be provided so that the controller can furnish the Accounting and Operating managements of the local plants or offices with copies, in order that they will be assured that their comments have been reported as agreed upon during the course of the audit.

With respect to follow-up, it must be remembered that the Audit Staff has no line or administrative authority in connection with the correction of their findings. However, it is the duty of the Audit Staff to determine what disposition is finally made of all recommendations so that management can be assured that their desires in this respect have been carried out. A suitable form of internal organization should be set up so that adequate record of follow-up activity is maintained.

No audits which are started should be "left up in the air." Adequate reasons should be furnished for the discontinuance of an audit and the failure to submit a report.

In most instances an audit report may be destroyed upon completion of the following audit report covering the same location, function, office, department, etc. However, audit reports containing recommendations which have not been acted upon should be retained until action is taken, unless the succeeding report contains the precise details of the initial reference.

CHAPTER 8

PLANNING AND MAKING THE AUDIT

The Over-all Program

1. Particular attention must be paid to the conventional responsibilities of the auditor, such as the prevention of significant and costly failures of internal control in such functions as cash, payroll, billing, and accounts payable. Many of the audits in respect to these functions will not appear to be productive, but they will be of psychological value and will reduce the possibility of failures in the system of internal control. These functions should be examined about once a year. Extent of coverage and method of approach are set forth below. Since many of the matters included in the foregoing types of audits are necessarily a part of the work performed by independent public accountants during the course of their balance sheet audit, it is necessary to coordinate the programs in respect to these functions very carefully with their manager at the beginning of the year before any of the work is done, in order that:

    a. Any of the work which they care to perform will not be duplicated.

    b. Their work will be augmented to the extent that has been mutually agreed desirable.

    c. Where each staff is doing a portion of the work, the timing feature will be coordinated.

2. In addition to these more or less basic responsibilities, the audit staff must perform a service to management with regard to all operations of the company's affairs having a bearing on the financial status of the company. This comprehends a very wide scope, and it would be uneconomical, as well as virtually impossible, to have sufficient auditors to cover all the items subject to audit in any brief period of time. Therefore, it is imperative that a very careful selection be made of the items to be placed on the audit program. This

is one of the most difficult jobs, and in so doing, the following matters should be borne in mind:

a. Responsibility audits should be confined to small outlying locations in which the time and expense of traveling do not warrant frequent visits and to occasions when management desires to obtain a bird's-eye view of the general effectiveness of certain responsibilities. This restricted use of responsibility audits is advisable because of their tendency to cover too broad a field and to sacrifice a sufficient intensity of coverage to permit an adequate evaluation of conditions.

b. Functional audits which permit an intensive coverage have produced the best results. In determining which functions or portions of functions are to be audited, concentration should be primarily on those in which internal control weaknesses could result in actual losses. Generally, those audits concerned merely with account distribution or review of compliance to established procedures should be considered as secondary audits which must wait until adequate coverage of the primary functions is completed. Of course, during the review of these primary functions, any deviations from general accounting procedures should be noted and reported. Finally, functional audits should not become too large in scope, or take too long to complete because coverage then becomes too thin, as in responsibility audits.

c. A general over-all review of the internal control of a company's operations should assist in the selection for audit of those functions where internal check is weakest and where, consequently, the danger of loss is greatest. However, if it soon becomes apparent that little benefit is to be derived from the audit, it should be broken off promptly.

d. There are many functions, most of which have a direct bearing on the company's profit, in which control is lodged in departments other than Accounting; i.e., control of appropriation expenses by the Engineering Department, control of pricing by the Sales Department, and control of timekeeping reporting by the Operating Department. A study of these departments and others, such as Traffic or Purchasing, offers an opportunity for the Audit Division to do a productive job for management. Again these audits must be approached, not from the viewpoint of adherence to clerical procedures, etc., but rather from the viewpoint of effective internal control and adherence to sound business practices which will result in the lowest cost to the company.

e. Trends in Accounting, Statistical, and Cost reports should be reviewed and used to obtain leads as to where time can be spent to the best advantage. For example, in a case widely publicized in the newspapers, it was found that an excessive increase in inventory, as indicated by monthly reports, was ignored by the management, although investigation would have resulted in prompt disclosure.

3. Audit Supervisors should appraise the results of each audit and determine which are unproductive and the reasons therefor, such as:

a. Whether the audit has been searching enough to reveal unsatisfactory conditions.

b. Whether the auditor actually got into the core of the problem, or merely reviewed the obvious matters.

c. Whether the auditor was capable, on the basis of his knowledge and experience, to perform such a job.

If it is found that a given situation is being so well handled that an audit report is not productive of material improvement, consideration should be given not only to assigning less time to future audits of this function, but also to the continuance of progress already being made in the correct application of internal controls.

4. Time should be allotted to reviewing procedures from an internal control viewpoint before they are installed and otherwise, generally, to collaborate with the procedure staff and line management.

5. Members of the audit staff should be assigned to various jobs, in order to broaden their experience.

Subjects for Audit

1. *Standard Reports.* Periodical review of all standard reports will suggest many subjects for audit. The Audit Division should analyze these reports and understand the nature of the transactions included in them. It should ascertain the sources of entries and the procedures involved in originating, recording, and controlling them. It should be familiar with the sources of all income and expense. It is not sufficient to know that all expenditures for a certain class

of expense were charged to the proper accounts and that the expenditures were properly authorized; the Audit Division should also ascertain that the company received full value for the expenditure and that the company benefited from it. There is no limit to the extent to which these subjects can be extended.

2. *Contracts and Agreements.* The Audit Division should review contracts and agreements. These will provide many subjects for audit. In many cases, these subjects will represent transactions on which there are no regular controls or procedures and, therefore, are in need of auditing more than routine transactions.

3. *Procedure Instructions.* These should all be reviewed carefully to see that they provide adequate control of the company's assets, income, and expense. Review should suggest audits, not only of the execution of the procedure, but also of related subjects.

4. *Correspondence.* Occasional review of the correspondence received by various departments will suggest subjects for audit.

5. *Meetings*
   a. Audit Supervisors should attend all accounting staff meetings and thus gain information that should be helpful.
   b. Accounting officers should keep Audit Supervisors advised on subjects discussed in executive meetings and in conversations with other personnel.
   c. Audit Supervisors should maintain close contact with their staffs. This should be done by:
     (1) Field visits—working with the staff on audits.
     (2) Conferences—staff conferences when advisable.

6. *Plant Visitations.* Auditors should occasionally observe the physical operation of the plant. Such visits will enable them to make more intelligent audits and will also suggest further subjects to be audited.

7. *Periodicals, Books, etc.* Auditors should read current literature on auditing and accounting. When possible, Audit Supervisors should attend meetings with other company auditors and accountants.

Preparation for the Audit

A general program of work, which will provide for sound and beneficial objectives, should be prepared for each audit. It is not possible to prepare a complete audit procedure, nor is it desirable to do so, as individual thinking would be restricted during the course of the audit. Therefore, an audit manual should be used as a reminder only and not as a complete program.

An adequate background should be obtained by reviewing previous audit reports and work papers. In this connection, permanent files should be maintained and used, especially for those audits which are recurrent.

It is necessary to become familiar with current procedures applicable to the function or functions being audited. This will enable the auditor to proceed more efficiently, to reduce the time spent on the audit, and to require less time of the line personnel. Procedure deviations will be recognized more quickly, and analysis may reveal weaknesses of internal control which can be concentrated on during the audit.

Information concerning procedures may be obtained from such sources as:

1. Procedure staff surveys.
2. Procedures and letters of instructions which have been issued by the various departments of a function. (The auditor should familiarize himself with letters which may have been issued by Sales, Engineering, Production Planning, and Accounting Departments, etc.)

Extent of Test Checking

This is a matter of judgment of the senior auditor in charge. No exact percentages can be safely recommended. However, a supervisor should be satisfied that the senior's judgment is good.

There is opportunity here for preventing the expenditure of too much time in checking details. Unjustified duplication of line work is to be avoided. Generally, only enough of the detail should be checked to satisfy the auditor as to the principles involved. For instance, where an excessive number of errors are found, he is not primarily interested in them as such, but he is concerned with the principle involved—the lack of control over accuracy. The problem is to determine how to establish the necessary control to the greatest extent feasible at a reasonable cost.

Supervisors should make sure that there is no contradiction in the minds of their staff members between adequate coverage and avoidance of excessive detail. Adequate coverage should always be the primary goal, but it can be attained without excessive detail checking.

Management's Viewpoint

An objective point of view of the audit subject should be taken. If the auditor were the manager of the department, what would he want to know? Management will recognize the audit as the service it is intended to be and not as a check-up if the approach is from management's viewpoint.

Rotation of Auditors

Auditors should be rotated to a reasonable degree on recurring audits. A fresh point of view will tend to outweigh the disadvantage of breaking in a new man.

Correct Methods

Organizational lines must be carefully observed. Contacts must be made and information secured through supervisors. This rule should especially be observed in a plant, with the general superintendent having full knowledge of the audit objectives and being in general agreement as to the contacts to be made.

In order to be of service to management, the auditor should be concerned with obtaining the facts. The auditor's aim should be to avoid being regarded as a critic, but rather he should strive to assist supervisors in getting their particular responsibilities into the best possible condition.

Working Papers

1. It is essential that working papers be complete, insofar as support of the audit report is concerned. This is not only important to the Audit Supervisor, but also to the public accountants who may scrutinize them in the course of their annual audit.

2. Uniformity of working papers should be worked for throughout the Audit Division in respect to the following points:

   a. The same kind of paper should be used.

   b. All schedules should be indexed and cross-indexed.

   c. Clearly outlined work programs should be written up and initialed. The programs should be indexed to the relative work schedules.

   d. A brief summary of findings should be filed in front of the papers.

e. Upon completion of each engagement, the senior-in-charge should prepare a memorandum of work which he recommends be done on the next engagement or of things which should be followed up or investigated. This memorandum should be reviewed by the Audit Supervisor and a copy placed in the report file so that it will be reviewed prior to the next audit.

f. Working papers should be preserved until the next audit, after which any parts that will be of current interest should be transferred to a permanent file.

g. A permanent file should be built up over a period of years and should always be reviewed preliminary to starting a current audit.

h. Schedules should indicate exactly what work was done. This is facilitated by good planning of the schedule and the use of complete footnotes.

i. Working papers should be limited to essentials. A company's records or reports should not be copied.

j. Each schedule should be properly headed, showing the name, responsibility or department, subject matter, date, and initials of the staff member preparing it. No more than one type of subject matter should be covered on each sheet.

CHAPTER 9

CASH—FROM INTERNAL AUDITING STANDPOINT

The major objectives in an audit of cash and an examination of related transactions comprise the determination that:

1. Cash at the beginning and end of the audit period was in fact on hand and available and that it is in agreement with the books and balance sheet of the company.
2. All possible sources of cash are investigated and that controls are in existence to prevent its misappropriation before and after it has been recorded in the books of account.
3. All expenditures of company funds can be justified and are supported by properly approved evidence and that value has been received.
4. The system of internal control is so established that no one person is in a position to influence directly or indirectly all the records relating to receipt or disbursement of funds.

Before proceeding with a discussion of internal audit techniques, one caution is appropriate. The application of all the techniques contained in accounting literature would not of itself constitute a verification. It is requisite that the auditor carefully consider the aspects of each point audited to determine the existence of fraud or its possibility at some time in the future and then to see that proper controls are in effect or are instituted. This thought arises from the recollection of audits that failed to attain their objectives because the auditor had occupied himself with the application of mechanical techniques and hastened through his assignment without benefit, so to speak, of a stock taking—"a thinking out of objectives" —and a plan for their attainment.

Scope and General Preparation

1. It is important to determine at the outset what accounts and records should be audited. The choice should not be confined to

75

those accounts and records which deal directly with the actual recording of cash transactions, but may include stock records, royalty agreements, rental contracts, etc.

The auditor should determine the funds and accounts over which the responsibility under audit has full control. All funds, together with any other asset, such as securities, which can readily be converted into cash, should be audited simultaneously. The reason, which is obvious, is to prevent the transfer of funds from one account to conceal a shortage in another. If it is found, for example, that the petty cash custodian maintains a payroll working fund, then for the audit to achieve its end, both funds should be included in the examination. Similarly, if other related accounts such as deposits, savings bonds, or employe accounts receivable are maintained or affected by the same responsibility, they must be examined at the same time. On the other hand, where more than one fund is involved, an audit of the headquarters' treasury may, in respect to branch or plant funds, safely confine itself to a confirmation of the balance or balances controlled by the respective custodians. In such a case, a satisfactory verification of a particular fund or account may be made. However, there is no cut and dried rule, and the scope of each cash audit must be dictated by the prevailing circumstances.

2. Proper preparation is essential. Complete surprise may be desirable. The custodian's funds may consist of cash on hand and in several banks, cash at more than one location, a payroll working fund or advance account, or collections from miscellaneous accounts receivable. Statements and canceled checks must be secured from the banks, and balances must be confirmed. The services of more than one auditor may be required. A thoughtful appraisal of the prevailing circumstances and a careful planning of the requirements are essential to proper coverage.

Verification of Cash Balances

This involves the physical inventory of currency and vouchers pending reimbursement and a verification of cash in banks, which includes confirmations and reconciliation of the bank statements with the company's records and accounts:

1. *Cash Balances.* Immediately before beginning the audit, a record should be made of the first unissued check and of the last receipt issued to establish the point to which the reconciliation should

be made. The count of currency should then be made and listed. When the currency on hand is large, it is desirable that the count be detailed by denomination in the work papers. A detailed listing of all items other than cash should be made and subsequently verified to make certain that they are bona fide. Checks included in the fund should be carefully examined for date, payee, maker, amount, and where significant, the endorsements. Pay attention to details. Old checks, checks payable to the order of the company or the fund custodian, and those for abnormally large amounts should be questioned. Payroll checks bearing the endorsement of the paymaster or treasurer should be earmarked for conclusive follow-up. Such endorsement may reveal that unclaimed pay checks are being fraudulently cashed by the paymaster or treasurer. To determine conclusively that checks are good, the auditor should insist that they be deposited or cashed immediately. When this is done, the auditor should make inquiry at the bank within a reasonable time to determine whether any checks were refused by the bank of the maker.

Checks payable to the order of the company should not be included with petty cash funds. When found, the obligations which the makers intended to discharge should be ascertained and their liquidation carefully traced through the records.

The only checks payable by the company which have a proper place in the petty cash fund are those issued to reimburse or increase the fund. In such cases, the checks should not be payable to the order of Cash, but to the specific order of the cashier as custodian of the fund.

The practice of cashing payroll and personal checks should be prohibited. The reason for this is that the deposit of such checks in a fund bank account affords the custodian with the means of liquidating any checks of which he has come into improper possession. If it is the company's policy to render cashing service to employes, the auditor should satisfy himself that the custodian came into possession of such checks through cashing them for the designated payee and that the endorsement is genuine. In a recent case, a cashier was used as the paymaster on pay days, because of the location of his office at a convenient place where the employes could line up and because of the company's desire to use someone not connected with the Payroll Department to distribute the checks. Unclaimed pay checks were left in his possession for a period of 30 days. In addition, the checks were payable to the order of the employe "or bearer" to facilitate ease in cashing them in the community. There was nothing to prevent the cashier from cashing or depositing them and then abstracting an equivalent amount from his cash drawer. He was able to peculate considerable sums before he was detected.

Advances to employes should be carefully investigated for approval and authenticity. The best proof of their validity is to confirm them directly with the debtor. In this respect, the auditor should not be impressed with the importance of the official involved. Frequently there is no limitation as to the amount of advance granted, for example, to a president or vice president of a company. When an official has an excessive amount outstanding, the auditor should not fail to investigate whether it is legitimate or whether the amount has been increased by the cashier to cover deficiencies, because of his knowledge that no effort will be made to question the official involved. The confirmation of all outstanding advances due from major executives is recommended.

At the completion of the cash count and examination of supporting documents, the custodian should be requested to secure reimbursement for paid bills and petty cash slips in the fund. The reimbursement of such vouchers should subsequently be checked by the auditor.

2. *Bank Balances.* Bank statements and canceled checks should be secured directly from the bank as of the same date the cash funds are counted. By securing them directly from the bank, the auditor can eliminate the tedious examination of bank stamps, perforations, etc., necessary to make certain that no deletions, substitutions, or forgeries of the statements and checks have been made after they were received from the bank.

Canceled checks should be compared to and checked off on the check register or cash disbursement book, or the check book if it is used to serve the function of a register. Make certain that comparison is made to the record to which the check of postings and footings will be made. For example, in the reconciliation of payroll bank accounts the comparison should be made to the amounts shown on the payroll itself, in the Net Amount Due column.

Checks of prior period should be compared with the books and the prior listing of outstanding checks.

Particularly note that, irrespective of datings, all paid checks are recorded within the period ending as of the reconciliation date. One of the most common ways to cover a fraud is to deposit a company check in the bank account which is short and then to enter the check in the records of a subsequent period.

Within a reasonable time after the reconciliation date the auditor should secure a second bank statement with canceled checks for the interim period. This is done, not for the purpose of making another reconciliation, but to test certain components of the original reconciliation. By comparing the checks returned with the list of outstanding checks it is possible to determine whether the list, as originally prepared, was complete. Also, a check of deposits listed on the bank statement will indicate whether any portion has been charged back by the bank and reveal any undisclosed deposits in transit. In this connection, it is well to bear in mind that credits for deposits are conditional to satisfactory collection of individual items by the bank. The auditor should trace the deposits in transit to entry as of the next day, in the second bank statement, to ascertain that they were bona fide.

The importance of checking footings of cash receipts and disbursement records cannot be minimized. It must not be considered a clerical chore. A great number of fraudulent transactions are covered up by the simple expedient of plugging a cash book total and forcing it into agreement with the control account.

Postings should be traced to the subsidiary records, such as individual accounts receivable. A representative number of credits to customer accounts should be traced to the books of original entry and trial balances prepared, or checked, to detail accounts. One of the most crude, yet common, type of fraud is for a bookkeeper to confiscate a customer's payment and record it as a credit to the customer's account to avoid the customer's complaint. Failure to verify footings in cash books, or check a trial balance, would make the auditor, in turn, an additional victim of the fraud.

Confirmation of balances and other matters is an established and highly important audit routine. Confirmations from banks should include such things as notes or checks held for collection; liabilities or contingent liabilities of the company on any indebtedness of the company or others; authorized signatures and restrictions on balances, deposits, endorsements, and withdrawals; safe deposit boxes in the name of the company and existing instructions as to persons entitled to access thereto.

Confirmation of customer and employe accounts receivable and debit accounts payable often reveal uncredited payments. The auditor should arrange to review customers' statements before they are mailed, making certain that the detail agrees with the customers' accounts. He should also mail customers' statements personally.

The audit completed to this point will have adequately attained the first objective of a full cash audit, namely, the verification that the book balance agrees with the funds available.

However, such a determination is no basis for assurance on other and more important points. An account with a balance of $10,000 may be comprised of receipts and disbursements aggregating $100,-000 for the period under review. Payroll expenditures may very well run to several million dollars; yet the balance in the payroll account as of the date of audit may be insignificant. Too many auditors end their examination at this point, whereas it only constitutes the end of the first phase.

Verification of Receipts

The functions of receiving cash and disbursing funds should be segregated and not subject to control by the same person.

The verification of cash receipts is usually the most important part of the audit and at the same time the most difficult to accomplish. The inclusion of a cash receipt in a deposit entered in the cash book is no guarantee that the company will receive the benefit. Thus, an item entered in the cash receipt book, but retained by the custodian, could be cleared from the cash balance by issuing a company check for the same amount. Bank certified copies of detailed deposit slips offer a good start toward reasonable coverage of this point. A comparison of the deposit, per the cash book, with a copy of the deposit slip certified by the bank would disclose that the item confiscated had not originally been deposited.

Cash discounts allowed by creditors and to customers should be verified to determine that they conform to the rates established and that they were earned. Discount may be credited to a customer, when it has not been taken, or the amount of discount may be inflated. In one case, a customer paid a bill in cash, on which he was not entitled to and did not take cash discount. The bookkeeper credited the customer for the correct amount, entered the discount as being taken, but which he pocketed, and deposited the cash for the net amount. Several peculations of this type were discovered because of the auditor's persistence in finding out why discounts were allowed on payments received after due dates.

Receipts should be deposited promptly. It is desirable that someone other than the one who prepared the deposit take the receipts to the bank. Shortages may be concealed indefinitely by applying a portion of one day's receipts to those of another.

All persons handling cash should be bonded.

When a request is made to delay the audit to enable an employe to bring his records up to date, the auditor should be wary lest it is but an excuse for time to cover up deficiencies.

The verification of cash receipts is closely related to that of sales and other income. The determination that cash received has been properly recorded and deposited in the accounts is no assurance that the company has received all the revenue to which it is entitled.

The auditor should endeavor to discover all possible sources of miscellaneous income. An analysis of miscellaneous income reported is helpful in determining unusual sources. A review of the card of accounts usually indicates special types of revenue, such as interest, royalties, rentals, and commissions. Sources of income from the disposal of by-products, scrap, waste, and defective material can sometimes be detected, when they are not stated in the accounts, by a physical inspection of the plant and grounds. Sometimes waste and by-products are given away when it would be possible to secure revenue through disposal.

The auditor should make certain that interest, royalties, rentals, and other similar types of revenue are controlled and accrued on the books and not recorded only when received. Interest collected should be proved for accuracy, and the rates used should be the agreed to or legal rates.

Where rentals are a source of income, the auditor can test the amount reported by determining the period of occupancy times the rental charged.

Postage peculations, while usually in small sums, amount to importance over a period of time. The use of postage meters may be desirable. The auditor should examine vouchers, for the replenishing of postage funds, for reasonableness.

The auditor should determine whether the cashier, salesman, or Credit Department employes make collections on delinquent accounts or those which have been charged off and, if so, that they cannot misappropriate their collections.

Where prenumbered receipt forms are in use for the handling of employe or local sales, the full sequence for the period selected should be accounted for. However, the auditor should not assume that because a full sequence has been accounted for, all revenue has been reported. In a recent case, an employe was able to defraud his employer of a sizable amount by overlapping prenumbered receipt forms. Owing to the practice of the Accounting Department of "breaking off" the sales a week before month-ends, to expedite closings, the dishonest employe was able to apply receipts of the following month to cover the shortage. Another weakness in internal control, in this case, was failure of the cashier to pick up collections from the collecting employe. The fraud was discovered only when the income for one month was not sufficient to furnish enough cash to make up the accumulated deficiency.

The auditor should review existing instructions and established routines to detect loopholes and to make certain that they do not furnish positive means of affording an employe opportunities to accomplish fraudulent acts.

In a company operating a restaurant, a comparison should be made of cash register tapes and meal tickets. A count of the number of diners, times the average price per meal, compared to the cash receipts for the day or meal often reveals serious shortages. In a company-operated store, a comparison may be made of the retail value of the cost of sales with amount of store income. Where scrap is a recurring and consequential by-product of the company's operations, the amount of tonnage shipped might be determined from freight bills and the aggregate tonnage compared with that for which income was reported.

The auditor should thoroughly investigate return sales and allowances and returns and allowances to vendors.

Credit for customer returns should be checked to receiving reports, bills of lading, and inventory records. Returns to vendors should be similarly checked.

Cash receipts can be confiscated and fictitious credits made to customers' accounts by credit memorandums or journal entries. Credit memorandums should be approved by the chief accounting officer and by responsible persons in the Sales, Purchasing, or Operating Departments who possess the knowledge that the return has actually been made, or who are in a position to pass upon the propriety.

To disclose other points to check, the auditor must consider with some imagination the probabilities of fraud afforded by the attending circumstances. In this, the auditor's opportunities are unlimited, as no exhaustive listing of income sources is possible.

Verification of Expenditures

The auditor should determine what duties, relating to cash, have been delegated to officers and other employes of the company. He should ascertain to the best of his ability whether the persons who have the authority to approve vouchers for payment, sign and countersign checks, are in a position to influence the disbursements of funds for fraudulent purposes. The auditor should remember that this is a cardinal principle of internal control. No one person, particularly one in the position of a check signer, should be in a position to record transactions on the books of account, directly or through the preparation or approval of a basic document, and approve the amounts for payment.

The auditor should examine the routines and procedures step by step and, if possible, actually observe the preparation and approval of vouchers and the signing of checks. In this way the effectiveness of the procedures leading up to the actual signing and mailing of checks can be determined. For example, if a voucher is stamped "paid" before the check is signed, it might be possible for it to be submitted again for payment. It is desirable that vouchers be submitted simultaneously with the checks to the check signers, who should examine them to such an extent as to assure themselves that the approvals were made carefully and that, from the evidence on hand, the payment is in order. The checks should then be mailed by other persons direct to the payees.

The signing of blank checks should be strictly forbidden. This is a common practice and defeats the entire system of internal check and control. It presents an open opportunity for fraud. The auditor should severely criticize the practice.

Minutes should be reviewed to determine that all bank accounts used are authorized. A list should be prepared of check signers and co-signers authorized by the Board of Directors. Actual specimen signatures should be compared with those on checks to see that they are in accord with those authorized and as indicated in the banks' confirmation letters.

Checks payable to cash, fund custodians, the company, and to banks should be carefully traced and fully explained. Checks for unusually large amounts should be traced to the original documents. It is desirable that checks be limited in amount.

Expense reports should be carefully examined and checked to supporting detail, such as hotel bills, Pullman stubs, and airplane receipts. They should be approved by the affected employe's immediate superior, who should be familiar with the reason for the trip, its duration, and the number of calls made. The auditor should verify the mathematical accuracy and examine the form to see whether it is possible for additional expenses to be added after the expense account has been approved for payment, and whether changes have been made in amounts.

Journal entries are the most convenient means of accomplishing and covering up a fraudulent act. Explanations should be clear and concise. Charges to expense accounts, with a corresponding reduction in an asset account, such as notes receivable, accounts receivable, should be carefully investigated and explained. Journal entries should be approved, before entry in the accounts, by the chief accounting officer or a responsible subordinate who has a thorough knowledge of the accounts.

An examination of cash disbursements should conform to basic essentials of internal control prescribed in Chap. 12, Purchasing Departments and Accounts Payable. The student will do well to refresh himself with the principles and procedures outlined therein.

Summary

In respect to the verification of cash, the auditor should determine that:

1. The functions relating to the receipt and disbursement of funds are so delegated as to afford an adequate safeguard against loss and that the duties of one person act as a check on those of another.
2. All possible sources of income are investigated and recorded on the books of account at time of occurrence.

3. All expenditures are legitimate, properly supported, and value has been received.
4. Cash balances are correct and available and agree with the general books.

The auditor must remember that there are no rules which can be considered binding in all cases. The circumstances of each case must be considered as they are found. Above all, it is essential that the procedures be thoughtfully performed.

CHAPTER 10

CREDIT DEPARTMENTS AND ACCOUNTS RECEIVABLE

The objectives of an audit of Credit Departments and Accounts Receivable are to determine that:

1. The customers' reliability and financial ability to pay have been adequately measured before acceptance of the risk involved.
2. All amounts due the company are valid and are capable of being supported by documentary evidence having legal strength and force.
3. All balances due are in fact collectible items and are recognized as such by the customers and debtors.
4. Routines and procedures are in effect to review continuously the credit granted and the debtor's ability to pay, until the amount due has been redeemed.
5. Receivable accounts are classified as to type and are properly segregated on the balance sheet as to their current or non-current position.
6. Doubtful accounts are adequately reserved for and that uncollectible amounts are charged off.
7. The accounts charged off are properly approved, controlled, and reviewed periodically for collectibility and that cash payments received before and after the account has been written off as worthless have been recorded in the books of account.

Credit and Collections

The primary function of a Credit Department is to assist management in making a profit without undue risk of capital. To accomplish this, a Credit Department must be well-organized and staffed with trained personnel. It must be free of control or dictation by other departments, and at the same time, it must conform to the policies prescribed by management.

The work of the Credit and Sales Departments is closely related. Generally, these responsibilities are the only ones which have direct relationship with customers.

To attain the objectives of management successfully, there must be cooperation between the Sales and Credit Departments. Therefore, the policies of each department must be clearly defined and understood.

The chief duties of the Credit Department are the appraisal of the financial responsibility and ability to pay of potential and established customers and vendors and the collection of debts due the company.

The auditor should ascertain the established credit policies in effect, bearing in mind that changes are sometimes made to meet varying conditions. The class of risk to be accepted, the attitude toward returns and allowances, and enforcement of credit limits and terms of payment are all matters of company policy.

In reviewing the activities of the Credit Department, the auditor should determine that:

1. All customers' orders are approved for credit before acceptance.
2. Routines are in effect for securing and analyzing information affecting the financial responsibility, and other related matters, of potential and established customers, on a continuing basis.
3. Procedures are in effect to check the amount of credit granted and to notify the Sales Department or other authority promptly when the credit extended has reached the limit established.
4. Definite steps are taken to follow up past due accounts promptly and effectively and, when necessary, to instigate proper legal action for collection.
5. Accounts charged off are in fact uncollectible and that every effort has been made to secure payment.
6. Proper statistical reports are prepared concerning sales, credit, and collection activities.

Order Acceptance and Approvals

All customer orders and order changes should be approved for credit before acceptance and/or routing of the order through the manufacturing processes. The auditor should make certain that such approvals are secured on all orders received from a particular customer and not limited to the initial sale. Particular attention should be given to order changes, whether initiated by the customer or the company's production group. Such changes may cause the amount of the sale to exceed the credit granted. Routines should be established to assure the approval of changes before operations are performed to avoid possible rejection by the Credit Department, and loss. It is desirable that the auditor should examine a representative number of unfilled and completed customer orders to make certain that sales are not being made without proper approval. The auditor should be reasonable, however, when the amount of the order and total commitment is small.

In this category are included returns and advances to vendors. Before a return is made to a creditor, the credit receivable involved should be approved before the merchandise is shipped. Here the danger is that, if payment for the purchase has been made and the creditor goes bankrupt, full loss may be realized. Similarly, the credit of a vendor should be checked and approved where an advance payment is made or valuable tools, dies, and materials are delivered to him to assist him in carrying out the order.

Similarly, the credit responsibility of persons and firms with whom contracts are made should be determined and approved. This may include licenses to manufacture under patent rights, agreements to operate rental and restaurant facilities. The credits of trucking firms and other carriers should be investigated and approved before these carriers are permitted to transport goods, whether or not a contract is signed, to ensure the collection of transportation claims.

When reviewing contracts or other legal documents for credit approval, the auditor should make certain that the approval of the Legal Department has also been secured.

The auditor should determine the possible sources of loss which may arise due to inability on the part of an existing or potential debtor to make good on his obligation.

Credit Department Activities

Adequate sources of credit information must be maintained. Reference manuals published by the various credit agencies, such as Bradstreet's, Poor's, and others, should be available to persons approving credit.

Files of credit reports, customers' financial statements, and other data required to determine a rating should be maintained on a current basis. In case where commitments are small, in relation to high ratings in reference manuals, there should be little need to accumulate a comprehensive credit file. Up-to-date agency reports plus high ratings in published manuals should suffice.

The auditor should examine the credit files to make certain that the information contained therein is current and, to the best of his ability, that it is adequate for the credit man to determine the risk involved.

The work of approving credit should be separated from that of recording the sale and receiving collections. The Credit Department should not control, keep, or have possession of the detailed accounts receivable records.

The auditor should look for evidence that customers' financial statements have been thoroughly analyzed by a competent analyst. He should test a representative number of large accounts to the ratings listed in published guides, paying particular attention to those accounts to which credit has been extended in excess of the published ratings.

Routines should be in effect to notify the Sales Department what accounts are on the approved customer list and for the Accounting Department to open an account.

After an account is opened, the financial condition of the customer should be continuously checked. Financial reports and credit ratings should be secured regularly.

It is necessary for the Accounts Receivable Department to notify the Credit Department promptly of past due amounts.

It is important that the Credit Department be notified promptly of customer complaints regarding terms, defective material, or other reasons which may cause the customer to withhold payment. Loss of customer good will may result if the Credit Department notifies a customer that his account is delinquent when he has a legitimate complaint.

The auditor should examine all collateral, notes, mortgages, and trade acceptances furnished as security to see that they are properly drawn. He should pay particular attention to extensions of notes which may release endorsers, guarantors, and sureties. Chattel mortgages should be filed and recorded in accordance with the laws of the various states.   Life insurance policies should be assigned and followed to see that premiums are promptly paid.

The auditor should examine or prepare an analysis of the number of orders rated by the Credit Department and compare the number of orders rejected to the number approved for credit.

The Sales Department should be fully advised about customers' accounts.   Accounts can be rated so that the Sales Manager and his representatives in the field can be guided in their solicitation efforts. Credit Departments frequently develop industry and consumer analyses which indicate important trends.   This information can be very useful to the Sales Department in developing sales programs.

Similarly, sales programs should be formalized and well-planned and made known to the Credit Department.   A prompt and full disclosure of sales objectives to the credit manager will enable the latter to pass information along to the necessary levels of credit men for full and effective cooperation with the Sales Department.   Salesmen, by reason of their training and contacts, acquire a broad knowledge of the customers' products, competitive situation, nature and rate of operations, and backlog of orders.   This is the kind of information which is valuable to the credit man and which he attempts to develop from financial reports and other sources.   However, the auditor should make certain that the Credit Department treats such advices as auxiliary information in determining a credit rating.

The auditor should review the statistical reports prepared by and for the Accounting, Sales, and Credit Departments.   The following list is illustrative of some of the information which is required.

1. The relationship of actual losses to credit sales.
2. Collection costs.
3. Accounts charged off and a comparison of such amounts with the provision for bad debts.
4. Collections from accounts previously charged off.
5. Analysis of bad debts by class of product, customer, industry, and geographical location.
6. Amount of business rejected because of low credit ratings.

These reports should be prepared in comparative form to establish relationships with prior periods.   Tests should be made of mathematical accuracy and, wherever possible, reconciled to the accounting records.

Accurate and complete product costs and profits should be made available to the Sales and Credit Departments. The possession of such information by the Sales Department enables it to make better decisions in accepting orders and pushing sales activities of particular products. Likewise, the Credit Department may grant credit to a submarginal account when it is believed that the profit is worth the risk involved.

The auditor should remember that the granting of credit requires the use of experienced judgment and that the person most competent to decide whether an account is good, doubtful, or worthless is the credit manager. Nevertheless, the auditor should make such tests as he deems necessary and secure rational explanations for the decisions made. Charged off accounts should be approved by both the credit manager and a responsible accounting employe or treasury officer.

Accounts Receivable—Trade

Shipping records should be compared with copies of invoices and customer orders. It is important that no shipment be made without an authorized sales order. Individual items listed on the invoices should agree with the customer orders and the shipping papers as a proof that all items shipped have been billed.

Shipping and receiving activities should be segregated.

Unfilled orders should be examined to make certain that all shipments have been invoiced. It may be necessary to test check open orders to production and inventory records.

Invoices should be prenumbered and the full sequence accounted for.

It is desirable that bills of lading, packing slips, and delivery tickets be referenced on the customers' invoices. It must not be assumed that because a full invoice series has been accounted for and the individual sales proved to journals, ledgers, and customers' accounts, all shipments have been charged. The deliberate destruction or loss of shipping papers would result in failure to charge the customers.

Prices, terms, and extensions should be rechecked before the invoice is mailed. It is desirable that full pricing information be furnished to the Billing Department. Too often the construction of a sales price is considered to be the prerogative of the Sales De-

partment. Prices on invoices should not only be checked to customers' orders but also to pricing schedules, catalogs, and discount
sheets. Cash discounts, freight, and payment terms should conform
to the policies of the company. Unusual terms should be approved
by the credit manager or other responsible executives.

Invoices should be traced to sales records and individual customer
accounts. The auditor should test a representative number of debit
postings in the customers' accounts to sales records and supporting
data.

Customer returns should be approved for propriety by the persons
authorized to make adjustments with customers. Credits should
not be made until after the material has been received, and the
auditor should verify the actual returns by tracing them to receiving
reports and inventory records. Inspection of returned materials
should determine that the condition of the goods is commensurate
with the value allowed.

It is important that the original invoice be cross-referenced to
adjusting debits or credits to prevent the passing of duplicate allowances.

A representative number of credits, of all types, should be traced
from customers' accounts to the books of original entry. The auditor should be alert to detect the application of a payment received
from a charged-off account to an open account to cover a prior
fraudulent act. Debits should be traced for the same reason. The
auditor should be circumspect as to cash refunds charged to receivable accounts, unless the practice is characteristic of the type of
business.

Footings and cross-footings of sales journals and sales distributions
should be verified and reconciled with journal entries and postings
to the general ledger controls.

Trial balance of receivable accounts should be prepared or checked
to the individual accounts and totals verified to the control accounts.

The preparation of shipping documents, the billing of invoices,
the distribution of sales, the entry in books of original entry, the
posting of charges and credits to the debtors' accounts, and the
control of the general ledger should be performed by different
individuals.

It is recommended that charged-off accounts be maintained in
separate ledgers and be controlled by a separate general ledger or

memorandum control account. It is advantageous to place the bad debt ledger in charge of a person other than the one who keeps the regular accounts.

The auditor should make certain that amounts due from the officers and other employes are not combined with trade accounts receivable. Such treatment often prevents them from being noticed. Separate control accounts should be established for all amounts due from employes and should be classified as such on the balance sheet. The issuance of monthly reports to department heads and major executives is an effective way of currently controlling advances, loans, and receivables due from employes.

The auditor should see that routines are established to notify the Payroll Department promptly of amounts due from employes. Where deductions are made from employes' earnings, written instructions should be issued to that effect and approved by a responsible person other than the paymaster or person keeping the receivable records.

All loans and advances should be approved by responsible persons and promptly recorded as a receivable. Only those representing expense advances should be considered as part of a cash working fund. Even then it is best to transfer them to a receivable control account at month-end. Reversal entries can be made in the following month. Employe accounts should be charged for tools loaned for outside use in order to assure eventual return or payment therefor.

Miscellaneous Income Records

All sundry income should be analyzed as to source, and procedures should be in effect to assure receipt of all income to which the company is entitled.

Contracts, documents, and other records should be examined. Income from investments, rents, royalties, sale of real estate and fixed equipment, services rendered, interest on deposits, notes and mortgages, and quantity discounts should be recorded on the books of account as earned.

Consigned Stocks

Consigned stocks accounts should be reviewed to make certain that regular, periodic reports are secured from the consignees and that physical inventories are taken by the company's employes at

least once a year.   Consigned stocks should not be placed with customers to whom credit was refused on open account terms.   Conversely, consigned stocks should not be placed with customers when
the risk is good and it is possible to sell on regular open terms.

Shipments made on a consigned basis should be subject to the
same degree of control as those made on regular accounts.   The
auditor should test memorandum invoices and related shipping
papers to make certain that the shipments were actually made.
Adequate information should be furnished the Accounting Department when the goods are actually sold.

Notes Receivable

The auditor must establish that an adequate record is maintained
of all notes received.   In addition, he should make a physical examination of the notes themselves to determine that they have been
properly prepared and are valid.   The recording, safeguarding, and
collection of notes receivable should be performed by different
persons.

The Credit Department should issue acknowledgments to the
respective makers and immediately turn the notes accepted over
to the treasurer, or other official authorized by the by-laws, for safe-
keeping.   Upon receipt of a copy of the acknowledgments, the
Accounting Department should list all pertinent details of each note
in a register or individual ledger account. Checks and cash received
in settlement of notes must be promptly deposited by the cashier,
who should notify the Treasury and Accounting Departments, in
writing, attaching any remittance advices or other data received.

The Accounting Department should advise the Credit and Treasury Departments of the status of recorded notes at stated intervals.
Dishonored notes should be protested immediately as failure to do
so may release endorsers of their liability.

Extensions of notes must be carefully investigated.   Endorsers,
guarantors, and sureties may also be released from any liability when
an extension is granted to the maker.

Where a trade acceptance is used, the auditor should ascertain
that it has been properly accepted in writing across its face and that
it contains a statement to the effect that the debt arises from the
purchase and sale of goods.

The auditor should satisfy himself as to the reason for the acceptance of each note and that proper executive approval has been secured. When taken in lieu of a cash settlement of an open account, final collection cannot be made until maturity date of the note. The forgery of a note may also cover up the fraudulent confiscation of a payment on an account receivable.

Interest should be accrued as earned, and the auditor should make certain that it has been properly computed and that the rates used are the agreed-to or legal rates.

Paid or renewed notes should be marked paid or canceled and returned to the maker.

The Treasury Department should advise the Accounting Department of notes discounted, pledged, or deposited for collection. Possible liability on discounted notes should be reflected on the books of account and complete details retained on file.

Collateral should be recorded and endorsed only in favor of the company. Market values should be determined to see that the value thereof adequately covers the risk.

The auditor should subject the notes receivable records to the same tests as those recommended for regular accounts receivable. Footings should be verified, details checked, and reconcilement of subsidiary records made to the general ledger control account.

Write-off of Accounts and Notes Receivable

Accounts should be written off as they become worthless and not accumulated until year-end. Before the books are closed each month, all transfers from the accounts receivable to bad debts should be made.

The auditor should review all past due accounts and discuss them with responsible employes of the Sales, Credit, and Accounting Departments. He should review the correspondence files to make certain that they are followed effectively for collection. Charges to the bad debt account should bear the final stamp of approval of the Treasurer or Controller, in addition to that of the Credit Manager.

The adequacy of the reserve or provision for bad debts should be determined. The preparation of an aging schedule is helpful in determining whether the reserve is reasonably sufficient.

This schedule should disclose the names of customers; other debtors should be listed as at the close of the period selected for review. Accounts with credit balances should be segregated from those with debit balances. Space should be provided to show payments received subsequent to the end of the audit period. The unpaid items should be classified as to amounts due and overdue. Overdue accounts should, of course, be classified as to time overdue, such as 30, 60, 90 days, or over. Items in dispute should be shown separately. In this manner, the reserve requirements of the individual accounts can be built up in a special column on the work sheets for each type of accounts receivable. The auditor should not fail to include, in his analyses, debit balances appearing in accounts payable.

Confirmation of Accounts Receivable

When confirmations are used, it is desirable that the customers be circularized at the start of the audit to give the auditor the opportunity to examine the results and trace differences reported by the debtor through the books of account.

Verification by confirmation is best accomplished by sending statements to the customers with a request that they advise the auditor direct of any difference between their records and the amount shown on the statement. The auditor must maintain complete control of all statements. He should ascertain that they are in sufficient detail and agree with the name and address of and amount due from each debtor.

When confirmations are used, the number of accounts may be proportioned between negative and positive forms of verification. The negative form consists of a request to the debtor to reply only when he does not agree with the balance reflected on the statement. The positive form requires the debtor to advise whether he is in agreement or disagreement with the balance. For confirmations to produce the desired results the auditor should secure about a 90% coverage of the total unpaid balances. As replies are received, they should be coded and referenced to the auditor's work papers and all differences reconciled.

CHAPTER 11

INVENTORY CONTROL

Foreword

Inventory Control may be defined as a system of internal check and control to ensure that inventories of raw materials, stores, supplies, work in process, finished goods, etc., are protected against irregularities and that the information relative to inventories which is required in the preparation of operating and financial statements is authentic and reliable.

The fundamental principles of inventory control are no different from those set forth and continually emphasized in earlier chapters, several of which contain specific information relative to inventory control. The purpose of this chapter is to apply those principles to the inventory function.

Objectives

The principal objectives of and the benefits to be obtained from the inventory function and an adequate control thereover are:

1. The maintenance of suitable quantities and qualities of materials on hand at all times.
2. The safeguarding of materials awaiting use or disposition.
3. The determination and, in some cases, the anticipation of material requirements through proper correlation with operational activities.
4. The furnishing of cost figures on materials and supplies used in operations.
5. The furnishing of statistics as to quantities on hand, on order, consumed, required, etc.
6. The determination of the value of the inventories for the purpose of preparing financial statements.

Control Measures

The primary means of inventory control are:

1. Properly authorized and approved requisitions governing both requests for purchases and issuances from stock.
2. Accurate inventory records of all inventoried material.
3. Adequate physical safeguarding of material on hand.
4. Physical inventories performed as a means of control over perpetual inventory accuracy.

Responsibility of the Internal Auditor

It is the responsibility of the internal auditor to conduct sufficient periodic audits to determine that the administration of the inventory function complies with principles and established procedures, attains the desired objectives, and exercises effective control. In general, such an audit may be divided into several phases:

1. A review of purchase requisitions together with a review of the material receiving function.
2. A review of inventory records together with a review of the material requisitioning and issuance procedure.
3. An examination of the physical storage facilities.
4. A test of physical inventory methods and the accuracy thereof.

Purchase Requisitions

An examination should be made of the requisitions issued by the Stores Department to the Purchasing Department for a fixed period to determine that:

1. All requisitions are prenumbered and accounted for.
2. All requisitions are approved by authorized employes having knowledge of requirements.
3. Descriptions and specifications are correctly stated.
4. Quantities requisitioned and timing of issuance conform with established "quantities to order" and "order points."
5. All requisitions are promptly and properly posted to inventory records.
6. Unfilled requisitions are followed up and the reasons for delay in filling long outstanding requisitions are determined.

Receiving

The receiving function should be studied to determine that:

1. All material received is counted, weighed or measured, and recorded by employes other than those connected with requisitioning the material. The auditor should make test checks for accuracy immediately after counts, weights, or measures have been recorded. Where it is not practical to obtain actual counts, weights, or measures, the theoretical weights or other methods of calculated measurement used should be tested.
2. Scales are accurate and are inspected frequently, both by company personnel and by state officials, as evidenced by an examination of scale inspection reports.

The auditor's actions relative to the function of reporting material received may involve:

1. An examination to determine that receiving reports are prepared for all material received regardless of source and usage and that:
   a. Their numerical sequence can be accounted for.
   b. They are signed by persons who know the material was received.
   c. They are cross-referenced to requisitions, purchase orders, credit memos, invoices, etc.
   d. The method of shipment, routing, and car numbers are shown.
2. A comparison of receiving-report quantities with tally cards, scale tickets, etc.
3. The checking of receiving reports with requisitions and purchase orders and the ascertainment of reasons for differences in quantities, specifications, methods of shipment, etc.
4. A comparison of invoices with receiving reports. The method of handling discrepancies should be investigated to appraise the adequacy of the control exercised thereover.
5. A comparison of credit memos with receiving reports and a determination that the quantity and amount of the credit are proper.
6. A review of demurrage reports to ascertain that cars are unloaded promptly. Delays should be investigated for cause.

7. An examination of inspection reports on material received and the determination that claims were filed for defective material.

8. A check of receiving reports to inventory records to determine that correct postings have been made. In addition, a group of postings shown in the inventory records should be traced to receiving reports.

Issuing

The auditor's actions relative to the issuing function should include:

1. A study to determine that withdrawals from stock are made only on written requisitions approved by authorized employes qualified to do so by knowledge of the circumstances prompting the requisition. In this regard:

    a. A signature file of individuals authorized to approve requisitions should be maintained.

    b. Approvals must not be perfunctory.

    c. Requisitions should be signed by the individuals actually receiving the material and should be date-stamped at the time the material is issued.

    d. Where a duplicate requisition system is used, the duplicates should be used as a control medium.

2. A careful examination for possible alterations on requisitions and an investigation of any instances thereof.

3. A check of requisitions to inventory records to determine the accuracy of the postings. A group of postings should also be traced to requisitions.

4. The determination that materials issued but not used are returned to stock and are properly recorded on the inventory records.

Inventory Records

In addition to verifying the accuracy of postings, as set forth above, the study of inventory recording practices should determine that:

1. "Order points" and "quantities to order" are reviewed frequently in line with current and anticipated usages, prices, and quantity discounts.

2. Descriptions and specifications of materials are adequate for proper control.

3. The classifications of material are of sufficient number to ensure adequate control or, by contrast, are not unnecessarily large to the point of causing needless clerical effort.

4. The units in which materials are inventoried are consistent with the quantities in which the respective materials are issued.

5. If money balances are shown, the inventory accounts balance to the general ledger controls. Such a balancing should be performed regularly by the company as a control measure.

6. Requisitions are correctly coded and priced.

7. Inventory values, depreciation, etc., are correct on such items as are reduced in value on an arbitrary monthly basis.

8. Inventory records of balances on hand are correct, as indicated by test counts of selected items and by comparison with detailed records kept by the Production Planning Department, if such are maintained. Differences should be reconciled.

9. Physical quantities are checked throughout the year when stocks are low. Methods of handling any adjustments to records should be reviewed.

10. Extensions, additions, etc., on inventory records are correct, as evidenced by test checks.

11. Memorandum records of materials on hand, which have been charged off, are maintained and controlled.

12. Materials on hand but not recorded on inventory records are adequately controlled.

13. Adequate procedures have been established and are being utilized to determine when stocks are obsolete or slow-moving. The action taken to reduce such stocks should be reviewed.

14. Through a review of the latest physical inventory reports, no inventory adjustments are handled on requisitions as withdrawals or usage, but are properly made through variance accounts. Reasons for adjustments should be reviewed.

Handling and Storage Facilities

An examination of the facilities for handling and storing materials should determine that:

1. Materials are stored in a manner to prevent losses through theft, climatic conditions, etc.

2. Storage areas are accessible only to authorized employes.
3. The physical arrangement of stocks is such that it expedites receiving and issuing.
4. Adequate control is maintained over small tools or materials which are loaned to employes or which are used by storeroom employes.

Physical Inventories

Inventory taking is a very important phase in the administration of a business, not only as a medium of control over inventory records, but primarily by reason of its relationship to the financial statements which reflect the condition of a business.

Proper inventory taking requires certain actions on the part of the company and by the auditors observing the taking of an inventory and reviewing the results thereof. These are:

1. *Planning for the Physical Inventory.* Generally, inventories are planned for that time of the year when stocks are low or production can be stopped most economically.

The company should prepare written instructions in advance for all employes participating in the inventory. These instructions should be reviewed by the company's supervisors with each person involved so that his specific job is clear to him. These instructions should provide complete control by the Accounting Department of all counting, weighing, recording, pricing, and adjusting.

The mill, warehouse, etc., should be divided into sections in such a manner that each person can be told he is responsible for all the material in each section.

The plan should contain specific instructions for counting, weighing, marking, tagging, recording, etc., to assure that all material is properly recorded as to quantity, description, and condition. Pre-numbered tags, sheets, etc., should be issued and controlled by the supervisor in charge.

Adequate procedure must be outlined in the plan to control material flowing in or out of stock during the count and properly to adjust book inventory for materials in transit.

2. *Observation of Inventory Taking.* The auditors observe the taking of the physical inventory to satisfy themselves that the instructions are being followed. After the material has been counted,

the auditors should select certain materials to test the accuracy of the count and to determine that:

  a. Descriptions are correct and standard, thus permitting ready identification.
  b. Condition of material is properly recorded.
  c. Prenumbered tags and sheets are being controlled.
  d. All material in each section is being counted and tagged or marked to avoid duplication or omission.
  e. Material is arranged in such a way that an accurate count is possible.

  3. *Review of Compilation of Inventory.* At the conclusion of the inventory taking, the auditors will determine that the company supervisor in charge is properly accounting for all prenumbered tags and sheets, that any transcriptions and coding from the original inventory are being properly made, and that the inventory is properly classified as indicated by tests of production records, receiving reports, and inspection reports.

Careful examinations will be made to determine that:

  a. Material on hand belonging to others is not included in the inventory.
  b. All invoices, for material on hand and that which has been included in the inventory, have been entered on the books.
  c. Material billed to customers includes all the material, and only that material, shipped up to the cut-off time for the physical inventory.
  d. Material in transit at the date of the inventory is recorded as such.

  4. *Pricing the Inventory.* The auditor will test check the prices used in extending the inventory values to authorized lists of standard prices, or current purchase prices and current costs, depending on the basis of pricing in effect. Tests of freight and handling charges added to purchased materials should also be made.

If inventories are carried on a LIFO basis, the proper identification to LIFO pools, and proper application to base periods and acquisition months should be examined.

It is important that material reduced in value or written off in prior periods be properly identified so that improper revaluation will not occur. Memorandum records of charged off materials should be examined and sales or other dispositions tested. Material inventoried as being in sub-standard condition will be reviewed to determine that reasonable effect is given to this condition in the pricing.

Limited tests of extensions and additions of inventory sheets and recapitulations may be performed.

5. *Adjustments.* The auditors will test that the physical inventory quantities and valuations are properly used in revising detailed inventory ledgers, controls, and adjusting journal entries.

At the time of the review of the detailed records, slow-moving items may be observed. Reasons for and proper valuation of such materials should then be ascertained.

6. *Causes of Differences.* Analysis of the physical and accounting handling of items on which major differences have occurred should assist in correction of improper practices which result in such differences.

7. *Consigned Stocks and Materials Held outside the Plant.* Consignees should be requested to take physical inventories at periodic intervals and submit reports. If the quantities are substantial, a representative of the company should observe the taking and listing of the inventory.

The auditor will test that all such inventory differences are billed to the consignee.

CHAPTER 12

PURCHASING DEPARTMENTS AND ACCOUNTS PAYABLE

In a small business enterprise, particularly one operated as a single proprietorship, purchasing and the payment of obligations are usually performed, or closely supervised, by the owner-manager. The owner is thoroughly acquainted with his stock and other needs; he orders the materials and services his business requires and consummates the transactions by signing the checks in payment of the obligations.

As the size of the business increases, the amount of time and attention that must be given to these duties requires that the owner delegate them to others. When the duties of the owner are entrusted to the care and management of another, the person to whom they are assigned is clothed with the legal power to act as an authorized agent. It is then that management relinquishes direct control and must depend upon the integrity and business sagacity of others.

The functions of purchasing and accounts payable concern almost every transaction necessary for the operation of a business and therefore offer innumerable opportunities for the commission of inefficient and fraudulent acts. It is of utmost importance that management establish routines and procedures that will maintain an effective control over the purchasing and payable functions.

Objectives

The objectives of an audit of the purchasing and accounts payable operations are to determine that:

1. All purchase orders, contracts, and commitments are genuine and that they have been approved by responsible and properly delegated employes before the company is obligated.
2. The goods and services were received and were in the amounts and of the quality for which the company incurred a liability.

3. The acquisitions have been made at the lowest ultimate cost.
4. The liabilities incurred have been settled in such a manner as to prevent loss to the company.

Basic Essentials of Internal Control

The following responsibilities should be established independent of each other and not performed or controlled by the same person:

1. The original request for the material or service desired.
2. The approval of the request.
3. The negotiation with sources of supply.
4. The issuance of orders and contracts.
5. The receipt and inspection of the goods or services ordered.
6. The checking and approval of terms, prices, discounts, and special charges on vendors' invoices, before payment.
7. The matching of the vendor's invoice with proof of the receipt of the goods or services.
8. The recording of the liability.
9. The distribution of the charge.
10. The payment of the liability incurred.

Purchase Requests

The first step in the acquisition of an item is the verification of the need. This may not necessarily be based upon an immediate need, but may be a matter of policy or sound business judgment, such as placing an order to take advantage of current prices in anticipation of higher costs or because of an anticipated scarcity of materials. In any event, management must have means of establishing the fact that the goods or services are actually required and that they will result in benefit to the business. A proper control at this point will impede and obstruct fraud and the misapplication or misappropriation of company assets.

The request for purchase should be in writing. It is important that specifications as to material or services and the date of delivery be complete and clearly stated. Each request should be approved by a responsible, authorized employe who is thoroughly familiar with the needs of his responsibility. The Purchasing Department should have on file current instructions and specimen signatures designating whose approval shall be accepted. Provision should be made for the prompt withdrawal of an authorization when the delegated employe leaves the employ of the company or has a change in responsibility. To test the genuineness of signatures, the auditor should secure new specimens directly from the persons listed in the official authorization and a new certification as to their propriety from the major executive.

Requests should be limited in amount and to type of purchase to avoid giving the authorized employe unconditional powers to commit the company and to restrict the extent of a possible fraud. The auditor should examine the minutes for such restrictions and, if they are lacking, make such recommendations as he will deem necessary properly to safeguard the interests of the company.

The auditor should explore the possibility of requests being used repeatedly. Cancellations should be preserved for audit and voided in a manner to prevent further use. The use of initials or a rubber stamp in lieu of a signature should not be condoned.

The auditor should examine groups of purchase orders to see that they are supported by approved requests. Missing and altered requisitions should be listed and accounted for to make certain that the Purchasing Department is not making unauthorized purchases. Collusion between members of the Purchasing Department and those of other responsibilities is not apt to be widespread but confined to one person or department. The auditor should therefore make tests of requests and orders originated by each authorized employe.

Purchase Orders

Purchase orders should be in writing and should be based upon properly authorized requisitions. Verbal orders should be promptly confirmed in writing. The agreement should be clearly set forth as to quantity, specifications, price, terms, time and method of delivery, and special conditions such as inspection, penalties, and guarantees.

It is desirable that all orders be priced and that the approval of invoices be the dual responsibility of the Purchasing and Accounting Departments. The Purchasing Department should make a comparison of the unit prices, description of merchandise, terms, etc., shown on the vendor's invoice with the corresponding items on the purchase order, and the Accounting Department should make a similar comparison and, in addition, check extensions and amounts. However, to reduce clerical effort a definite reference to quotations, catalogs, and discount sheets should suffice.

Frequently, it is contended that the Purchasing Department is best qualified to verify invoices. In such cases, the negotiation and placing of an order with a vendor and the checking of invoices should be sufficiently distributed in the Purchasing Department to prevent collusion.

Purchase orders should be serially numbered. If numbered as issued, the blank forms should be safeguarded, to the same extent as checks, to prevent misuse. Verbal modifications should be confirmed in writing. Changes involving factors other than price, terms, discounts, and routing should be approved by the originating responsibility. Changes should be numbered, referenced, and attached to the original order. All documents pertaining to an order, such as requisitions, quotations, summaries of bids, and correspondence, should be filed together.

The auditor should check to see that all special terms and conditions have been complied with. For example, when a vendor is required to carry insurance, such as Fire, Workmen's Compensation, or Liability, there should be evidence in the form of insurance certificates.

A careful examination should be made of all orders placed on a cost-plus and escalation basis and those containing termination and cancellation clauses. Such orders should be analyzed for clarity of terms and definition of costs and the bases for determining overhead and profit fees. Provisions should be included in such orders for an audit of the vendor's or contractor's records pertaining to the charges involved. The auditor should examine the controls established by the Accounting Department for the verification of the vendor's or contractor's charges.

Emergency orders should be sent through the same channels as regular orders and the invoices approved by the Purchasing Department. The auditors should prepare analyses of intermittent purchases to determine whether there is sufficient volume to secure the advantages of lower prices through volume discounts or the issuance of blanket orders. Frequently, it is possible to combine requests for magazines and periodicals which will result in savings from volume discounts and term rates.

The auditor should examine the routines established for determining the routing and the method of shipment. The choice of carriers and the manner of shipment, such as carload versus less carload, can result in important savings.

To avoid the responsibility for shortages, damages, and other losses occasioned by the carrier, inbound shipments, unless contrary to the policy of the vendor, should be made F.O.B. destination. The auditor should, however, consider the effect of F.O.B. point on Sales and Use Taxes. For example, in one state, the Use Tax regulations provide that the tax applies to the sales price at the F.O.B. point. If material is purchased F.O.B. destination, the transportation charges are included in the tax base. However, if the purchase is made F.O.B. shipping point, the transportation charges and Federal Transportation Tax are excluded from the tax base.

The auditor should examine orders to see that provisions are made concerning who is to pay Sales and Use Taxes. Exempt materials should be properly classified and vendors supplied with exemption certificates.

Contracts

Contracts are formalized agreements and are usually signed by officers authorized by the by-laws of a corporation or the principal of the company. The auditor should check for compliance. Purchases authorized by a contract should be covered by a purchase order.

A register should be maintained in which all pertinent data relative to the contract should be recorded, such as effective date, cancellation date, provisions for renewal and cancellation, and a brief description of the goods or services contracted for.

Original copies of contracts should be filed in a central place, and excerpts of the important provisions should be distributed to interested personnel and to the Accounting Department.

The auditor should examine the contracts for compliance and check to see that means have been established to control any unusual provisions.

Competitive Bids

In order to secure the best possible advantage in price, quality, or delivery, it is necessary that the Purchasing Department develop a number of sources of supply for each item or service required. Substantial savings can be made through the practice of securing competitive bids and placing the order with the best qualified, lowest bidder.

Bids should be received in suitable documentary form and should be preserved to support the selection of the successful bidder.

The auditor should check the bids received against the list of vendors from whom bids were requested. Missing and rejected bids should be fully explained by the Purchasing Agent.

Correspondence with a vendor should be examined to detect any arrangements not incorporated in the bid or purchase order, such as an intent to increase the price after the work is in progress. Special attention should be given to increases in price after award to the successful bidder.

Control and Verification of Invoices by Purchasing Department

Invoices should be time-stamped and assigned a Purchasing Department register number immediately upon receipt from the vendor. Checking of prices, terms, description, etc., should be performed by a person other than the one who negotiated and placed the order. If prices are shown on the order, the invoice should be checked to catalogs, discount sheets, quotations, and bids. Invoices covering services and intangibles for which there is no physical receipt should be approved by a responsible person who knows that value was received. The Purchasing Department should maintain records of invoices charged, by orders, to prevent the passing of a duplicate or fictitious invoice.

Negotiation of returns should be conducted by the Purchasing Department in order that it be familiar with all transactions affecting a purchase and to ensure the best possible arrangements. Frequently, returns are subject to rehandling and restocking charges, and the Purchasing Department should be in the best position to conduct negotiations with the supplier. Adjustments, whether in the form of accounts payable or accounts receivable debit or credit memorandums, should be approved by the Purchasing Department for price, terms, etc., to prevent collusion between members of the Accounting Department and the vendors.

The auditor should make a careful examination of vendors' invoices to determine that:

1. They are in full agreement with the purchase order as to name of vendor, order number, prices, terms, shipping instructions, and special provisions.
2. The prices paid are not in excess of those indicated by catalogs, discount sheets, quotations, and proposals.
3. They have been approved by the Purchasing Department before payment.

Receipt of Material

Material improperly received, such as erroneous counts and identification, may be due to fraud on the part of employes or the vendors.

Weak controls or the lack of definite procedures may result in the payment for goods not received and at a later date "buried" in an inventory adjustment.

The Receiving Department should be responsible for the receipt and identification of anything of a physical nature, such as material, supplies, and equipment. This function should be established as an independent department, free of control by the Accounting, Stores, and Purchasing Departments. All shipments should be checked for quantity and quality the day they arrive and delivered to Stores or consuming responsibility as soon as possible.

Freight car seals should be examined before opening the car. If the seals have been broken or tampered with, the car should not be unloaded without the approval of the carrier's representative. After the car is opened, it should be inspected for damaged conditions of the contents.

L.C.L., express, and motor shipments should be examined to see that packages, bundles, boxes, etc., agree with the quantities appearing on the freight bill or delivery receipt and that they are in good condition before signing for the shipment.

It is desirable that bills of lading, duplicate invoices, copies of purchase orders, shipping notices, packing slips, and delivery slips be controlled by a receiving clerk or by a representative of the Accounting Department stationed in the Receiving Department, who will retain them until the material has been checked in. Quantities should not be available to the person counting the material.

Shipments should be itemized on a serially numbered receiving report showing all other pertinent data such as date, vendor, order number, weight, carrier, freight charges, whether collect or prepaid, and any notation as to shortage or damage.   The receiving reports should then be checked to the packing slips, shipping notices, etc., by the receiving clerk; any discrepancies would necessitate a recheck.

Procedures should be instituted to ensure the filing of claims against carriers for shortages and damaged materials.

To place responsibility, the receiving report should be signed by the checker and approved by the receiving clerk.   Receiving reports should be forwarded promptly, and in serial number order, to the Accounting Department for matching with vendors' invoices.

Returns to the vendors should be made through the Shipping Department and subject to the same procedures as shipments to customers.   Returns should not be made until the vendor's credit rating has been approved by the Credit or Treasury Department and the Purchasing Department has been informed.

The auditor should review the receiving procedures to determine that proper precautions have been taken to ensure the receipt of the material in the proper quantity and quality.   In addition, the auditor should personally observe the actual receipt and counting of material.

To test the regularity of quantities billed on vendors' invoices, the auditor should select a number of items and prove their receipt by a physical inventory and a reconciliation of the affected perpetual inventory cards.   It is important that such records be kept by an employe other than the one who counted in the material.

Verification of Vendors' Invoices by the Accounting Department

It is desirable that the checking of invoices for prices, terms, discounts, etc., be performed by employes having no part in the matching of invoices with receiving reports.   If prices and terms have been checked by the Purchasing Department, the Accounting Department should examine each invoice for purchasing approval.   Each invoice should be checked for quantity and clerical errors.   Adjustments should be made only by the issuance of accounts payable or accounts receivable debit or credit memorandums, properly approved by responsible employes of the Accounting and Purchasing Departments.

Invoices paid before actual receipt of materials or services should be vouchered or entered in the purchase records.   It is preferred that such payments be charged to a special account, such as Material-in-Transit-Inbound, and that this account be analyzed at least once a month. Invoices paid in advance should later be subject to the same routines as regular invoices to see that the material or services are properly received.

If practicable to do so, different individuals should make the distribution of invoices and prepare a list of invoices, by due dates, which should be reconciled to the check register by the person who examines the voucher for payment or by some other independent party.

Where merchandise is purchased for direct shipment to customers, procedures should be established to ensure that the customers are charged properly. This can be accomplished by charging the vendors' invoices to an account such as Material-in-Transit-Outbound. Debiting such charges to regular inventory accounts can be easily covered up and disposed of by inclusion in a physical inventory adjustment. Credits to a customer should not be made for returns direct to a vendor until proof of receipt has been secured.

Adequate procedures should be established to control the payment of inbound and outbound freight charges. Owing to the requirements of the Interstate Commerce Commission regulation for the prompt payment of freight bills, freight charges are often paid before the actual receipt of the material. To prevent duplicate payment of freight charges it is best that such charges be made to Inbound and Outbound Freight control accounts. Clearance should be made to the ultimate account by comparing the freight charges shown on the receiving reports, invoices, and bills of lading. Each clearance should be referenced to the receiving report and voucher. Uncleared items should be investigated at least once a month and trial balances reconciled to the freight control accounts.

Adequate procedures must be instituted to control freight paid on purchases shipped "freight allowed" and, where freight is prepaid for customers, to ensure recovery of the amounts paid.

In-transit privileges for storing or processing materials en route are available for certain types of commodities. These privileges are known as "fabrication-in-transit," "milling-in-transit," "barreling-in-transit," etc. When advantage is taken of these privileges, a "through" or reduced rate applies. Control must be exercised to ensure proper arrangements with the carrier to avoid the payment of two rates.

To preclude the payment of excessive freight charges, all freight bills should be checked by an employe familiar with rates and tariffs or by an outside agency qualified to perform this service.

Payment of Invoices

All liabilities should be recorded on the books before payment is made. Vouchers should be approved for payment by an employe other than the persons who matched the invoices, checked prices and extensions, and entered them in the records. Where monthly statements have been received from vendors, they should be checked and reconciled to the payment. The person who approves a voucher for payment should make certain that all proper approvals are shown and that the required supporting documents are attached.

Paid invoices and all supporting documents should be marked or perforated in a manner to prevent their reuse.

Checks should be countersigned. The check signers should examine the supporting vouchers to such an extent as to assure themselves that the approvals were made carefully and that, from the evidence on hand, the payment is in order.

Monthly trial balances of detailed accounts payable should be prepared from vouchers and/or invoices and reconciled to the detailed accounts payable ledger, if kept, and to the general ledger control account.

The auditor should make test checks of paid vouchers and unpaid invoices to the extent possible by:

1. Comparing quantities on receiving reports to those shown on the invoices.
2. Checking the prices shown on the invoices to purchase orders and catalogs, discount sheets, quotations, and bids to make certain that they are not in excess of the agreed amounts.
3. Examining the vouchers as to date and name of both debtor and creditor.
4. Checking the mathematical accuracy of all calculations, such as extensions and additions of both invoices and vouchers.
5. Verifying the entry and distribution in the accounts.
6. Verifying the footings and cross-footings of purchase journal or voucher register.
7. Tracing all postings in general and subsidiary ledgers back to the original books of entry.

8. Inspecting all documents for completeness and propriety of approval.
9. Determining that all documents have been properly voided.
10. Comparing a representative number of paid vouchers with canceled checks returned from the bank.

The auditor should compare statements submitted by vendors to a trial balance of the individual creditors' accounts which he has personally prepared and reconciled to the general ledger control.

The auditor should also prepare a list of the outstanding liabilities as of the latest possible date and should preserve it in his work papers for verification on the next audit.

CHAPTER 13

SALES ORGANIZATION—AUDIT OF SALES OFFICES AND SHIPPING AND INVOICING CONTROLS

ORGANIZATION

Generally, there are two types of sales organizations whose principles are briefly stated as follows:

1. *Centralized.* This type comprehends the function of accumulating, processing, and preparing consumers' orders which have been solicited by sales offices and agencies throughout the country and entering them at the factory for production.

2. *Direct Entry or Decentralized.* This system comprehends all functions stated above, except that the functions are performed in the sales office and orders are entered directly to the factory from that point.

Certain fundamentals and controls are common to the proper functioning of both types of sales organizations. The important fundamentals of a sales organization are found in the development of sales prices and policies.

Sales prices are determined by management and are predicated on forecasts of probable total available business under prevailing market conditions, indicated economic trend of the future, and costs of product manufactured.

When prices have been established, they are officially issued in a "price list," or some sort of price brochure, and are distributed to all interested departments throughout the company. As prices are officially changed, revisions are made to the lists accordingly.

Generally, sales policies fall into two categories:

1. Those relating to the development of markets, price mainte-

nance, product distribution, quotas, product improvements, and other activities that are necessary to attain the ultimate objective of profitable sales. The responsibility for the development of these policies is vested in a group immediately subordinate to sales management, and these policies are usually established on a divisional or product basis, or any basis compatible with the organization as a whole. Their primary function is the correlation of relevant factual data, procured from information and statistics from various sources and sections of the country, into recommendations or reports to management.

2. Those relating to the control over functions of application and execution at sales office level, and including those relative to personnel, solicitation activities, customer order entry and service, and miscellaneous functions pertinent to the successful operation of a sales office. The development of the policies for these functions, as a rule, falls within the influence of the group mentioned above, but these policies may also be developed and controlled by a collateral or staff group of a sales organization.

Sales offices operated under the system of direct entry will require more extensive auditing, and more time will be spent than would be required under a centralized order entry arrangement.

ADMINISTRATION

It is impossible to define sales policies for all of a company's products, since, very frequently, because of unusual circumstances relative to the sale or manufacture of a product, special handling by management must be accorded such a situation. To develop policies for handling, in such instances, would be impractical. Usually, 90% or more of consumers' orders can be entered and processed at the district sales office level if manufacturing processes have been largely standardized. Accordingly, 90% administration occurs at this point.

Audit Objectives

In the course of sales office audits it should be verified that:
1. The administration of responsibilities is in accordance with company policies.
2. Prices as developed and prescribed by management are properly applied to customers' orders.
3. The company is securing all the revenue to which it is entitled.

District Sales Offices

A district sales office operating under a direct entry system is divided into two functions: solicitation and order service. The responsibility of coordinating these functions lies with the management of each office. This management usually consists of a Sales Manager, who is assisted in solicitation by assistant managers and salesmen; an order service, consisting of an Office Manager or Chief Clerk, assistants, departmental supervisors, and their assigned personnel. The organization of a district office is responsible for the solicitation of consumers and servicing of customers in such a manner that sales objectives are realized and that satisfactory customer relationship is maintained.   It is the official contact between the company and the consumer.

Personnel

The variety of duties performed by district sales office personnel makes it necessary for the auditor to approach the over-all picture from a responsibility point of view and to become familiar with office routine as it is indicated by the individual duties of employes.

1. *Position and Duties.* The survey of sales office personnel and their duties should be performed on a basis of complete coverage, if at all possible, but in any event, in sufficient scope and degree to determine:

a. That the authorization of personnel assigned to the office is evidenced by personnel records which, in turn, support the payments of wages made.

b. That the employes are actually performing the duties ascribed to their respective positions.

c. That the employes are being paid at the rates indicated for their positions.

d. The identity of each employe.   This may be effectively done by observing the distribution of salary checks.   If the pay observation is made in the early phases of the audit, not only will it permit the auditor to account for absentees, but, also, will aid him in associating employes with departmental and organizational routines, thus facilitating other phases of the sales office audit.

2. *Personnel Records.* The auditor should test personnel records to determine that they have been properly prepared with respect to employment transfers, temporary and substitute personnel,

promotions and demotions, terminations, retirements, etc., and that they display adequate information to permit compliance with governmental regulations and requirements of unions. Frequently, employes are provided with company property, such as brief cases, manuals, price books, identification cards or letters, or keys, and in some cases, cash funds. Records should be reviewed to ascertain that employes have been charged with the assigned materials and that these have been returned or accounted for in the event of termination or transfer.

3. *Attendance*

a. *Exempt Personnel.* Certain minimum attendance records are required relative to this type of personnel in order to establish eligibility for vacations, pensions, benefits, etc., and the auditor should satisfy himself that these objectives have been achieved.

However, the method of accumulating and recording hours worked is established at the discretion of the Office Sales Manager. The auditor should review the attendance records to ascertain compliance with local office direction and in the light of Federal, state, and municipal regulations that may apply.

b. *Nonexempt Personnel.* Companies operating on an interstate basis come under the Federal Labor Standards Act. Nonexempt personnel are governed by the provisions of this act, and company attendance policies are patterned accordingly. The controls and practices in effect for the accumulation and reporting of time as worked by this class of employes under the Fair Labor Standards Act should be reviewed and tested to ascertain their effectiveness in securing accuracy and propriety of such hours. Proper signatures and approvals are necessary on the Fair Labor Standards Report since it becomes the authentic record in the settlement of employe benefits and/or disputes.

4. *Vacations.* Since the eligibility requirements of vacations differ with respect to class of employes, length of service, etc., and are subject to changes from one year to another, it is incumbent on the internal auditor to acquaint himself with the vacation requirements prior to audit. He is then in a position to determine whether the office under audit is complying with vacation policy provisions. In the review of service and attendance records, he can readily establish exceptions, if any, relative to vacation eligibility, payments, allowances, etc.

Solicitation. This function of a sales office comprises all personnel actively engaged in the solicitation of accounts and the selling of products of a company to consumers.

A salesman's activity is often developed from a "Budget of Calls." The budget is based on extensive sales surveys and sales research projects designed to assure continuous contact with potential business. It is intended as a quota and guide by which a salesman is expected to schedule his itinerary of calls on customers on a systematic basis in the solicitation of business and the development of important information covering the account. Accordingly, the internal auditor has the responsibility of checking this function to determine that:

1. A budget is being assigned to each salesman.

2. The salesman is planning and executing his calls in accordance therewith.

3. The salesman reports pertinent information with respect to the customer and the company.

4. Such information has been received and noted by delegated authority.

5. The reports are being recorded and entered into proper related records.

6. Such reports and records are current and kept in such shape that a quick and complete report can be given whenever management may request it.

7. All claims and complaints reported through this medium are brought to the attention of responsible personnel for immediate processing in order to maintain good customer relationship.

8. Information and activity are properly correlated into reports for top-level management as requested.

Since the Sales Manager cannot confine his activities solely to the checking of performance of solicitation personnel, any conclusion that the internal auditor may make as a result of his test checks of this function should be discussed with the Manager to the end that he may improve, correct, or revise solicitation practices accordingly.

Order Service

In the main, order service comprehends the handling of the customers' inquiries and orders so as to convert them to manufacturing orders, service them during interim period of production and shipment, and assure the proper application of pricing data for ultimate invoicing. It may be discussed under the following headings:

1. *Handling of an Inquiry.* The customer makes known his wants through the medium of an inquiry, which usually asks for information concerning price, quantity, quality, delivery, etc. In most cases, particularly where standard products are desired, a company can give a quick reply. However, if nonstandard products which require special manufacturing are involved, certain facts must be developed before an intelligent reply can be made to the inquiry or a quotation given. Thus, in the examination or review of the practices of handling an inquiry, the internal auditor should ascertain that it flows through the various processes without undue delay and that a reply is sent to the customer as quickly as possible. Delays that are occurring constantly should be noted and the causes analyzed by the auditor so that he is fully prepared to discuss these exceptions with the Sales Manager and offer constructive suggestions for improvements in this particular function.

2. *Handling of an Order.* The majority of products are manufactured to certain standards and are commonly regarded as "standardized" products. The customer orders certain quantities of these, which, when received in the district sales office, are routed through a department or through a series of departmental steps for the application of each department's portion of manufacturing, shipping, and invoicing data, ultimately emerging as a manufacturing order.

In reviewing these orders, the auditor should ascertain the degree of efficiency attained in order processing, the accuracy and adequacy of manufacturing information indicated thereon, and that pricing data has been accurately and fully stated for final invoicing.

Some of the departmental applications which merit audit emphasis are as follows:

a. Pricing. Because of policy reasons, the manufacturing order does not, as a rule, display a monetary amount which is to be charged for a particular item, but indicates essential data, through the use of symbols and codes, which will assure proper pricing of an order after shipment. On the premise of good internal control, the application of prices to codes and symbols in accordance with official price brochures is usually performed by a designated group under Accounting Department responsibility. Where such function is performed by the Sales Department, as well as applying essential pricing data to the order, the Accounting Department performs the function of checking invoices against sales orders to assure full assessment of established prices.

Thus, the application of price codes and symbols to the manufacturing order is a very important function of order handling. Codes and symbols are also associated to the respective manufacturing data, as indicated in paragraphs to follow.

To the internal auditor, however, the pricing function assumes number one position from the audit viewpoint. Extensive checks and tests should be made to determine that codes and symbols are properly interpreted and applied in accordance with applicable prices.

b. Estimating. A broad consideration of this function comprehends the classification of ordered items into product types.

Less than maximum accuracy in this connection not only would contribute to a decrease in office efficiency, but, also, would add unnecessarily to office burden because of the corrections required.

c. Specifications. The application of specifications to manufacturing orders, in effect, comprehends all manufactured products; *i.e.,* all products must be produced to meet certain standards, be it quality, strength, or capacity, or to meet special requirements.

The auditor's concern in this instance should be to ascertain the accuracy and adequacy with which this information has been transcribed to the manufacturing order. Any performance short of perfection could easily result in losses, or at least erroneous production of the order, as well as necessitate corrections which in themselves create a source of potential error.

d. Packaging. This portion of manufacture, like specifications, is usually performed to certain standards. Therefore, the applying of proper information to the manufacturing order concerning packaging, wrapping, bundling, etc., as required by the particular product standard, is of special significance since separate standards usually apply for almost each type and size of product.

This function calls for a diligent review by the auditor since the slightest inadequacy often adversely affects ultimate shipping and pricing.

e. Credit Terms. It is necessary to emphasize the importance of the correct application of credit terms to the manufacturing order. The auditor should note that this phase is fully complied with in accordance with the company's credit provisions.

f. Special Instructions. This step in order handling is a "catch-all" for other information which must be shown on the manufacturing order. It is primarily instructive and statistical in nature but, nevertheless, important.

It is comprised of information concerning manner of shipment, *i.e.,* carload, less than carload, truck, etc.; delivery carrier, date and point of shipment, consignee; and much other information necessary for completion of the manufacturing order.

Careful review of this information is required of the auditor since much of it affects final invoicing.

Continual neglect in specifying such information causes the customer needless irritation, and necessary repeated requests from him for correction of these details makes for customer bad will, as well as adding unnecessarily to office burden.

g. Order Changes. During the interim period of order receipt and shipment, changes are often made to an order. These are requested either by customer or by the factory if the manufacturing order is incorrect. In such cases, a notice of change is prepared identifying the order and the item affected.

Alertness on the part of the auditor to the possibility of error in this connection is necessary. It must be ascertained that not only have changes been manifested to the respective orders at all points of production and pricing, but, also, that such changes have been properly recognized in final invoicing.

h. Order Status. Since the interim period of order receipt and shipment may be a long one, considerable data may have been accumulated pertinent to its present status. Such information must be correctly and properly noted on the order so that any reference thereto will immediately reveal the status of the order in its entirety without resorting to the review of voluminous files for the information desired. This is also an aid to the auditor in making a review of the order files. He can establish the efficiency of the party responsible for servicing the order; it is an indirect clue to filing efficiency, and it will give an insight into the manner in which the original manufacturng order was prepared.

Filing System

It is impossible to evaluate properly the efficiency of a filing system by merely examining its function. During the course of the audit the auditor should be able to observe the degree of efficiency attained by those responsible for order files. For example, order files accumulate considerable correspondence or memorandums from the time of order receipt to the time of shipment. If the file has been efficiently maintained, every piece of paper should be in the file in substantiation of information on the order. If the contrary is true, it indicates that the data have not been filed, have been misfiled, lost, or destroyed.

The methods of "charge outs" and "follow-ups" should be reviewed. Exceptions taken in this respect should be reported to management for corrective consideration.

Tests should be made with respect to retention and disposition of file material. Prepared schedules are usually available for "retention time" of records, and these should be reviewed to determine if they are all inclusive and reasonably current, since the requirements are changing constantly and new records are frequently added. Where such schedules are not in evidence, the auditor should be guided by Federal, state, and municipal regulatory requirements and prudent judgment concerning retention and disposition of records.

Working Funds

The majority of sales offices are assigned a cash fund for the purpose of transacting petty and emergency expenditures and to provide funds for traveling and solicitation expenses.

In addition to reconciling the fund and making usual tests of fund administration, the auditor should determine that sums advanced to employes are authorized and signed for, that periodic accounting is made therefor, that items on expense statements have been properly classified, and that expense statements are properly signed and approved before reimbursement.

Salary advances should be aged and reviewed for frequency. Exceptions that are taken should be discussed with office management, and if possible, necessary procedures should be recommended to strengthen the controls.

Idle Office Equipment

The auditor should be alert in the observance of idle equipment. He should prepare a list of such equipment and initiate steps with the office under audit which will permit this fact to become known throughout the entire company. In this manner, the equipment may be utilized elsewhere or properly disposed, thus preventing needless utilization of company funds, as well as releasing additional space for more productive purposes.

SHIPPING AND INVOICING CONTROLS

Manufacturing orders are received at the factory as previously prepared and entered by the district sales office. They contain all the essential data necessary for production, shipment, and pricing. The following paragraphs will consider the controls with respect to the two latter functions only.

Shipping

The Shipping Department has notification that certain orders are scheduled to come off the production line on certain dates. Shipping arrangements are made accordingly, and freight cars and trucks are ordered to be spotted for loading. Products are routed to the loading platform, and loading proceeds as follows:

Railroad Cars. As the material is loaded in accordance with the factory sales order, a loading report or tally is prepared, usually by operating personnel. This shows the number of units, weights, sizes, etc., which are obtained from the production records or tags accompanying each unit package or bundle of product. After the load has been rechecked to the tally, a bill of lading is prepared authorizing the release of the car. All shipping documents are forwarded to the Billing Department where they are accounted for, usually through the checking of numerical sequence of numbers assigned to each document, and listed on a shipping register.

Truck Shipments. These are handled in a manner similar to that of railroad shipments, except that, in addition, control is exercised over the entry to and the departure of the truck from the factory premises.   Gate control records are also developed and become a part of the shipping documents.

Audit Objectives

Since the function of shipping is an important intermediate step between production and invoicing, it demands considerable audit attention to determine that:

1. The system of control over the shipping function is basically sound and adequate.
2. Instructions to the Shipping Department are synchronized with production schedules.
3. The loading and load checking operations are evidenced by authorized signatures.
4. Shipping instructions and tally sheets are in agreement and are complete in detail.
5. Bills of lading and load reports are in agreement with product classifications, weights, and rates.
6. All shipping documents are forwarded to the Invoice Department under an adequate control system, *e.g.*, a sequentially numbered shipping register.

Invoicing

As stated earlier in the chapter, in the interest of good internal control, the invoicing function should be performed by a group unrelated to sales office routine, preferably under Accounting Department responsibility.   Usually all invoicing is done at a centralized point, whether at factory level or at the General Office of a company. However, to facilitate invoicing, certain preliminary work is performed which converts the sales production order and shipping documents into invoice information preparatory to pricing.   This is commonly referred to as billing.

Billing.   On receipt of the shipping manifests, the Billing Department compares the documents with its copy of the sales production order.   The information displayed on both is correlated, and that which is not necessary for final invoicing is omitted from the bill. Copies of the bill serve as shipping notices, but ordinarily indicate no prices or amounts.

In reviewing the function of billing, the auditor should ascertain that:

1. The shipping documents have all been accounted for under the system of control.
2. Freight car movement records have been reconciled to bills of lading and that truck movements have been reconciled to gate records.
3. Order changes have been processed to the factory order, shipping instructions, etc., in order that proper pricing may be assured.
4. The loading tallies are in agreement with the sales order.
5. The transcription of correlated information to the bill is accurate, complete, and adequate for correct invoicing.
6. The bills are controlled through numerical sequence, or by any other equally effective method.

Pricing. Pricing is the application of monetary amounts to shipped product items preparatory to the extension and final compilation of invoice amounts.

The audit objectives in the review of this function should comprehend:

1. The verification and accounting for all bills by checking to an invoice register, etc.
2. The verification of corrections which have been made to production and shipping documents prior to shipment and the determination that such corrections have been processed into the final price.
3. The determination that errors disclosed by audit have been corrected.
4. The reviewing of records for all errors arising during the course of transcription and preparation of all records relative to billing and pricing.
5. The review of the application of prices as established by official price lists, discount sheets, extra lists, etc., and the association of these prices to respective product description quantities, sizes, etc.
6. The review of freight terms and rates, credit extension, terms of sale, etc.
7. The verification of extensions and footings.
8. That for composite prices, all elements have been properly accumulated and applied to the respective product units.

General Audit Objectives

In addition to the specific audit procedures already discussed, there are certain other audit conclusions which may be arrived at based upon such procedures.

The functions of billing and shipping are the natural results of previous activities, such as order solicitation, conversion, order entry, and production. Any improper handling of an order during these prior activities will be reflected in what is actually shipped and billed, unless corrected. Thus, the auditor should put his finger on the guilty responsibility and make recommendations for correction of procedures at the point indicated. In order to do this, the auditor will have to evaluate the controls over orders accepted and entered, order changes, and production performance in the light of promises, diversion of materials to other orders, and other considerations having a bearing on efficient fulfillment of orders.

CHAPTER 14

PAYROLL CONTROL AUDITS

Objectives and Scope

The objectives of a payroll control audit are:

1. The determination that the procedures established for handling the various phases of the payroll utilize the applicable principles of internal control set forth in Chap. 3.
2. The determination that these procedures are being complied with in practice and that the resulting payments are correct.
3. The determination that the stipulations of Union agreements are complied with.
4. The determination that applicable government regulations, such as the Fair Labor Standards Act, Workmen's Compensation laws, and state and local laws regulating hours for women and minors are complied with.
5. The observation of opportunities for reduction of unnecessary labor costs and simplification of payroll accounting methods.

As in all types of audits, the objectives will be accomplished by test checks. We do not believe it is possible to lay down definite rules covering the extent of test checks which should be made of each of the various operations involved in payroll preparation. Particularly on payroll work, because of the many entries and calculations, the test checks will be relatively limited. The objectives, as outlined above, do not comprehend determination of the clerical accuracy of the payroll except when a tendency toward an abnormal amount of clerical inaccuracies is indicated during the course of the audit. In other words, verification of clerical accuracy is confined to that portion of the work involved in the examinations covered by the above objectives.

Preparation for the Audit

In preparation for the audit:

1. The auditor should review all the written procedures and the forms and records employed in order to learn the approved methods of payroll handling. To the extent that written procedures do not exist for all or a portion of the payroll operation, and to the extent that the permanent file of work papers does not include a brief description of the existing practices, he should prepare a skeleton flow chart for the permanent work paper file.
2. He should then review the written procedures and/or his skeleton flow chart in order to determine indicated general weaknesses of internal control.
3. In order to attain certain of the objectives above, the auditor must familiarize himself with the provisions of the labor agreement and the government regulations applicable.
4. If the auditor is not already familiar with the physical layout of the plant, location of time recorders, etc., he should make such an inspection.
5. He should prepare a tentative audit program outlining each of the steps contemplated and establish a tentative time budget on each. In the preparation of the program and selection of the periods and departments tested, care must be exercised that they are representative as to employe classifications, bases of pay, and representative of the work of the several clerks or groups in charge of the various phases. As the audit progresses, the extent of coverage in various steps of the audit may be shortened or expanded to the extent that the auditor finds it necessary to do so in order that he can satisfy himself as to the adequacy of each phase.

Making the Audit

The important features of a payroll system in an industrial company are:

1. *Authorization and Control of Rates.* Wage scales and/or rate cards will be examined to determine that the rates coincide with those established by labor agreements, or other authorizations, and

that authorized changes are properly given effect to. **Proper approvals** must be evidenced on these wage scales and/or rate cards and observation made that access to these records is confined to authorized persons.

2. *Attendance and Time Reporting.* A study of attendance and time reporting practices should be made to determine that the feature of internal control exists by which independent employment office records may be compared with payroll records to establish that all employes listed on the payroll are authorized by the Employment Department.

The procedure for reporting of hours worked should be analyzed to determine that the person so recording is in a position to have knowledge that the employe did work the hours shown and on the occupation indicated. For example, the operating foreman should be in such a position, or a departmental clerk who spends approximately his entire time in and around the department near the men may also be in such a position. However, traveling time-takers who travel a route through the plant and may see each man only once or twice a day for a few seconds, if at all, are not in such a position. In the case of the use of such time-takers, the time records should be approved by the operating foreman in more than a perfunctory manner. Normally, an operating foreman will have charge of relatively few men, possibly 5 to 50, in a large plant. Therefore, there will be many such foremen reporting time. Since, as already mentioned, they are in a position to report the time accurately and properly, attendance recording therefore depends primarily upon the integrity of these foremen. The fact that there are many such foremen tends to reduce the possibility of cases of large payroll padding. The majority of these foremen will be honest; and, if any are not honest, the extent to which a small group can be padded without detection is limited. Accordingly, the auditor's approach to determination of the adequacy of this time reporting will be through:

a. Comparison of time reported with independent reports of production on various operating units used as the basis of incentive plans.

b. Comparison of time reports with independent reports of time on maintenance or production job orders.

c. Comparison of time reported with hours worked by facilities or occupations requiring fixed crews.

d. Comparison of the remainder of the employes who are not working on incentive, maintenance, or fixed crew occupations by comparison of trends of the number of employes in each such occupation or gang. Inasmuch as this latter group, which may approximate 10% to 20% of a normal industrial payroll, is the most difficult to control, the auditor will concentrate a considerable portion of his time on this phase and will determine that levels of supervision higher than the reporting foreman regularly observe trends and approve the number of men on each such occupation.

As a secondary check on the time reported, as discussed above, limited review of time registered by time clocks, gate control records, etc., should be made by the auditor.

The auditor will conduct tests to establish to his satisfaction that the time thus reported and approved is properly transcribed into the payroll records.

As noted above, the distribution of labor costs by expense classification is established at the same level as the reporting of time. Other than to determine that the procedure for such accumulation of cost by classification is adequate and is being followed, little verification of actual distribution will be made by the internal auditor.

3. *Payroll Preparation.* A test examination of the selected portions of the payroll will be made to determine that proper regular, shift differential, piece or other incentive, overtime, or other rates are being applied. If there are any special rates of allowances, such as reporting allowances or medical treatment on company time observed, the authorizations, reasons, or approvals therefor should be carefully examined.

Determination of accuracy of extensions, footings, balancing of payroll hours, etc., will be reviewed only to the limited extent previously referred to in this chapter in connection with verification of clerical accuracy.

Each class of deduction from gross earnings should be reviewed to determine that the deduction is properly authorized by the individual employe, by duly recognized Unions, or by law, as the case may be. Final distribution of the total amount deducted for each class of deduction should be confirmed. For example, deductions for withholding taxes should be traced into payments to the Federal government for these taxes; deductions for group life insurance premiums should be traced into payments to the insurer, etc.

Deductions, generally, comprise such items as social security taxes, withholding for Federal income tax, group life and hospital insurance, pension plans, credit unions, savings plans, Union dues, savings bonds, employe purchases, wage advances, assignments, and garnishments. The auditor will review the practices in use in case insufficient hours prevent full deductions for all such items to determine that proper control is exercised to ensure ultimate deduction.

4. *Disbursement of Payroll.* During the course of his audit, the auditor will observe the disbursement of a current payroll to determine that:

   a. The employes making such disbursement are independent of the group which reports time and production or prepares the payroll.
   b. Disbursement is made only upon careful scrutiny of proper identification.
   c. Adequate protection is accorded cash involved during the pay-off.
   d. Unclaimed wages at the conclusion of the pay-off period are recorded and returned to the Treasury Department or cashier for redeposit or retention for the established period for payment when called for by properly identified employes.
   e. Disbursement is made only upon proper receipts from the employes, or such other records are maintained as are deemed adequate by top accounting management.
   f. As indicated by limited test checks, the amounts disbursed agree with net payroll calculations, and in the case of check payrolls, the bank accounts are reconciled by employes independent of the paymaster or the Payroll Department.

5. *Vacation Allowances.* Determination of the procedure followed in the calculation of vacation allowances will be made by test reviews to determine that the company vacation policy and Union agreement have been complied with as related to such matters as service eligibility rules and that the amount paid is in accordance with the prescribed method of calculation.

6. *Payroll Adjustments.* An analysis of adjustments of overages, shortages, errors, etc., by type and frequency, should be made in order that corrective actions can be recommended to reduce such adjustments.

7. *Separations.* A study should be made to determine that practices relative to separations comprehend adequate control to ensure that all obligations to the company are satisfied before final wage payment is made to the employe and that any additional compensation such as severance pay is properly computed in accordance with prescribed company policies.

The general principles of internal control and audit procedures, as indicated above, apply both to wage and salary payrolls. Special clearance with top management is usually required, however, for the internal auditor to review certain confidential salary payroll records.

CHAPTER 15

INCENTIVE PLANS AND CONTROL OF PRODUCTION REPORTING

Objective and Governing Policies

The realization of the benefits to be obtained from a program to secure the uniform return of a fair day's work for a fair day's pay, through the medium of incentive applications designed to establish the requirements of a fair day's work and to provide for the payment of incentive earnings for the performance of work over and above the requirements of a fair day's work, necessitates the establishment of and adherence to policies and procedures based on the fundamental principles governing the development and application of incentives.

Responsibility and Objective of the Audit Division

It is the responsibility of the Audit Division to conduct sufficient periodic audits to determine compliance with the established policies and procedures.   The specific objective of such audits is the determination that incentive applications are in accord with established policies and procedures and are being correctly applied, adequately controlled, and properly maintained under changing conditions.

Requirements for Effective Auditing of Incentive Plans

The discharge of this responsibility and the attainment of the desired objective require the possession of certain knowledge, some general and fundamental, other detailed and specific, of the governing policies and procedures, including a working knowledge of certain phases in the development of performance standards.

While the procedure in an incentive audit requires the performance of certain routine examinations and verifications, the nature and purpose of incentives, their relationship to the pay envelope, and their subjectiveness to human elements demand that the auditor analyze all phases of the incentive application, recognize the inherent weaknesses therein, employ every available control tool, and correlate all the details of his investigation.   Such a correlation may reveal inconsistencies, the further investigation of which may lead to the disclosure of irregularities which are obscure on the surface.

The Audit Proper

Provisions of Plan.   The brochure which formally presents the provisions of an incentive application is the base reference point for all aspects of an incentive audit.   It is of prime importance, therefore, that a careful analysis be made of the provisions stated therein in order to determine their compliance with existing policies, to verify, later, that application practices are in conformance therewith, and to note for detailed investigation those items which can get out of line, be misunderstood, be misreported, or be misapplied. The items of particular significance to be noted will become evident as the related phases of the audit are presented below.

This analysis should determine also that the respective provisions are adequately and clearly stated to permit a ready application thereof.

An outline brief of the plan should be prepared for inclusion in the work papers.

Development and Maintenance of Performance Standards.   The determination, accumulation, and correctness of the elements comprising a performance standard are the responsibility of the Industrial Engineering Department.   Although most of these elements are not susceptible to audit by the Audit Division, standards development should be reviewed to the extent required to ascertain that:

1. The composition of these elements into a final performance standard and the incorporation therein of allowances for rest and personal needs, delay allowances, and process allowances are in conformance with established policies and procedures.
2. Where inherent delay and/or process allowances are built into the standards, no opportunity exists for the performance of work during stand-by time that would inflate incentive performances.

The fundamental principle that performance standards shall cover a specified set of conditions only, and must be voided when and if those conditions are changed, requires the determination of the applicability of the established standards under current conditions. Depending on the nature of the incentive application, this determination may involve:

1. A review of established standard practices covering the materials, tools, equipment, processes, speeds, products, crew sizes, etc., upon which the performance standards were based.
2. A review of the work elements comprehended in developing the performance standards.
3. Field studies of actual operating conditions.
4. An analysis of incentive performance trends.
5. A review of any accounting functions not directly related to incentive application that may provide warning signals, such as appropriations, cost revisions resulting from revised product specifications, or relocating and rearranging charges.

Reporting. A detailed study will be made of the methods employed to convey to the Payroll Department the data required for application of the incentive plan to determine that:

1. The reporting functions are performed by nonparticipants of the incentive plan. In this regard, the perfunctory recording of data furnished by a participant should not be construed as nonparticipant reporting.
2. Reports (production, inspection, or rejection, time, etc.) are properly prepared to facilitate incentive application.
3. Items on the respective reports are adequately identified and/ or described to facilitate auditing and control.
4. Reports bear the signatures of the preparers and the authorized approving supervisors.

Controls. A detailed study will be made of the controls established and exercised over reported data, and of the past applications of such controls, in order to judge their effectiveness and to determine that:

1. The independent records used for verification of reported production quantities are authentic and are adequately controlled.

2. Quantities produced cannot be reported as less than actual in order to report the held-out production at a more advantageous time from an incentive earnings standpoint.
3. Where performance standards are classified by the number of units processed per operating cycle, or by the number of passes, or other similar classification, per unit of production, adequate protection is provided against misreporting of these classification factors.
4. Those items reported on an occurrence basis, if not subject to direct verification, are controlled through test observations.
5. Reported time and the allocation thereof between measured and unmeasured work are adequately controlled.

The study of control methods should determine that:

1. To the greatest degree possible, controls are exercised by personnel other than those performing the reporting function.
2. Where controls must be exercised on a test check basis, the frequency is consistent with the degree of control required.
3. Applications of standards and provisions of plans and calculations of incentive earnings are adequately controlled to ensure clerical accuracy.
4. Performance charts and related reports are maintained and analyzed to detect unusual trends.
5. Means are provided for ascertaining changed conditions affecting the applicability of the plan.

Application and Calculation. It is not possible to designate a specific number of application periods for which the application of the provisions of a plan to reported data and the calculation of resulting performances and incentive earnings should be audited. The examination need be only as extensive as is required to assure, primarily, that principles, policies, procedures, and provisions are being adhered to, but such analyses as are made should be intensive and complete, with supposition and imagination being employed constantly. The accuracy of the calculations is secondary in importance, but if numerous errors are noted, the principle of control over accuracy is involved.

The items to be covered will vary depending on the nature of the plan, but this phase of the audit should determine that:

1. Correct performance standards are applied to reported productions, set-ups, size changes, etc. In this regard, the vulnerability of all "per occurrence" standards must be recognized.
2. Provisions for the exclusion from pay production of rejects caused by the participants of the plan are applied.
3. Unmeasured work reported is not covered by the performance standards applied to reported productions, etc.
4. Delays are not paid for on an hourly rate basis, either as delays or as unmeasured work, where the performance standards contain allowances for such delays.
5. Standard crew sizes are adhered to. This is particularly important on plans covering crews whose performance standards contain process allowances comprehending inherent stand-by time for certain positions.
6. Performance and earnings calculations are correct.

Internal Control Principles

General Principles. The primary objective of an incentive control program is to ensure that payments under the respective plans properly reflect productive effort when related to the principle of a fair day's work for a fair day's pay. Administered by the Accounting Department, the program should conform, to the greatest degree possible, with the following general rules:

1. Reporting functions shall be performed by nonparticipants of the incentive plan. In this regard, the perfunctory recording of data furnished by a participant should not be construed as nonparticipant reporting.
2. Controls shall be exercised by personnel other than those performing the reporting functions.
3. Controls shall be designed to prevent rather than correct irregularities and shall be practical, effective, and economical relative to cost versus possible loss.

Principles Governing Control Methods. While the controls required will vary depending on the conditions surrounding the individual incentive applications, the principles governing specific control measures are:

1. The independent records used to verify production quantities and to determine the accuracy of all reported data shall be authentic and shall be controlled adequately.
2. Controls exercised, of necessity, through periodic test checks of records, actual observations, or special audits shall have a frequency consistent with the degree of control required.

Control Consciousness. The success of a control program depends not only on the establishment of adequate direct and indirect controls wherever possible, but also on the development of control consciousness in all employes engaged in the various functions relating to the application and administration of incentives. A complete understanding of duties and responsibilities, familiarity with plant operations, and an appreciation of any weaknesses in the control methods are essential elements of control consciousness which, together with the establishment of benchmarks relative to production quantities, force requirements, percentages of unmeasured work, incentive performances, etc., will increase the ability to detect irregularities and initiate prompt investigation.

CHAPTER 16

PRODUCTION PLANNING AND COSTS OF MANUFACTURING

In order to control production and thereby produce the desired quantity and quality of product for a minimum amount of material labor and other manufacturing expense, it is essential that production activities be planned.

To plan production properly, it is necessary that each step in the production cycle be determined in advance in order that each operation can be performed at the maximum efficiency.

Planning encompasses the following:

1. The determination and budgeting of machine and equipment capacity and of work force required.
2. The maintenance of accurate, up-to-date inventory records.
3. The maintenance, and direction of the use, of specification and practice files and customer approved product practices.
4. The translation of incoming orders into production schedules.

In the auditing approach, consideration should be given to the over-all matters which will be of primary interest to management, rather than attempt any detailed technical reviews of methods pertaining to development of plant and equipment capacities. Any attempt beyond establishment that equipment and departmental capacities have been determined by engineering studies and that bottleneck operations are properly considered in scheduling could result only in controversy.

The objectives of an audit of the planning functions are to determine that:

1. Customers' orders are properly controlled.
2. The backlog of sales orders is so controlled that it furnishes management with sound data for developing sales forecasts.

3. Inventory controls are adequately maintained.
4. Established manufacturing practices are being followed.
5. Production schedules established by the Production Planning Department are being followed so as to attain the objective of economical operation.
6. Customer relationships are not impaired owing to chronic failure to meet promised shipping dates.
7. The consumption of material and the use of labor as production moves through the prescribed manufacturing processes are adequately recorded so that a complete history of goods produced is provided.
8. Accounting controls are established to verify the production reported and that the cost accounting system is established on a responsibility basis.

Prior to beginning the audit, the auditors should thoroughly acquaint themselves with the procedures and operations performed. The actual flow of materials should be observed in order to understand the problems relative to the storage and release of raw materials, the control over materials through the various operations, and the warehousing conditions.

Receipt of Orders and Order Changes

The auditor should review the procedure being followed to determine the extent of control over receipt of orders and order changes. Tests should be made to satisfy the auditor that orders and order changes are promptly acknowledged to the entering office.

A number of order changes should be reviewed to see that they are properly authorized and are handled in accordance with company policies if cost and/or selling prices are affected. Checks should be made to ascertain that copies of changes are submitted to all departments affected and that the changes have been recorded on job or production orders. It is of utmost importance that all changes be serially numbered and referenced to the original order. Provisions should be in effect for the Billing Department to review such changes to detect any effect on sales price. Similarly, all orders should be reviewed by the Cost Department for changes affecting costs.

Order Entry

The auditor should determine that the flow of orders and related papers is efficiently performed so as to avoid unnecessary delay in handling and delivery.

Quota records should be checked to make certain that orders are not accepted by the Sales Department in excess of allotted tonnage. General sales authorizations in support of changes in quotas should be on file.

An examination of the uncompleted order files should be made to determine whether the Production Planning Department is advising the Sales office currently as to the status of unscheduled orders, revised promise dates, etc.

Scheduling of Orders

All orders should be included into a broad advance schedule, and the auditor should ascertain that the detailed weekly schedules are in accordance therewith.

1. *Inter-mill and Inter-company Orders.* In some plants the production of a mill unit may represent end product to be shipped to customers and also raw materials of another mill unit; *e.g.,* rods may be shipped to customers as finished product or may be used as raw material in the production of wire. Particular consideration should be given to the coordination of the scheduling by the individual mill units to ascertain:

  a. That the mill unit placing orders for material is not suffering equipment downtime as a result of failure to receive materials.

  b. That order requirements are not being placed by the mill unit to build up inventory when material could be shipped to customers.

The first condition would tend to lower profits in the company, not only because of increased costs due to downtime, but also because of failure to realize the further profit which would accrue from the additional operations. Broken promises and impairment of customer relations may develop as a result of not according proper attention to inter-mill and inter-company orders.

As a result of the second condition, immediate loss of revenue is sustained and the further possibility of loss due to obsolescence, damage in the course of warehousing, and inefficiency due to overstocking is presented. This matter is of prime consideration when the auditor reviews inventory controls in effect.

2. *Load Charts.* A review of load charts will be required to ascertain if they are properly maintained, with due consideration to the level of operation. The auditor should determine the reason for the variance between loading and rated capacity of equipment. Overacceptance of orders and the resultant overloading of equipment can result only in broken promises and customer dissatisfaction. In the event that equipment centers are only partially loaded, a "want order" condition may exist. If such is the case, the auditor should determine if the Sales Department has been advised so that sales efforts may be concentrated on those items necessary to fill the unused capacity.

3. *Canceled Orders.* Recently canceled orders should be checked to the load charts to determine that space is immediately released. In the event that processing has begun prior to cancellation, determine that action has been taken as follows:

   a. That the Production Planning Department has notified the Sales Department that the order is in process and that an effort has been made to persuade the customer to accept the order, or

   . That work was stopped at the most convenient and economical point of operations and that the Sales and Accounting Departments were informed as to all costs incurred prior to the Sales Department's determining the action to be taken for the incurred costs.

   c. If it is decided, in view of the facts presented, to continue operations on the canceled order, it should be determined that such action will not result in stocking unauthorized quantities or that such material was applied to open orders not in process.

4. *Adherence to Standard Practices.* The permanent file records showing data necessary to schedule each product should be compared with orders in process to determine that established manufacturing practices are adhered to. Particular attention should also be directed to standard material requirements, both as to quantity and quality, versus actual material put into process. During a period of shortages a deliberate attempt to manufacture overruns due to customer partiality could result only in disruption of the company's quota system. Normally a customer may refuse to accept

an overrun. If the material is of a specialized nature and restricted as to salability, a slow-moving stock item often results.

Deviation from standard practice by substitution of material may result in a higher percentage of rejections or scrap than would have been developed if the standard practice had been observed.

The auditor will check the standards set for the most economical grouping of orders and compare them with current scheduling. Failure to adhere to economical runs of material requires unnecessary unit changes and reduced production. Reasons should be secured for the deviations.

5. *Completed Orders.* A test check of completed orders should be made to determine the following:

a. A comparison of promise dates, scheduled completion dates, and the actual shipping dates. Reasons should be procured for significant variances.

b. If additional operations are performed which are not scheduled, the auditor will check the costs incurred for the additional work to charges to the customer. Reasons for failure to make such charges will be ascertained.

c. In the event that an individual job order accounting system is in effect, comparison of production versus shipments should be made.

d. If orders are of such quantity that shipment in carload lots is indicated, any L.C.L. shipments should be noted for further check. This condition may indicate ineffective scheduling or material delays in process.

6. *Carry-over Orders in Weekly Schedules.* Weekly schedule carry-over should be reviewed, and repetitive items should be noted. The reason for recurring carry-over items and the effect upon the backlog should be determined. Possible lack of cooperation between operating and planning personnel could be a significant factor at this point. If such a condition prevails, the objectives of the Production Planning Department could not be attained.

7. *Material Delays in Process.* In-process order files should be reviewed to reveal the occurrence of material delays at any stage of the operation. Procedures should be in effect to determine the cause and its immediate correction. The auditor should pay special attention to "lost" or "sidetracked" material which often results in increased cost due to:

  a. Additional treatments.

  b. Rejections.

  c. Additional movements of transportation.

  d. Reduced production at centers where congestion develops.

  e. Downtime of equipment and idle workers.

  8. *Equipment Utilization.* Equipment utilization reports should be reviewed and idle hours analyzed to determine if low utilization is directly associable to the scheduling function.

  9. *Effect of Credit Department "Holds" on Scheduling.* A comprehensive and thorough check should be made to determine the effect on production scheduling and shipping of "holds" entered by the Credit Department at both the production and shipping levels.

The following points should be specifically covered:

  a. Frequency of holds. If the holds are numerous, a ratio to the total orders scheduled or shipped should be developed.

  b. Frequency and importance of changes in production schedules due to holds. In this connection, it will be noted that, where a production hold is entered and withdrawn by the Credit Department prior to the time the order is entered into production, no scheduling effect will be sustained. If, however, the Credit Department does not cancel the hold before the scheduled production date, two effects will be sustained:

  (1) Necessity of displacing the hold order with other orders to maintain productive efficiency.

  (2) Possible displacement of subsequently scheduled orders to permit the re-entry of the hold order at a later date.

  c. In connection with loading or shipping holds, points similar to the above should be considered in their effect on prior operations.

  d. Statistical development should be made of the number of orders scheduled or loaded where the material has been produced and the hold subsequently results in a cancellation at the direction of the Credit Department or by the Sales Department for credit reasons.

In brief, establish, by statistical presentation, what effect is sustained on operating practices by the present direct entry order system which requires entry and scheduling of an order before the receipt of credit approval.

10. Peaks and valleys in daily shipments contribute to inefficient performance. Often a review of shipments during a month will reveal upward trends on week and month-ends. This usually results from a last-minute attempt to meet production directives.

Consideration should be given to the improvement of the scheduling to avoid these peak loads. Failure to level shipping schedules reasonably results in imposition of excessive work loads on the invoicing and accounting functions and, in most cases, the incurrence of additional payroll expense.

11. *Demurrage.* An analysis of the reasons for demurrage costs should be made to determine whether they are attributable to inefficient planning and scheduling.

Inventory Control

1. *Duplicate Inventory Records.* The auditor should ascertain if more than one set of detailed inventory records are being maintained. In those plants where the accounting is decentralized, the opportunity for eliminating duplicate records is presented. When considering this, however, the auditor should weigh the following points:

   a. The purposes they serve.

   b. Differences in content.

   c. Reasons for not consolidating into one record.

2. *Surplus Material.* Inventory records should be reviewed to determine activity of the various materials. Stock build-ups should be given particular attention, and the reasons therefor will be questioned. The file of unfilled orders requisitioning materials should be considered in conjunction with inventory balances. As mentioned previously, surplus material may represent loss to the company due to deterioration, necessity for special treatments before it can be used or shipped, and warehousing costs entailed.

3. *Purchases of Raw Materials.* The auditor should review methods in effect to determine that coordination of material requirements with order placement is effective.

4. *Slow-moving Stock.* Slow-moving items should be listed at regular intervals and submitted to the Sales and Purchasing Departments for appropriate action in the form of special sales promotions and/or return to the vendors. The auditor should compare such lists with inventory records to see that all items are included. An

observation should be made of slow-moving stock to determine whether or not it has deteriorated to a condition where it should be physically scrapped.

5. The reason for increase in finished goods inventory balances must be considered. Such increase may be due to normal production of an item which has wide salability or to overruns on customers' orders. In the latter instance, if the material has restricted salability because of special specifications required by a particular customer, potential loss exists.

Correspondence Files

Correspondence files will be reviewed and analyzed for reflection of customers' attitude toward:

1. Overshipments.
2. Undershipments.
3. Broken shipping promises.
4. Defective material.
5. Nonadherence to shipping instructions.

Order Backlog

The backlog reflecting unshipped orders which enters into the development of sales forecasts and production directives should be reviewed and test checks made to determine that the quantities reflected are legitimate. The validity of orders in files should also be established.

Production Recording

The auditor should review the system of recording production to make certain that:

1. Wherever possible, production records are prepared by an independent person who derives no benefit from the amount of production reported.
2. The responsibility for the production recorded has been definitely established and that the reports are signed by the preparer and approved by the responsibility head.
3. The production reports are accurate.
4. Production is recorded at those points where it is most feasible to collect information for use in determining costs and establishing budgetary and inventory control.

5. Procedures are in effect to verify continuously the production of one center by the consumption or production of another.

6. All scrap, defective material, and other losses are reported at the points at which they occur.

The accurate recording of material consumption and resulting production, in each operational phase, is of vital importance. Unless a high degree of accuracy is attained, and maintained, costs and operating statistics presented to management can be misleading and sometimes valueless. Physical inventories should be used only as a check of balance sheet values and of profit and loss results. It should not be necessary for management to keep its fingers crossed or to correct its interpretation of accounting information after the physical inventories have been taken and recorded in the accounts.

The consumption of material and its movements through the manufacturing processes should be adequately recorded so that a complete history is provided of the goods produced. This history should include the sequence of operations performed. The auditor should be able to trace the finished product back through the production records to the original raw materials and, at the same time, determine that specifications are being met and that the production records provide adequate proof.

Sometimes there is a tendency on the part of recording personnel to be careless in recording consumption and production. Because of incentive payments or operating performance goals, figures are deliberately distorted or incorrectly reported to attain personal objectives. It is therefore desirable to have production and consumption reports prepared by independent recorders, preferably under the jurisdiction of the Accounting Department. These independent recorders should be able to verify the figures they record, by test checks of actual counts and reference to production reports of prior or subsequent operations. However, it is often not practicable to use independent recorders, and operating personnel must make their own recordings. In such instances, independent tests or checks must be provided to assure control over accuracy and to ensure the validity of the production reported.

Testing the Production Records

The auditor should test at least one production order for each product selected for examination.

Either of two methods can be used to test the accuracy of production reports:

1. The auditor may find it desirable to begin with the finished product shipped to the customer and trace it back through the operational phases to the original raw material.
2. The auditor may find it more expeditious to begin with the raw material stage and follow the order through to its completion.

Material produced by one operational unit should be accounted for by consumption on other operational units.

After accounting for total production to consumption on various orders the auditor should continue to follow only that material which applies to the order included in the audit test.

Material consumed by each operating unit should be completely accounted for as good product, scrap, defective product, or scale.

Taking normal losses into consideration, whenever it is found that the material consumed by an operating unit has not been completely accounted for, the reason for the difference should be determined. Additional tests may be desirable for checking consumption and production of this unit.

Material produced and consumed is measured and expressed in the production records as weight, pieces, bales, bundles, etc. Accuracy of recording is, of course, necessary and can be determined only by observation, actual measurement test, and comparison with measurements on previous or subsequent operating units.

While the auditor is reviewing and testing production records, he should constantly keep in mind the internal control objective of independent record preparation by personnel who are not part of the operating group.

Comparison of Actual Production Methods with Anticipated or Budgeted Methods

The auditor should compare the actual operations performed, for a given order, with the specifications and practice instructions. Deviations should be noted and reasons secured.

In standard cost plants the performance and deviation variance accounts should provide much valuable information as to differences between anticipated or planned and actual methods used.

Test of Basic Operating Detail Records

Production reports are necessarily prepared from car tickets, scale weights, lift reports, and other basic detail operating records of production. These records should be verified on a test basis. The auditor should list the weight or quantities shown on the forms attached to the material and trace the information to production reports to see that it is accurately reported. Physical counts of the material in the bundle, lift, or other container should be made. Scales should be tested in the presence of the auditor, and mechanical counters should be observed in operation, keeping in mind questions as to how the count could be falsified or made in error.

Usually tare weights of buggies, cars, tote boxes, etc., are painted on the container. Dirt, moisture, additional material added for repair, and pieces lost or worn off will change the tare weight. Care should be taken to determine the accuracy of all tare and gross weights used.

Where the quantity of material is based upon weights or number of units, the auditor may find succeeding operating units accepting the counts of preceding units without performing an independent count. Where production or consumption is based upon estimates, it is important that an independent measurement be made at some operational phase after the estimate.

Scrap, Defective Material, and Other Losses

A minor amount of scrap, defective material, scale, and other losses are inevitable. However, the auditor should check the actual yield of the orders examined with that prescribed in the standard practices. Reasons should be obtained for unusual or out-of-line losses.

The auditor should check a representative number of production reports to the inventory control records maintained by the Production Control group. In addition, he should select a number of items posted to the control records and trace them to the source data. Production reports should be balanced by the recorders and forwarded in chronological sequence to the Cost Department.

Cost of Manufacturing Reports and Statistics

The objective of any cost system is to develop and present accurate and complete costs and statistics to management so that it may attain the most effective control over its operations. It therefore follows that the internal auditor should review the cost reports and statistics in order to ensure management that the information is accurate and dependable and can be used as a proper basis for managerial decisions.

To determine that the information is authentic, the auditor should probe the existence and reliability of the basic documents, such as production reports, labor force reports, material yields, and scrap reports. He should prove the clerical and mathematical accuracy and, wherever possible, see that the information agrees with the general ledger accounts. For example, reports presenting labor statistics should agree with the number of employes, hours worked, and wages earned as compiled in the payrolls and reconcile to the monthly journal entry. Where payroll accruals affect the report, the auditor should make certain that estimates are not used, both in the report and in the journal entry, which may destroy the value of the information.

Schedules of inventories and rates of turnover should be examined. The development of inventory trends may lead the auditor to the disclosure of deliberately padded figures or entries made by the Accounting Department to "bury" costing errors or to eliminate credit balances in inventory accounts. Frequently, scrap inventory accounts develop credit balances due to failure, intentional or otherwise, on the part of the operating organization to report scrap on production reports at the time of incidence. Entries are then made to bring the scrap account up to some "guesstimated" figure and credits made to the work-in-process account for fictitious values.

In a recent case, work-in-process figures presented to a governmental agency were subsequently proved to be overstated. It was discovered that, although a trial balance of job orders agreed with the general ledger work-in-process account, effect had not been given to partial deliveries to the finished goods account. It had been the practice of the Accounting Department to make adjustments to the accounts only when a job order had been completed. The auditor was aware of the correcting entries but failed to see that effect had not been given to the partial deliveries, on open or uncompleted orders, at the time of audit.

In another case, recently discussed, fraud was accomplished through the submission and payment of fictitious invoices for the purchase of various commodities. The amount embezzled was sizable, and the greater part was charged to inventories. Procedures were in effect which are usually considered to constitute adequate controls over accounts payable. However, alertness in determining the reasons for fluctuations in inventory, through comparisons, might have prevented the fraud or limited the amount involved.

Turnover rates often reveal the accumulation of slow-moving, obsolete, and surplus materials. Turn rates for a total inventory are not sufficient to exercise proper control. The auditor should see that the inventory is classified into product groups and that turn rates are developed for each group. Turn rates should be properly computed. Turnover of raw materials should be based on the average raw material inventory and the amount charged to work-in-process. Rates for work-in-process should be computed on the average work-in-process inventory and the value of completed product. Turnover of finished goods should be based on average inventory at cost and cost of sales; turnover of supplies, on average investment in supply stocks and the amount of supplies expensed for the period.

Comparisons of unit costs should be made, and the auditor should see that the accounting records provide adequate information relating to product costs and sales. An analysis of the elements comprising unit costs should be made. Where standard costs are in use, the authenticity, origin, and approval of the data used in building the standards should be determined.

Cost estimates used for pricing new products and special orders should be analyzed and compared with the actual costs developed and the return realized.

Sales should be costed at the same values charged and carried in the finished goods inventory account. The auditor should test a representative number of sales invoices by comparing the unit costs of sales to the values used in pricing transfers from work-in-process to the finished goods account.

Management's attention should be brought to costs carried in inventory which are higher than the established selling prices. When unit costs of items in work-in-process are higher or comparable to the amount to be realized, the auditor should determine the cause.

Where a job order system is in use, routines should be in effect and properly policed to record transfers from one job to another.

The auditor should determine the reasons for the development of each report. Discussions with the executives for whom the reports are prepared will often indicate that the information is incorrect or should be enlarged, revised, or curtailed. In interpreting cost figures the auditor should constantly be on the alert to detect unfavorable conditions and, if they exist, to find out what action has been taken to investigate and correct them.

Bases for computing overhead and burden rates should be studied. Overhead charges should be segregated between controllable and fixed expenses. The distribution of service charges to cost centers and products should be checked to see that it is fair and reasonable. The auditor should check to see that entries are classified in accordance with the manufacturing card of accounts.

Journal entries and supporting work papers should be carefully reviewed. Explanations should be concise and clear. Work papers should be preserved. The preparation and approval of journal entries should be delegated to responsible individuals who have an adequate knowledge of the manufacturing processes and the system of accounts used. Subsidiary records should be in agreement with their respective controls.

In general, the auditor should determine that management is presented with accurate, factual cost figures and statistics and that they tie in with the general accounts; that the accounts are established to reveal production costs in detail and total for each cost center and product; that the figures submitted by the Accounting Department can be reconciled to statistical information submitted to management by other departments; that trends in unit costs, inventories, labor, yields, etc., are developed; and that effective steps are taken to correct unfavorable conditions.

CHAPTER 17

TRAFFIC AND TRANSPORTATION AUDITS

The objectives of an audit of traffic and transportation activities should determine that:

1. Transportation and its related services are purchased at the lowest possible cost, consistent with other factors, such as time and the safety of the commodity in transit.
2. Proper records are maintained to assist in the control, prior to the incidence of plant transportation cost, with particular emphasis on demurrage, switching, and weighing.
3. Adequate procedures are in effect for the verification of transportation and accessorial service charges.
4. Procedures are in effect to ensure the prompt and proper filing of all claims and their recording in the accounts at the time of filing.
5. Transportation functions, both intra-plant and with contract or common carriers, are supervised and coordinated by centralized Traffic and Transportation Departments.
6. Procedures, at the Traffic Department level, ensure compliance with published tariff regulations and statutory requirements.

Purchase of Transportation

The Traffic Department should check method of shipment, routings, and type of equipment before bids are selected or purchase orders placed with the vendors. The auditor should make certain that routines are in effect to ensure the approval of all purchase orders.

Orders for cars should specify the exact size and type of car or motor truck in order to keep the payment of freight charges at a minimum.

Procedures should control the shipping of freight to make certain that less-than-carload or less-than-truckload shipments are classified and grouped to take advantage of carload or truckload rates or carload forwarding services.

Where compliance with customer's request regarding routing and type of equipment results in costs which exceed those comprehended in the sales price, routines should assure the recovery of excess costs.

Wherever possible, the policy of making shipments on a "freight collect" basis should be followed to avoid the expense of paying the carrier's charges and the use of company funds.

Proper weighing practices should be followed and adequate weighing facilities made available for the check of questionable weights on inbound and outbound shipments.

Accounting for purchased transportation and plant transportation services should be established on a responsibility basis. The auditor should examine the card of accounts to see that they are in sufficient detail to be of value in determining and controlling costs.

Plant Transportation Control Records

The auditor should determine the adequacy of records covering:

1. The ordering of inbound freight cars and their placement at the spots where they are to be unloaded.
2. The ordering and placement of empties of the size and type required.
3. Switching of cars within the plant for further loading or unloading.
4. The release of loaded and empty cars to the carrier.
5. The control and supervision of cars subject to demurrage.
6. The coordination of plant transportation facilities to prevent congestion which may result in costly delays.
7. The control of weighing and check weighing costs.

Switching

For effective control, requests covering empty and loaded cars, intra-plant switching, and reweighs should be transmitted to the Transportation Department and issued to the carrier in the form of a serially numbered switching order.

Orders should be specific as to car initial and number, time, date, type and size of equipment, and the location where the car is to be spotted. When weighing of a car is desired, it should be so indicated on the switching order. When intra-plant switching is involved, the order should include the tracks from and to which the car is to be moved. Provisions should be made for yard checks, on a test check basis, to verify the fact that a move has been completed.

Control records should be kept by the plant Transportation Department on which is accumulated all information relative to switching and demurrage. Routines should be established to account for all switching orders and their use to verify the carrier's charges.

Demurrage

Separate records are desirable for control of demurrage. Information pertaining to actual or constructive placement should indicate the car number and initial, as well as exact time and date of placement. Similar information covering the release of cars should be recorded.

Demurrage is a penalty charge assessed by the carrier for the detention of a freight car beyond a free period of time allowed for loading or unloading. A consignee is usually allowed 48 hours of free use. Charges are then made at a rate per car, per day. Rates increase in severity the longer a car is held. For example:

First 48 hours	(Excluding Sunday and holidays)	Free time
Third and fourth days	(Debit days)	$ 3.30 each
Fifth day	(Arbitrary demurrage)	5.50
Sixth day	(Arbitrary demurrage)	11.00
Subsequent days	(Arbitrary demurrage)	16.50 each

When the supply of cars changes, demurrage tariff supplements may increase or decrease the penalties involved.

In actual practice, a consignee will release some cars before the expiration of the free time allowed. Unless special arrangements are made, the prompt release of a car will not reduce demurrage incurred on other cars.

If there is sufficient volume, the consignee should make what is known as an "average demurrage agreement" with the carrier. Under such an agreement, credits are allowed for the release of cars within the first twenty-four hours of free time. The consignee is then permitted to use these credits as offsets to charges made against cars detained in excess of the 48 hours of free time. As a rule, one credit is required to offset one demurrage debit. Credits can be applied only against demurrage debits which, in the above example, are the first two days after the expiration of the free time. Also, they cannot be applied against demurrage assessed at increased rates, known as "arbitrary demurrage," nor carried over to offset debits of the following month. Credits on loading cannot be applied to debits on unloading, and vice versa. Free time is usually computed from the first 7:00 A.M. following actual or constructive placement, and charges are assessed for each day or portion thereof.

Control of demurrage, however, goes beyond that of verifying the carrier's charges. Much demurrage is attributable to operating inefficiencies, such as poor planning. Arrivals schedules should be prepared by the Transportation Department and issued to the receiving and operating responsibilities sufficiently in advance to ensure the availability of unloading and storage facilities. Conversely, the Transportation Department should be notified of the exact date and time that empty cars will be needed in order that they will be on hand and available for use.

Routines should be in effect to notify department heads when free time has elapsed and as demurrage accrues. Effective action should be instigated to release cars subject to the arbitrary rates.

While examining demurrage charges, the auditor should be on the alert to detect any unusual circumstances and errors or neglect on the part of the railroad which may affect the charges. For instance, allowances may be made for "run-arounds" attributable to errors or failures in switching or when made for the railroad's convenience. This type of allowance is made for cars held in excess of the first two debit days or against arbitrary demurrage charges only. The two debit days, however, may be offset by the regular demurrage credits.

Weighing

Track scales should be used to verify the weights of empty and loaded cars as they enter or leave the plant to verify the tare weights. Records should be maintained by a clerk or weightmaster stationed in the scale house, showing the gross, tare, and net weight and the identity of each car. The auditor makes certain that this information is used to verify the freight charges billed and the weights used for billing purposes. These weights should also be used by the accounts payable and receiving departments to verify material purchased on a weight basis.

Control should be exercised over reweighing practices. The auditor should examine the respective tariff to make certain that the rules are being complied with by both carrier and consignee. When carload freight is check-weighed, the carrier's charges should be compared to the original weight to make certain that they do not apply to cars whose check-weight varies from the original weight plus the specified tolerances.

Internal Check and Verification of Transportation Charges

In examining the system of internal check and verification of transportation charges, the auditor should make certain that procedures are in effect to:

1. Determine that carrier's charges are valid and that the services billed have been rendered.
2. Ascertain that rates and weights charged on transportation bills are in accordance with published tariffs, classifications, and agreements with private carriers.
3. Establish that the functions of quoting, rating, and checking of transportation rates are sufficiently distributed to reveal errors and to prevent collusion between members of the Traffic Department and the carrier.
4. Control charges and allowances billed and allowed on vendors' and customers' invoices.

All freight bills should be approved for rate and classification by the Traffic Department. Rates should be checked to effective tariffs by a person other than the one who rated and classified commodities.

Errors in rate are usually due to the application of the wrong rate through a clerical error, improper or inadequate description of the commodity, or the application of a class rate where a commodity rate applies. The auditor should test check rates to effective tariffs or to contracts with the assistance of qualified Traffic personnel.

Errors in overcharges and undercharges for weight are usually due to errors or omissions in the preparation of bills of lading or other shipping documents, failure to weigh freight accurately, the use of incorrect tare weights stenciled on cars, or failure to deduct allowances for dunnage, snow, etc.

The auditor should determine that routines are in effect for checking weights shown on freight bills to shipping papers, invoices, and weight reports. Adequate procedures should be in effect to control freight paid on purchases shipped "freight allowed" and, where freight is prepaid for the account of customers, to ensure recovery of the amounts paid.

The auditor should be sure to extend his examination to credits to and deductions by customers for freight charges paid by them. Such adjustments should be approved for propriety by the Sales or other department authorized to make arrangements with customers, and for rate and commodity classification by the Traffic Department.

In some areas, "pick-up" and delivery service is offered without charge on less-than-carload shipments and may be allowed on rail shipments hauled 300 miles or less within the area covered by the tariff. The auditor should make certain that allowances have been made or claims filed against the carrier when this service is performed by the company's own trucks.

In-transit privileges are provided by the railroad for the storing or processing of materials en route. For example, "milling-in-transit" privileges are granted to the grain industry, "barreling-in-transit" to the oil industry, and "fabrication-in-transit" to the steel industry. Controls should be in effect to ensure the recovery of excess charges paid, under the provisions of the respective tariffs.

Settlement of freight charges should be so controlled in the accounting records as to prevent the payment of duplicate or fictitious bills. Transportation charges should be compared and cross-referenced to basic documents such as bills of lading, invoices, and other debit and credit memorandums.

The auditor should compare theoretical mill scale and railroad scale weights to make certain that they are within the prescribed tolerances.

It is important that repairs made by the carrier to company-owned tracks be adequately controlled. Provisions should be made for the determination of the need for and the extent of such repairs, which should be covered by job and purchase orders.

Control should be exercised over material and labor furnished to the railroad through the issuance of accounts receivable invoices or the determination that proper allowances have been made on the carrier's invoice.

The auditor should make test checks of freight charges by:

1. Comparing weights to bills of lading, scale tickets, invoices, and other documents.
2. Verifying the accuracy of all calculations, such as extensions and additions, on freight bills and vouchers.
3. Verifying the entry and distribution in the accounts.
4. Inspecting all freight bills and charges for propriety and completeness of approvals.
5. Determining that the payment of freight bills is subject to the same degree of control as regular accounts payable.

Claims

In examining claims, the auditor should establish that:

1. Responsibility for the filing of freight claims is placed with the Traffic Department.
2. Procedures are in effect to ensure the filing of all claims and their prompt recording in accounting records.
3. Claims have been filed in accordance with tariff provisions and followed for settlement.
4. Effective measures are being taken to determine and eliminate the causes of losses, damages, and overcharges.
5. Costs used in computing claims are based upon accounting records and are in accordance with sound accounting principles.

The auditor should examine receiving routines to make certain that every piece of freight receipted for is delivered by the carrier.

Shipments should be promptly counted in by the Receiving Department to detect concealed loss and damage.

The carrier's local representative should be notified within the time limits prescribed by the tariffs and should approve the discrepancies in accordance with proper claim procedures.

Claims arising from inbound shipments, made F.O.B. destination, should be promptly charged against the vendor and referenced to the invoice covering the shipment concerned. Transportation charges, when they apply, should be assessed against the vendor.

The auditor should examine settled claims to make certain that the carrier has included interest on overcharges, unless payment has been received within the 30-day period prescribed in the tariffs.

Cash or checks in payment of claims should be received and entered by the cashier.

Rejected claims should be brought to the attention of a responsible official, who should decide whether the claim should be canceled or prosecuted.

The auditor should trace a representative number of settled and unsettled claims to the accounts receivable records.

CHAPTER 18

CONTROL OF MAINTENANCE AND CONSTRUCTION APPROPRIATIONS

American corporations annually appropriate, in one way or another, huge sums for maintenance and the acquisition of new plants and equipment. These expenditures form such an important part of total outlay that it is necessary that top management formally approve, either in the minutes of the company or by special appropriation forms, etc., that such application of funds is economically justified. The funds must be made ready and available according to plan as the maintenance and construction program progresses. In other words, because of their size and long-term implications, such expenditures must be made under an appropriate internal control system that will provide all the necessary safeguards which will be outlined in the following pages.

Objective

The objective of an appropriation audit is to determine that full value is received and accurate accounting records are established for all expenditures under a properly authorized program. In attaining this objective it must be ascertained that all responsible groups are properly performing their duties. Therefore, the objective becomes a matter of ascertaining the effectiveness of internal control by means of a series of test checks of functions necessary in the planning, purchasing, and performing of work under an appropriation, as well as the accumulating of accurate accounting records. The extent of verification will vary somewhat. Usually, a test check to determine that controls are adequate is considered sufficient, but in some cases, as much as 100% verification will be required.

Internal Control

Good internal control requires a procedure whereby no one individual or department has complete control of a transaction, or group of transactions, without being checked by some other individual or department. Basically, there are two types of appropriation expenditures to be considered, one for outside purchases and the other for services performed by company personnel. Obviously, the control of expenditures for outside purchases is of greater importance, but the need for adequate control over the second category should not be minimized. Therefore, in order to comply with good internal control principles, the procedure should be adequate for the control of either type of expenditure, or a combination of them.

It is impractical to attempt to set forth in detail a procedure which would be suitable for the various types and sizes of organizations utilizing the appropriation method of planning and controlling expenditures. It is considered, however, that an adequate procedure should designate:

1. The types and sizes of expenditures for which appropriation requests are required.
2. What levels of management are authorized to approve the various types and sizes of expenditures.
3. That supplemental requests be submitted in the event of overruns, underruns, changes in plans, or postponements.
4. The Engineering Department's responsibility to provide necessary technical data; determine that the proposal is based on sound and economical fundamentals; check estimated costs and savings; maintain necessary checks on the progress of work being performed and/or approve the completed project.
5. The Purchasing Department's responsibility to obtain equitable prices and terms on outside purchases by means of impartially solicited quotations or bids.
6. The Accounting Department's responsibility to provide an independent control of expenditures as well as maintain records which are in accordance with sound accounting principles.
7. The Engineering, Purchasing, Accounting, and Legal Departments' responsibility to collaborate in determining that

the provisions contained in outside contracts are fundamentally sound and provide maximum protection of company interests.

It is considered that if these basic designations are set forth in such a manner that no one individual has complete control of a transaction or group of transactions without being checked by some other individual or department, an acceptable internal control will be effected.

Review of Appropriation Request

It is necessary to review the request in order to become familiar with the proposed project. Inasmuch as the proposal is the basis of estimates, specifications, approvals, accounting distribution, etc., the auditor must develop a clear understanding thereof if he is to perform a satisfactory audit.

Review of Detailed Estimate

As indicated above, the estimate is based on a request for an appropriation. Ordinarily, the Engineering Department prepares the estimate because it is the group best qualified to provide technical data.

Prior to authorization, the estimate is the principal source of detailed information on the proposed project and presents the approximate expenditure required. Also, it probably will be used by the controller's office in providing for the distribution of expenditures to the proper Capital Investment or Operating Cost Accounts.

Once the request is approved, the estimate is probably the only detailed document which can be referred to, in following the progress of the work, by anyone not located at the site of the work. Therefore, if the estimate is inadequate or ambiguous in nature, loss of control may result because those in whom the responsibility for control is vested will not be fully aware of the actual conditions involved.

Occasionally, the estimate will be used as a basis of payment on outside contracts. This condition is most common when unit price contracts are involved.

Considering the above facts, it becomes apparent that the estimate is a very important part of an appropriation; therefore, the auditor should become thoroughly familiar with it. This will provide a means of testing the degree of compliance with the original proposal, the adequacy of contract provisions, the accuracy of accounting records, etc.

It should be kept in mind that the estimate which accompanies the request usually cannot contain complete details of work to be done because the volume of such a document would be prohibitive. Therefore, it is considered essential that the "condensed" estimate be supported at the source by adequate detailed information to substantiate quantities, requirements (quality, performance, etc.), physical location, and any other information necessary to permit a comprehensive review of the contemplated project. If this requirement is met, the auditor can use the information to good advantage; if it is not, the fact should be reported as a weakness in the appropriation procedure.

Specifications

The fundamental purpose of an engineering specification is to explain to the supplier, or contractor, what the purchaser wants to buy. Consequently, the specification and the estimate will both contain practically the same details. The notable exceptions are that the specification will not contain estimated costs whereas it will contain more specific reference as to quality of work, performance, requirements, etc., necessary for final acceptance of the project. In fact, the specification usually becomes the basis of requesting bids on outside contracts.

Thus, the auditor must refer to two documents (the estimate and the specification) in order to become thoroughly familiar with the details of the work to be performed under the appropriation.

Outside Contracts

A work paper should be set up showing:

1. Appropriation number and a brief description of the work.
2. Appropriation amount authorized (including any supplements).
3. Appropriation amounts expended and committed as of the date of the audit.
4. Vendors, purchase order numbers, and a brief description of the work authorized by the purchase orders.

5. Type of contract involved.
6. Original contract price and any subsequent increases which have been authorized.

The information contained in this work paper provides a ready reference to the main parts of work to be done under the contract and therefore can be used as a basis for outlining the audit program. It is particularly desirable to audit a large and complex appropriation in small sections, in order that progress reports can be issued periodically on those portions, or phases, which have been completed.

The construction ledger detail should be balanced with the controls regardless of how the audit program is broken down. This will facilitate a comparison of the ledger accounts with the card of accounts approved by the controller's office. It will also constitute a test check of clerical accuracy.

In the course of the audit, a test check should be made of invoices which have been posted to the ledger. It should be noted that the invoices are submitted in ample detail to permit accurate distribution. It is undesirable for invoices to be submitted in such a manner that arbitrary distributions are necessary. The invoices should also be checked for proper approvals and correctness of extensions. The Purchasing Department should approve the invoices for price and terms; the Engineering Department should approve the quantity of work performed; the Accounting Department should recheck the prices, approve the distribution and clerical accuracy, and determine that there is a purchase order on file authorizing payment of the invoiced items.

In addition to the above review of invoices, it should also be determined that proper controls have been set up to prevent the possibility of duplicate payment of an invoice.

It then remains to review charges for compliance with contract provisions. This review is very important and will probably be the most difficult for the auditor to conduct. It is this phase of the audit which will lead into the determination that engineering detail is complete and accurate and that contract provisions are adequate. Inasmuch as each type of contract involved will require different coverage, the following discussion will treat each type separately.

Lump-sum Contracts

A lump-sum contract is generally used where it is possible to specify the quality and quantity of work and where working conditions will be such that bidders may submit reasonably priced proposals. From an audit standpoint, a lump-sum contract presents fewer problems than any other type because the price is fixed on a completed project.

Although a lump-sum contract is not considered difficult to control, there are five basic tests which should be made in order to assure that reasonable control has been maintained.

1. It should be determined that any payment for extras was properly authorized and was justifiable.
2. A review of maintenance or shop labor and materials requisitions should be made to ascertain that services furnished the contractor were charged back to him.
3. A review of any escalation charges should be made. (Escalation is discussed in more detail in a following section.)
4. It should be determined that any specified retention of progressive billings is being complied with.
5. A review of premium time charges should be made to ascertain that they were properly authorized and adequately controlled. It should be determined that the work week (40 hours or 48 hours) used as a basis for the lump-sum bid is stated in the contract.

Unit-price Contracts

A unit-price contract is generally used when the quality of work to be performed can be specified but where final quantities are indefinite. This type of contract requires close control by the Engineering Department because payment is based on the number of units of work actually performed rather than on a fixed price for a completed project.

In auditing a unit-price contract, it should be determined whether (1) the quantities contained in the contract are actual and are to be used as a basis of payment, or (2) the quantities are merely estimates with payment to be based on actual field measurements. This is important because it determines the scope of the review to be made.

If the quantities contained in the contract are to be used as a basis of payment, they should be supported by detailed drawings and lists of materials, which, generally, will be on file in the Engineering Department. Although the auditor is not expected to have technical engineering training, he should be able to test check the clerical accuracy of some quantities contained in the contract. Also, by physical observation of the work it should be possible to determine that the engineering detail is based on up-to-date drawings or specifications.

Under this basis of payment, the invoiced quantities should be compared with those contained in the contract. Any differences should be supported by revisions of detailed drawings and a complete explanation of the reasons for the revisions.

It should be noted that the above review is based on data compiled before the fact, and for this reason special emphasis is placed upon the need for accuracy in compiling the quantities contained in the contract. Consequently, engineering field notes are used only as a means of verifying that the work is being performed in accordance with contract provisions and to determine that the contractor's progress billings are reasonable.

If the quantities contained in the contract are merely estimates, with payment to be based on actual field measurements, the above situation will be reversed. The field notes will be of greatest importance, while the need for accuracy in compiling the quantities contained in the contract will be relatively unimportant. Therefore, the auditor should place more emphasis on the procedure followed by the field engineers in verifying the units of work actually performed. Here again the auditor should utilize detailed drawings and physical observations in testing the accuracy of unit quantities paid for.

Under this basis of payment, there is little to be gained by comparing the invoiced quantities with those contained in the contract. Inasmuch as the contract quantities are known to be rough estimates, it is to be expected that discrepancies will exist. Therefore, the test check will be based on engineering field notes made after-the-fact.

In addition to reviewing the method of arriving at quantities and testing the clerical accuracy of the supporting data under either basis of payment, it should also be determined that:

1. The progress of the job is controlled and recorded on a current basis.

2. Work for which there has been no authorized unit price is not paid for by applying an arbitrary rate.

3. There is no duplication, or other discrepancy, in applying unit prices to similar types of work (such as applying the rate for cubic yards of hand excavation to cubic yards of machine excavation).

4. Proper methods of controlling escalation payments have been established.

5. Proper methods of controlling premium time payments have been established.

6. Retentions are being made in accordance with contract terms.

7. Payment for extras has been properly authorized and that such work is not comprehended in the original unit prices.

8. The cost of materials or services which have been furnished the contractor but were originally comprehended in the unit prices is charged to the contractor's account.

9. The work week (40 hours or 48 hours) used as a basis for arriving at unit prices is stated in the contract.

Cost-plus Contracts

A cost-plus contract is generally used when it is impossible to secure fair prices because of the unknown conditions involved in the proposed project. Also, during a period of fluctuating markets in both material and labor, it is probable that cost-plus contracts will predominate.

There are two basic types of cost-plus contracts: (1) cost plus a fixed fee and (2) cost plus a fee based on a fixed percentage of the costs. Experience has disclosed that the former type of contract is preferable, particularly when accompanied by a provision whereby the contractor receives a bonus for underrunning but is penalized for overrunning an estimated cost which has been mutually agreed upon. The equity of this type of contract depends on a reasonably accurate estimate, but at any rate, it creates an incentive for the contractor to keep costs down.

Under either type of contract the audit will be based primarily on the determination that charges are confined to costs which are admissible under the terms of the contract. Ambiguity and omissions are the two factors that cause most controversies and negotiations after the placing of the contract. Therefore, in testing the adequacy of the contract and the extent of control over payments, it should be ascertained that the intent of the contract provisions is fairly applied:

1. The cost of material is based on suppliers' invoices subject to approval by purchaser, applicable market prices, or indices, etc., as agreed to.
2. Labor rates are based on Union or other rates approved by purchaser.
3. A provision has been made as to whether or not supervisory personnel are to be included in direct labor charges or in overhead.
4. Labor charges (including premium time) are supported by a copy of the contractor's payroll.
5. A provision has been made regarding the reimbursement of payroll taxes and insurance.
6. A provision has been made regarding the reimbursement of fees, permits, licenses, etc.
7. A provision has been made regarding admissible overhead charges.
8. A provision has been made regarding the contractor's fee or profit.
9. A provision has been made regarding equipment rentals.
10. A provision has been made regarding the disposition of cash and/or trade discounts on material purchased by the contractor.
11. A provision has been made regarding the recovery of salvage from materials charged to the contract.
12. An acceptable procedure is being followed by the Engineering Department and/or Accounting Department in making test checks of contractor's personnel and equipment for verification purposes.
13. Retentions are being made in accordance with contract terms.
14. The cost of materials or services which have been furnished the contractor is not duplicated in the contractor's charges to the purchaser.
15. A provision has been made regarding required approvals for subcontracting any portion of the work.

It is impractical to set forth hard and fast rules governing the provisions listed above because circumstances and conditions very often justly influence the final negotiation of a contract. The auditor is required to analyze these provisions and thereby determine their adequacy. However, a following section will contain some desirable contract controls and administrative features suggested by actual audits.

Escalation

An escalation clause provides for the adjustment of prices if labor and material costs fluctuate appreciably during the course of a contract. Theoretically, the price should be adjusted either up or down depending on the trend of costs. Therefore, an escalation clause should clearly state whether decreases as well as increases in costs shall be considered in determining the final price.

Escalation clauses will be contained in lump-sum and unit-price contracts but not in cost-plus contracts. The reason for this is that the cost-plus contract, as indicated by its title, is based on actual costs and any increases or decreases in costs are automatically reflected in the contractor's billings.

In order to control escalation effectively, it is essential for the base labor rates, material costs, etc., to be clearly defined at the time the contract is let. Without this base determination, it would be difficult to arrive at actual increases, and considerable negotiation would be required to arrive at an equitable settlement of the adjustment.

The escalation clause should specify that copies of payrolls and vendors' invoices, or such other data pertinent to verification of compliance with the contract provisions, be submitted in support of escalation invoices.

The local organization should be set up to test check the contractor's personnel in order to facilitate verification of escalation invoices.

In addition to reviewing the above phases of escalation control, the auditor should consider the advisability of visiting the contractor's office in order to verify the validity of the data which has been submitted in support of invoiced items. In the event of escalation on work performed in the contractor's shop, it will be necessary to make such a visit.   This condition is generally encountered when escalation applies to machinery and equipment purchases.

Premium Time Payments

The payment of premium time is, in reality, another form of escalation when the contract is on a lump-sum or unit-price basis. In other words, the contractor is reimbursed for costs which were not considered when the lump-sum or unit-price bids were submitted. This does not mean that all premium time incurred by the contractor is reimbursable, but only that portion which the contractor is authorized to incur in order to expedite the completion of a project or meet an emergency.

If the contractor is actually performing work which he had originally considered on a straight time cost basis, reimbursement should be confined to the premium portion of overtime hours worked.

The Purchasing Department should approve all rates to be used in calculating premium time and also what classes of labor, or supervision, are covered by the agreement.

Payroll taxes are admissible charges on taxable wages.   Workmen's Compensation, as a general rule, is assessed on gross payroll earnings, whereas Public Liability and Property Damage Insurance is payable only on straight time earnings.

The auditor should ascertain that local management has established a procedure for adequate verification of premium time incurred by the contractor.

Premium time invoices may be supported by copies of the contractor's payrolls.   Consideration should be given to the advisability of examining the earnings statements of the contractor's employes to ascertain that the premium time was actually paid.

Premium time under cost-plus contracts should also be governed by most of the principles stated above.   The only notable exception is that both the straight time and the premium time will be reimbursed.

Construction Work Performed by Company Personnel

The audit of an appropriation which involves only company labor, material, and equipment does not present the complex problems usually connected with outside contracts. Generally, the audit will be initiated by reviewing the request, approvals, card of accounts, and engineering specifications in the same manner as appropriations involving outside contracts. After this phase is completed, the audit is usually confined to a review of payroll charges, direct purchases, stores requisitions, etc., which are charged to the appropriation. In many instances, it will be found that previous functional audits of the responsibilities involved can be used as a guide in ascertaining that adequate control exists.

It is not the intent to minimize the importance of auditing this type of appropriation. It is apparent, however, that the absence of a two-party agreement does not necessitate the rigid controls which must be present when outside contracts are involved.

General Items

The following items are general in nature and should be included in all appropriation audits:

1. Note that appropriations are closed to property or profit and loss accounts promptly upon practical completion of the job.
2. Ascertain that unexpended parts of an appropriation are not used for other purposes.
3. Review charges to Repair and Maintenance which did not go through appropriations, and determine if any of these should have been charged otherwise.
4. Physically observe new facilities to ascertain that they are properly identified.
5. Ascertain that properties and/or facilities to be retired under the appropriation have been properly disposed of.
6. Ascertain that local management has established a procedure for controlling appropriation material receipts on company purchases and also on materials to be used on cost-plus contracts.

CHAPTER 19

PURCHASE OF A BUSINESS

Introduction

When it becomes desirable for a company to purchase another business in order profitably to supplement its existing facilities and markets, the advisability of such a project necessitates decisions on a number of important considerations in order to arrive at the manner of acquisition and whether or not the expenditures involved are justified.

The necessary investigation and appraisal of a seller company would be undertaken only after the President and Executive Committee of the buyer company had approved the desirability of considering the purchase. However, even before such consideration could be given, certain other preliminary investigations and negotiations would have to be made.

The Market Research Department should accordingly make a survey of the industry which is being considered. This survey might consist of a complete review of the available markets, existing competition, present participation of the buyer (if any), freight rates, profits, etc. A report should be prepared by the Market Research Department in collaboration with the Statistical Department, Traffic Department, Purchasing Department, and other related interested departments. The Sales Department should ascertain which particular businesses are most desirable and what the asking prices are.

This information, along with the report, is then submitted to the Executive Committee for approval that it is desirable to enter into this type of business.

It is recommended that a preliminary investigation of the seller company be jointly made by the Engineering Department and the Audit Division and a report prepared presenting all factual data, together with reasons for unusual conditions and conclusions as to the value of the business based upon an analysis of the available facts.

Preliminary Investigation and Report

The following steps should be taken, with emphasis being placed on those items in relation to their importance for the particular circumstances at hand.

1. *Principles of a Balance Sheet Audit* (without detail verification).

    a. *Cash.* List and tie up bank balances to book balances; are any funds earmarked or restricted; closed banks; excessive working funds.

    b. *Securities.* If involved in sale, list; examine; evaluate.

    c. *Notes and Accounts Receivable.* (1) Examine aging; (2) bad debt experiences; (3) tax policy; (4) major old accounts; (5) claim record; (6) reserve.

    d. *Inventories.* (1) List and analyze by product and compare with cost records, sales prices, and gross profit ratio; (2) system for maintaining; (3) rate of turnover; (4) obsolescence; (5) test inspect.

    e. *Operating Parts and Supplies.* (1) Summarize; (2) inspect lay-out; (3) turnover by classes; (4) system of control; (5) large items and their usage; (6) inactive items; (7) basis of value.

    f. *Fixed Assets.* (1) Summary of book values and reserves; (2) depreciation policy compared with Tax Department allowances; (3) analysis of acquisition of properties by dates; (4) maps of locations and lay-out; (5) idle; (6) fully amortized facilities.

    g. *Intangibles.* List and analyze basis of value and estimate actual; patents.

    h. *Other Assets and Deferred.* Analyze major accounts and evaluate.

    i. *Current Liabilities.* Confirm reasonableness; observe subsidiary company or offices; determine liabilities not of record; compensation claims, contracts, leases, trucking, royalties.

    j. Long-term Debt. Examine indenture provisions.

    k. Contingent Liabilities. Get details; any lawsuits; retroactive increases, inequities.

    l. Reserves. Analyze and determine necessity therefor.

    m. Capital Stock. List types and holders thereof; dividend policy and requirements and any deficiencies due.

    n. Surplus. Analyze surplus accounts.

2. *Analysis of Income and Expense.*

    a. Analysis of Profit and Loss for extended period.

      (1) Detailed Profit and Loss by Product, Department, or similar available breakdown.

    b. Sales (for such periods as deemed appropriate).

      (1) List products sold and volume and profit on each.

      (2) List selling prices, ceilings, and trends.

      (3) Analysis of sales deductions (including buried) and causes.

      (4) List existing sales contracts to determine if any unprofitable.

      (5) Analysis by territory; freight absorption.

      (6) List major customers and type of sales to each.

      (7) Description of sales organization and policies.

      (8) Analyze competition; advantages of each; competitors' sales activities.

      (9) Management's forecast of sales.

      (10) Sales to buyer company, and profit.

      (11) Royalties paid on sales or received as income.

      (12) Discuss sales advantage of any new items which purchase of seller company would cause to be added to existing lines of buyer.

      (13) Determine by sales area the total requirements for company's products, and estimate respective sales volume of competing companies.

      (14) Terms of sale.

      (15) Trends on orders received and unfilled order volume by products.

    c. Costs.

      (1) Determine adequacy of cost system: analyze production records, cost statements by plants and products and basis thereof, cost trends, reasons for changes.

      (2) Payroll statistics and trends.

      (3) Long-time trend of repair and maintenance expense.

      (4) Analysis of tax expenses, ad valorem, sales, use, franchise, etc.

      (5) Analysis of selling and administrative expense and officers' compensation.

    d. Analyze major "other income and expense" items.

3. *History and Trends.*

    a. Corporate structure and history; charter; by-laws.

    b. Comparative balance sheets, profit and loss statements, cost statements, and sales analysis over a reasonable period.

    c. Review of past records as follows:

      (1) Independent auditors' reports (and work papers).

      (2) Management engineering or appraisal surveys.

      (3) Tax returns and examiners' reports and settlements.

      (4) Stockholders' reports.

      (5) Minutes of directors and stockholder's meetings.

      (6) Corporate books—note condition.

4. *Purchasing Data.*

    a. List major suppliers and quantities bought from each.

    b. Prices at which major purchases made.

    c. Adequacy of purchasing personnel.

    d. Availability of materials and transportation.

    e. Review purchase contracts for necessity of paying a higher price than available from buyer company.

5. *Personnel and Industrial Relations Data.*

    a. Organization chart and normal complement of employes.

    b. Union agreements and relations; variation from buyers.

    c. Review seller company's wage and salary brackets, incentive plans, work schedules. Note variation from buyers.

    d. Determine liabilities under pension or welfare plans, group insurance.

    e. Adequacy of personnel and available labor supply (supplied by Engineering Department except as to Accounting Department).

    f. Local living conditions for personnel.

6. *Legal Data and Miscellaneous.*

    a. List existing contracts.

    b. Description of recent lawsuits or pending litigation.

    c. Effect of government regulations and restrictions, zoning laws, etc.

    d. Leases in effect; patents; royalties received and paid.

    e. Encumbrances to property titles, etc.

    f. Description of easements, right of way, etc.

    g. Adequacy of insurance in effect.

7. *Major Classifications of Subjects Handled Wholly by Engineering.*

    a. Description and appraisal of properties, equipment, patents, etc.

    b. Description of operating methods; capacities.

    c. Description of safety and sanitation facilities.

    d. Evaluation of inventories.

    e. Description of transportation facilities.

    f. Description of changes which should be made, estimated cost of same and results to be secured.

    g. Estimate of remaining useful life of facilities.

    h. List of surplus or obsolete equipment.

    i. Investigation of utility services.

    j. Comparison of facilities with competitors.

Based upon the foregoing work program, the joint report of the Engineering Department and Audit Division is prepared and is reviewed by interested departments who may request additional information and add their comments thereto. The report is then returned to an appraisal committee consisting of the chief executives in charge of finance, engineering, sales, operating, and accounting. A representative of this committee should contact the owner of the business and ascertain the purchase price.

The appraisal committee should then prepare a brief summary based upon all the data submitted to it and make recommendations as to purchase price and desirability, after which its report, together with the joint report of the Engineering Department and the Audit Division, is submitted to the President and Executive Committee for approval.

Conclusion

If approval of the Executive Committee is obtained and the buyer and seller agree as to price, the following remaining steps will ensue:

1. A detailed verification of assets to be purchased (by Audit Division).
2. Preparation of purchase contract (by Legal Department).
3. Examination of deeds, contracts, etc., and assignment of titles (by Legal Department).
4. Determination of key organization and personnel (by President of Buyer Company).
5. Notice to trade and employes (by Legal Department).
6. Open new books of account (by Audit Division).
7. Provide cash for new operation (by Treasurer).
8. Meeting of new officers with corresponding officers of buyer company to instruct relative to each function, define policies, and coordination of organizations.

APPENDIX

CASE PROBLEMS IN INTERNAL AUDITING

CASE PROBLEM 1

CONSTRUCTION AUDITING

The *X–Y–Z* Corporation, Pittsburgh, Pennsylvania, is engaged in the manufacture of metal products. Branch factories are maintained in Oil City, Pennsylvania, and Cincinnati, Ohio. As part of its expansion program the Corporation has decided to erect a power plant at its Cincinnati Works. The cost of this project was estimated to be $1,650,000. Funds were authorized and appropriated by the Directors as follows:

Building	$1,150,000
Machinery and Equipment	500,000
	$1,650,000

Separate contracts were made for the construction of the building and the purchase of equipment.

The Erecto Construction Company was employed as contractor. Abstracts from the contract with the Erecto Construction Company are as follows:

1. Construct and erect building to be used as a power plant, in accordance with *X–Y–Z* Corporation's specifications and drawings and contractor's proposal dated November 1, 1946.
2. The Erecto Construction Company is to be reimbursed for the net actual cost of all materials, labor, tools, and other facilities necessary for the execution of the work.
3. The contractor is to be reimbursed for his main office overhead at a rate of 10%, not including premium time and applicable payroll taxes and insurance.
4. A fee of 10% is to be allowed for profit.
5. The contractor is to be reimbursed for Federal Old Age Benefit Tax, Federal and State Unemployment Compensation, Workmen's Compensation, and Public Liability and Property Damage Insurance.

6. When it is deemed expedient, the *X–Y–Z* Corporation will purchase, store, and deliver materials to the construction site.

7. The contractor is to furnish an estimate of the proportional value of the work completed and of acceptable material furnished and delivered upon the Corporation's property, at the construction site, within 10 days after the end of each month.

8. The contractor is to render billings for labor on a weekly basis and for material on a monthly basis.

9. Eighty per cent of each invoice will be due and payable within 10 days of the date thereon. The balance will be paid within 30 days of the completion and acceptance of the building.

Excavation for the building foundations began early in January 1947.

According to information contained in the contractor's progress report, dated January 10, 1948, work was 80% complete as of December 31, 1947. A summary of the detail charged to the construction accounts, as of the end of the year, is as follows:

Contractor's Gross Charges	$ 964,040.84
X–Y–Z Corporation's Charges	183,810.00
Total Charges to Construction Ledger . .	$1,147,850.84

Mr. H. J. Jones, Controller of the *X–Y–Z* Corporation, has requested his Internal Audit Supervisor to verify the charges submitted by the contractor and to review the system of internal accounting control of construction activities, commenting on any weaknesses.

You are assigned to verify the contractor's charges by audit of his records at the construction site and his general office and to review the degree of control exercised over construction activities by the Cincinnati Works management. Preparatory to beginning the audit, assume that you have prepared, from the records of the *X–Y–Z* Corporation, the summary of contractor's charges, per Exhibit 1A.

Upon arrival at the construction site you find that the following routine has been established:

The contractor's clerical work at the site is performed by a field clerk. Daily labor reports are prepared by the foreman of each craft. Weekly payrolls are prepared by the field clerk from the daily labor reports and are paid in cash. Payrolls are then forwarded to the contractor's general office, where labor billings are prepared by his bookkeeper. Overtime requirements are determined by the foreman of each craft and require only the approval of the contractor's superintendent. Labor billings reflect only the total straight time and overtime hours worked by each craft and are not accompanied by copies of payrolls. You observe that there is no field check of construction employes by the Corporation's timekeepers and that the contractor's employes are permitted to enter or leave the Corporation's premises at any time by merely displaying their badges.

Material purchased by the contractor and delivered to the job site is received by the field clerk, who initials accompanying packing slips or delivery tickets to indicate receipt of the shipment. These documents are then forwarded to the contractor's general office for matching with his vendors' invoices.

Materials furnished by the X–Y–Z Corporation are disbursed on the basis of unapproved requisitions and are billed to the contractor once each month on a "no charge" basis, reflecting actual costs plus a mark-up of 15% to cover purchasing, accounting, and warehousing costs. Charges for this material are made directly to the Construction Ledger Accounts by the X–Y–Z Corporation. The contractor is permitted to remove materials from the premises without approval. The contractor's material billings are rendered once each month in summary form and are unaccompanied by any detail.

Construction accounting details are handled by the Accounts Payable Bureau at the Cincinnati Works. It was evident that considerable confusion existed owing to insufficient knowledge of construction matters and the lack of authority to investigate construction charges.

Payroll rates in effect during June 1947 are as follows:

Ironworkers	$2.75 per hour
Bricklayers	$2.25 per hour
Carpenters	$2.75 per hour
Laborers	$1.35 per hour

Saturday work and overtime is paid for at double time.

Assuming that you have prepared the schedule of hours worked, per Exhibit 1D, from daily labor reports of the contractor, reconstruct the payroll for the week ended June 14, 1947.

You make a 20% test check of each payroll, but when comparing the individual payroll totals as taken from the contractor's records (Exhibit 1B attached) with the weekly labor billings, you observe a difference, which is localized to the following:

1. The reconstructed payroll you have prepared for June 14, 1947.
2. Erecto Construction Company's Invoice No. 62 of June 21, 1947, for $3,798.94 (Exhibit 1E).
3. Erecto Construction Company's Invoice No. 72 of July 31, 1947, for $623.32 (Exhibit 1F).

You find that a general increase of $.15 an hour has been granted to the contractor's construction employes, effective Sunday, July 17, 1947, in accordance with an agreement, dated Sunday, July 10, 1947, between the Union and the Erecto Construction Company.

As part of your procedure, you examine the contractor's accounts payable to support the validity of the material charges made to the X–Y–Z Corporation. Representative test checks indicated proper billing except on Erecto Construction Company's Invoice No. 81 of September 10, 1947, for $10,576.17 (Exhibit 1G, page 195). The invoices (Exhibits 1H and 1N, pages 196 and 202) paid by the Erecto Construction Company were examined in support of above-mentioned Invoice No. 81. A representative check was made of materials disbursed from the stores of the X–Y–Z Corporation. No exceptions were found.

An inventory taken on January 21, under your supervision, revealed that the following items had been removed from the job site by the contractor because they were no longer needed for the work, but no allowance had been made.

| | | Purchase Cost | |
	Quantity	Unit Price	Total
Returnable Drums on Deposit	25	$ 5.00	$125.00
Wheelbarrows	17	14.75	250.75
Shovels	73	2.75	200.75
Picks	18	1.65	29.70
Various Other Small Tools	—	—	273.71
			$879.91

An agreement reached by the contractor and the Chief Engineer set a value of 50% for this material (drums excluded) because of its used condition.

Two grades of lumber had been used for the job, as follows:

1. First grade—for permanent construction only.
2. Second grade—for making forms for pouring concrete.

Lumber was not charged to the job as purchased but on a requisition basis as used. All lumber in the contractor's inventory accounts had been purchased specifically for this job.

After taking an inventory of both grades of lumber and analyzing the contractor's purchases, the following facts are determined:

		Board Feet		
	Price	Inventories	Purchases	Charged
First Grade	$150.00 M	60,000	555,500	504,171
Second Grade	$110.00 M	3,000	57,142	75,799

From personal observations you note that the contractor frequently reused lumber from dismantled concrete forms.

Premiums of $4,984.92 were paid to the State of Ohio for 1947 for Workmen's Compensation Insurance. The Mutual Risk Company had billed the contractor $7,746 for Public Liability and Property Damage Insurance on straight time payroll only.

The roof had been painted by a subcontractor and billed by the Erecto Construction Company on a unit price basis of $3.20 per square for 4,800 squares. You examine the building blueprints and note the following:

	Squares
Metal Surface	3,456
Openings for Glass Skylights	1,344
Total	4,800

You learn through discussion and an examination of correspondence that the Corporation had made several complaints to the contractor about the progress of the work and the disorganized way in which construction activities were conducted. Repeated requests that the contractor replace his superintendent with an efficient manager were finally heeded, and a new superintendent was appointed on November 1, 1947. These conditions have resulted in higher construction costs and the payment of increased profit to the contractor.

Reference to the Erecto Construction Company's Invoice No. 462

of October 15, 1947, for $884.74 (Exhibit 1C, page 191) revealed
that changes had been made in electrical wiring specifications on the
basis of verbal instructions of the Chief Engineer. No change
order had been issued by the Purchasing Department as they were
unaware of the change.

To determine the reasonableness of the costs of large items purchased by the contractor, you arrange for the Purchasing Department to secure bids from competitors of the suppliers, with the following results:

Purchased from the Steel Sash Company,
F.O.B. Detroit, Freight Collect:

400 Steel Window Frames @ $27.00 . .	$10,800.00
Freight Charges	378.00
	$11,178.00

The Harris Company would have furnished these frames at the
same price, F.O.B. Cincinnati, Freight Allowed.

A bid secured indicated that the roof could have been painted for
$2.80 a square.

*   *   *

As the audit progresses you will prepare necessary working papers
which will include your work program and related analyses in support of your findings. From your working papers you will prepare an audit report addressed to Mr. H. J. Jones, Controller of the
X–Y–Z Corporation, in which you will report your findings and
make recommendations for the correction of internal control weaknesses, etc.

CASE PROBLEM IN CONSTRUCTION AUDITING

EXHIBIT 1A

THE ERECTO CONSTRUCTION COMPANY

SUMMARY OF CHARGES BILLED TO THE X-Y-Z CORPORATION
FROM JANUARY 1, 1947 THROUGH DECEMBER 31, 1947

Labor at Straight Time	$ 262,326.23
* Payroll Taxes and Insurance @ 10.8%	28,331.23
Premium Pay	40,616.30
* Payroll Taxes and Insurance @ 10.8%	4,386.56
Material Purchases	329,842.73
Lumber	83,964.00
Material Furnished on a "No Charge"	
Basis by X-Y-Z Corporation	183,810.00
Painting - Roof	15,360.00
	$ 948,637.05
Overhead @ 10%	94,863.71
	$1,043,500.76
Fee @ 10%	104,350.08
	$1,147,850.84
Less Value of "No Charge" Material	183,810.00
	$ 964,040.84
Less "Holdback" @ 20%	192,808.17
Total	$ 771,232.67

* Federal Old Age Benefit Tax	1.0%
State Unemployment Compensation Insurance	2.7
Federal Unemployment Compensation Insurance	.3
Workmen's Compensation Insurance	3.1
Public Liability & Property Damage Insurance	3.7
	10.8%

CASE PROBLEM IN CONSTRUCTION AUDITING

EXHIBIT 1B

THE ERECTO CONSTRUCTION COMPANY

SUMMARY OF CONSTRUCTION PAYROLLS FOR 1947

Month	Straight Time Earnings	Premium Pay Earnings	Total Gross Earnings	Earnings In Excess Of $3,000	Net Taxable Earnings
January	$ 23,494.16	$ 3,993.94	$ 27,488.10	$	$ 27,488.10
February	22,645.06	3,624.20	26,269.26		26,269.26
March	23,651.34	3,902.42	27,553.76		27,553.76
April	22,991.04	3,678.66	26,669.70		26,669.70
May	23,204.82	3,480.60	26,685.42		26,685.42
June	18,692.76	2,897.26	21,590.02		21,590.02
July	19,880.22	3,180.80	23,061.02	2,213.86	20,847.16
August	21,131.24	3,592.27	24,723.51	2,546.68	22,176.83
September	24,210.40	3,389.40	27,599.80	4,140.00	23,459.80
October	23,920.02	3,588.00	27,508.02	5,639.14	21,868.88
November	18,702.32	2,992.32	21,694.64	12,193.03	9,501.61
December	19,173.90	2,109.03	21,282.93	15,610.93	5,672.00
Totals	$261,697.28	$40,428.90	$302,126.18	$42,343.64	$259,782.54

Actual Rates Paid

Federal Old Age Benefit Tax	1.0%
State Unemployment Compensation Insurance	1.8
Federal Unemployment Compensation Insurance	.3

CASE PROBLEM IN CONSTRUCTION AUDITING

EXHIBIT 1C

THE ERECTO CONSTRUCTION COMPANY
221 Fifth Avenue
Pittsburgh, Pennsylvania

Invoice No. 462

To: X-Y-Z Corporation   Date   10-15-47
11 Grant Street
Pittsburgh, Pennsylvania

To charge you for additional costs incurred due to change in electric

wiring requested by your Chief Engineer.

Material	$	397.88
Labor - Straight Time		456.73
Premium Pay		59.37
	$	913.98
Overhead @ 10%		91.40
	$1,005.38	
Fee @ 10%		100.54
	$1,105.92	
Less Holdback of 20%		221.18
	$	884.74

CASE PROBLEM IN CONSTRUCTION AUDITING

EXHIBIT 1D

THE ERECTO CONSTRUCTION COMPANY

CONSTRUCTION HOURS WORKED DURING WEEK ENDED JUNE 14, 1947
AS SHOWN BY DAILY LABOR REPORTS

Badge No.	Occupation	Mon.	Tue.	Wed.	Thu.	Fri.	Sat.
1	Ironworker	8	8	8	8	8	8
2	"	8	8	8	8	8	8
3	"	8		8	8	8	8
4	"	8	8	8	8	8	
5	"	8	8	8	8	8	8
6	"	8	8	8	8	8	8
7	"	8	8	8			8
8	Bricklayer	8	8	8	8	8	8
9	"	8	8	8	8	8	8
10	"	8	8	8	8	8	8
11	"	8	8	8	8		
12	"	8	8	8	8	8	
13	Carpenter	8	8	8	8	8	4
14	"	8	8	8	8	8	4
15	"	8	8	8	8	8	4
16	"	8	8	8	8	8	4
17	"	8	8	8	8	8	4
18	"			8	8	8	8
19	"			8	8	8	8
20	Laborer	8	8	6		8	8
21	"	8	8	8	8	8	
22	"	8	8		8	8	8
23	"	8	4	8	8	8	
24	"	8	8	8	8		8
25	"	8	8	8	8	8	8
26	"	8	8		8	8	8
27	"	8	8	8	8	8	4
28	"	8	8	8	6	8	4
29	"	8	8	8	6	8	4

CASE PROBLEM IN CONSTRUCTION AUDITING

EXHIBIT 1E

THE ERECTO CONSTRUCTION COMPANY
221 Fifth Avenue
Pittsburgh, Pennsylvania

Invoice No. 62

To: X-Y-Z Corporation
11 Grant Street
Pittsburgh, Pennsylvania

Date   6-21-47

To charge you for construction payroll for week ended 6-14-47.

Straight Time Wages

Seven (7) Ironworkers @ 48 hrs.	336 hrs. @ $2.75	$ 924.00
Five (5) Bricklayers @ 48 hrs.	240 hrs. @ 2.25	540.00
Seven (7) Carpenters @ 48 hrs.	336 hrs. @ 2.75	924.00
Ten (10) Laborers @ 48 hrs.	480 hrs. @ 1.35	648.00
	1,392 hrs.	$3,036.00

Premium Pay

Ironworkers	56 hrs. @ $2.75	$154.00	
Bricklayers	40 hrs. @ 2.25	90.00	
Carpenters	56 hrs. @ 2.75	154.00	
Laborers	80 hrs. @ 1.35	108.00	506.00
	232		$3,542.00

Payroll Taxes and Insurance @ 10.8%	382.53
	$3,924.53
Overhead @ 10%	392.45
	$4,316.98
Fee @ 10%	431.70
	$4,748.68
Less Holdback of 20%	949.74
	$3,798.94

CASE PROBLEM IN CONSTRUCTION AUDITING

EXHIBIT 1F

THE ERECTO CONSTRUCTION COMPANY
221 Fifth Avenue
Pittsburgh, Pennsylvania

Invoice No. 72

To: X-Y-Z Corporation   Date   7-31-47
11 Grant Street
Pittsburgh, Pennsylvania

TO CHARGE YOU FOR RETROACTIVE WAGE INCREASE FOR JULY 1947.

| | HOURS | |
	STRAIGHT TIME	PREMIUM
WEEK ENDED JULY 16, 1947		
IRONWORKERS	486	72
BRICKLAYERS	376	41
CARPENTERS	428	55
LABORERS	373	76
	1,663	244
WEEK ENDED JULY 23, 1947		
IRONWORKERS	437	53
BRICKLAYERS	378	44
CARPENTERS	345	57
LABORERS	369	48
	1,529	202

SUMMARY

WEEK ENDED JULY 16, 1947			
STRAIGHT TIME HOURS	1,663 @ $ .15	$ 249.45	
PREMIUM HOURS	244 @ .15	36.00	$ 286.05
WEEK ENDED JULY 23, 1947			
STRAIGHT TIME HOURS	1,529 @ $ .15	$ 229.35	
PREMIUM HOURS	202 @ .15	30.30	259.65
PAYROLL TAXES AND INSURANCE @ 10.8%			$ 545.70
			98.23
OVERHEAD @ 10.8%			$ 643.93
			64.39
FEE @ 10%			$ 708.32
			70.83
LESS 20% HOLDBACK			$ 779.15
			155.83
			$ 623.32

CASE PROBLEM IN CONSTRUCTION AUDITING

EXHIBIT 1G

THE ERECTO CONSTRUCTION COMPANY
221 Fifth Avenue
Pittsburgh, Pennsylvania

Invoice No. 81

To: X-Y-Z Corporation   Date   9-10-47
11 Grant Street
Pittsburgh, Pennsylvania

For materials purchased for construction of building - August 1947.

Stationery	$ 270.00
Cement (450 bags)	382.50
300 Rolls - Tar Paper	3,816.00
Nails	48.00
2-1/2 x 2-1/2 x 1/4" - Angle Iron	2,610.50
Steel Plate	148.33
1/2" Round Reinforcing Bars	247.15
Wheelbarrows, Shovels, Picks, and Handles	583.35
Cost of Material Furnished by X-Y-Z Corp.	
(on a "No Charge" Basis)	11,542.73
Electrical Supplies	816.68
	$20,465.24
Overhead @ 10%	2,046.52
	$22,511.76
Fee @ 10%	2,251.18
	$24,762.94
Less Material Furnished by X-Y-Z Corporation	11,542.73
	$13,220.21
Less Holdback of 20%	2,644.04
	$10,576.17

CASE PROBLEM IN CONSTRUCTION AUDITING

EXHIBIT 1H

THE ELECTRICAL SUPPLY COMPANY
102 First Street
Pittsburgh, Pennsylvania

Invoice No. A-56742

To: Erecto Construction Company   Date   8-5-47
     221 Fifth Avenue
     Pittsburgh, Pennsylvania

Terms 2% - 10th Prox. Delivered

7,350 ft. of 3/4" BX Cable	$ .085 ft.	$591.68
5,000 ft. of Electric Cable	.45 ft.	225.00
		.$816.68
Less 2% Cash Discount		16.33
		$800.35

Paid 9-10-47
Ck #5160

CASE PROBLEM IN CONSTRUCTION AUDITING

EXHIBIT 11

IRON AND STEEL SUPPLY, INC.
775 Second Avenue
Pittsburgh, Pennsylvania

Invoice No. S-4263

To: Erecto Construction Company   Date   8-3-47
     221 Fifth Avenue
     Pittsburgh, Pennsylvania

Terms 2% - 10 Days - Delivered

2-1/2 x 2-1/2 x 1/4" Angle Iron	6,908 lbs. @ $3.74 cwt.	$261.05
48 x 12.75# x 360" Plate	3,490 lbs. @ 4.25 cwt.	148.33
1/2" Round Reinforcing Rods	8,672 lbs. @ 2.85 cwt.	247.15
		$656.53
Less Cash Discount @ 2%		13.13
		$643.40

Paid 8-13-47
Ck #4168

CASE PROBLEM IN CONSTRUCTION AUDITING

EXHIBIT 1J

THE HARDWARE SUPPLY COMPANY
902 Main Street
Pittsburgh, Pennsylvania

Invoice A-5610

To: Erecto Construction Company   Date   8-22-47
221 Fifth Avenue
Pittsburgh, Pennsylvania

Terms 1% - 10 Days - Delivered

25 Wheelbarrows	$14.75 ea.	$368.75
144 Shovels	2.75 ea.	121.00
24 Picks	1.65 ea.	39.60
72 Pick Handles	.75 ea.	54.00
		$583.35
Less Discount @ 1%		5.83
		$577.52

Paid 9-1-47
Ck # 4324

CASE PROBLEM IN CONSTRUCTION AUDITING

EXHIBIT 1K

THE BLANK STATIONERY COMPANY
1011 Center Avenue
Pittsburgh, Pennsylvania

Invoice No. 201

To: Erecto Construction Company   Date   8-19-47
221 Fifth Avenue
Pittsburgh, Pennsylvania

Terms 2% - 10 Days - Delivered

Company Letterheads	10,000 @ $15.00 Per M.	$150.00
Company Envelopes	7,000 @ 10.00 Per M.	70.00
Earnings Record Cards	1,000 @ 50.00 Per M.	50.00
		$270.00
Less Discount @ 2%		5.40
		$264.60

Paid 8-29-47
Ck # #376

CASE PROBLEM IN CONSTRUCTION AUDITING

EXHIBIT 1L

PENN BUILDERS SUPPLY COMPANY
1715 Market Street
Pittsburgh, Pennsylvania

Invoice No. 8-3213

To: Erecto Construction Company   Date   8-7-47
     221 Fifth Avenue
     Pittsburgh, Pennsylvania

Terms 2% - 10 Days - Delivered

400 Bags Cement	.85 Bag	$	340.00
50 300-ft. Rolls Tar Paper	12.72 Roll		636.00
12 Kegs 10 P Nails	4.00 Keg		48.00
			$1,024.00
Less Cash Discount @ 2%			20.48
			$1,003.52

Paid 8-17-47
Ck #4529

CASE PROBLEM IN CONSTRUCTION AUDITING

EXHIBIT 1M

THE ELECTRICAL SUPPLY COMPANY
102 First Street
Pittsburgh, Pennsylvania

C.M. No. 1893

To: Erecto Construction Company
221 Fifth Avenue
Pittsburgh, Pennsylvania

Date 8-21-47

CREDIT MEMORANDUM

To credit you for the return of the following material on 8-16-47.

3,750 ft. of 1" BX Cable @ $ .115 ft.	$431.25
Less 2% Cash Discount	8.63
	$422.62

Paid 9-10-47
Ck # 5160

CASE PROBLEM IN CONSTRUCTION AUDITING

EXHIBIT 1N

THE ELECTRICAL SUPPLY COMPANY
102 First Street
Pittsburgh, Pennsylvania

C.M. No. 2147

To: Erecto Construction Company
221 Fifth Avenue
Pittsburgh, Pennsylvania

Date 8-16-47

CREDIT MEMORANDUM

To correct our invoice number A-56742 of 8-5-47.

We Charged:

    7,350 ft. of 3/4" BX Cable @ $.085 ft. $ 591.68

Should have been:

    3,750 ft. of 3/4" BX Cable @ $.085 ft.   <u>318.75</u>

                                       $ 272.93

        Less 2% Cash Discount   <u>5.46</u>

                                       $ 267.47

Paid 9-10-47
Ck #5160

CASE PROBLEM IN CONSTRUCTION AUDITING

AUDIT WORK PROGRAM

| | WORK PERFORMED | | |
	DATE	BY	SCHEDULE

GENERAL

1. SECURE A COPY OF THE CONTRACT AND MAKE SUCH EXCERPTS AND ABSTRACTS AS YOU DEEM NECESSARY.

2. PREPARE A SUMMARY OF ALL CHARGES INVOICED BY THE CONTRACTOR.

3. SUMMARIZE THE CHARGES TO THE CONSTRUCTION LEDGER ACCOUNTS OF THE X-Y-Z CORPORATION AND COMPARE WITH THE AMOUNT APPROPRIATED FOR THE PROJECT TO DISCLOSE POSSIBLE UNAUTHORIZED OVERRUN.

LABOR

1. REVIEW METHOD OF TIME REPORTING EMPLOYED BY CONTRACTOR, AND DETERMINE EXTENT OF CHECK MADE BY THE CORPORATION OF CONSTRUCTION EMPLOYES ON THE JOB. FIELD CHECKS SHOULD INDICATE THE CRAFT OF THE WORKERS.

2. TEST CHECK THE PAYROLLS OF THE CONTRACTOR TO UNDERLYING RECORDS SUCH AS, DAILY LABOR REPORTS, RATE SCHEDULES, ETC. TEST CHECK EXTENSIONS AND APPROVALS.

3. OVERTIME SHOULD BE PRE-SCHEDULED BY THE CONTRACTOR AND APPROVED BY A REPRESENTATIVE OF THE CORPORATION. LISTS OF EMPLOYES WHO ACTUALLY WORKED OVERTIME SHOULD BE SUBMITTED BY THE CONTRACTOR AND APPROVAL SECURED FOR ANY CHANGES.

4. PERSONALLY OBSERVE THE CONSTRUCTION WORKERS ENTERING AND LEAVING THE CORPORATION PREMISES DURING REGULAR WORKING HOURS. TRACE TO PAYROLL RECORDS TO SEE THAT TIME IS ADJUSTED ACCORDINGLY.

CASE PROBLEM IN CONSTRUCTION AUDITING

AUDIT WORK PROGRAM (Continued)

| | WORK PERFORMED | | |
	DATE	BY	SCHEDULE

LABOR (CONTINUED)

5. PREPARE A SUMMARY OF WEEKLY PAYROLL TOTALS FOR STRAIGHT TIME EARNINGS, PREMIUM PAY, GROSS EARNINGS, AND EXEMPT EARNINGS. COMPARE WEEKLY TOTALS TO LABOR BILLINGS, RECONCILING ANY DIFFERENCE.

6. TEST THE ACCURACY OF INDIVIDUAL EARNINGS TO SOCIAL SECURITY EARNING CARDS.

7. SECURE COPY OF LABOR AGREEMENT BETWEEN UNION AND CONTRACTOR, AND NOTE IF WORKERS ARE PAID IN EXCESS OF PROVISIONS MADE.

MATERIAL

1. REVIEW THE CONTRACTOR'S PROCEDURES AS TO MATTERS RELATING TO VENDORS' INVOICES, SUCH AS PURCHASE ORDER ROUTINE, RECEIPT OF GOODS, APPROVALS, ETC. ALL REQUISITIONS FOR PUR- CHASES SHOULD BE APPROVED BY A REPRESENTATIVE OF THE X-Y-Z CORPORATION BEFORE PURCHASE ORDERS ARE PLACED. COPIES OF PRICED PURCHASE ORDER SHOULD BE AVAILABLE TO THE ACCOUNTING DEPARTMENT FOR CHECKING TO COPIES OF VENDORS CHARGES SUPPORTING THE CONTRACTOR'S MATERIAL BILLINGS.

2. PREPARE AN ANALYSIS OF THE CONTRACTOR'S JOB CONSTRUCTION ACCOUNT, LISTING SEPARATELY ITEMS WHICH ARE OF AN OVERHEAD OR INDIRECT NATURE, AND CREDITS FOR RETURNS. RECONCILE TO BILLINGS.

3. REVIEW THE RECEIVING PROCEDURES AND RECORDS. ARE ACTUAL COUNTS AND INSPECTION MADE OF THE MATERIAL RECEIVED, AND IS A REPRESENTATIVE OF THE X-Y-Z CORPORATION PRESENT FOR VERIFICA- TION?

CASE PROBLEM IN CONSTRUCTION AUDITING

AUDIT WORK PROGRAM (Continued)

	WORK PERFORMED		
	DATE	BY	SCHEDULE

MATERIAL (CONTINUED)

4. WHENEVER POSSIBLE, IN ADDITION TO THE EXAMIN-
ATION OF INVOICES, EXAMINE VENDORS' MONTHLY
STATEMENTS AND ASCERTAIN THE EXISTENCE OF
CREDITS NOT REFLECTED IN THE JOB ACCOUNT.

5. CHECK INVOICES FOR FREIGHT TERMS, TRADE AND
CASH DISCOUNTS, PRICES AND EQUITABLE DISTRI-
BUTION OF CHARGES. ASCERTAIN WHETHER TRADE
AND CASH DISCOUNTS, AND FREIGHT ALLOWANCES
HAVE BEEN DEDUCTED FROM THE COST OF MATERIALS.

6. VERIFY THE CORRECTNESS OF THE INVOICES BY COM-
PARISON WITH RECEIVING REPORTS, PURCHASE
ORDERS, ETC.

7. LIST LARGE PURCHASES AND CHECK TO CATALOGUES,
PRICE LISTS AND FILES OF PURCHASING AGENT TO
DETERMINE WHETHER ORDERS HAVE BEEN PLACED ON
A COMPETITIVE BASIS TO SECURE THE LOWEST POS-
SIBLE COST TO THE X-Y-Z CORPORATION.

8. OBSERVE THE DEGREE OF CONTROL EXERCISED BY
THE X-Y-Z CORPORATION OVER THE REMOVAL OF CON-
STRUCTION MATERIAL FROM THE PREMISES. DOES
THE CONTRACTOR SECURE APPROVAL AND IS THE MA-
TERIAL CHECKED AT THE GATE? DOES THE ACCOUNT-
ING DEPARTMENT FOLLOW UP FOR CREDIT?

9. ARRANGE FOR AND PERSONALLY OBSERVE PHYSICAL
INVENTORIES OF TOOLS, SUPPLIES, LUMBER. REC-
ONCILE TO DETERMINE OVERCHARGES OR FAILURE TO
ALLOW CREDIT FOR ITEMS REMOVED BY THE CON-
TRACTOR.

10. PREPARE A LIST OF ALL VOUCHERS PAID FOR MATE-
RIAL IN TRANSIT CHARGED TO THE JOB CONSTRUC-
TION ACCOUNT, AND VERIFY SUBSEQUENT RECEIPT.

CASE PROBLEM IN CONSTRUCTION AUDITING

AUDIT WORK PROGRAM (Continued)

	WORK PERFORMED		
	DATE	BY	SCHEDULE

OVERHEAD

1. CONSIDER THE APPLICATION OF THE OVERHEAD RATE TO ITEMS NOT ALLOWED BY THE CONTRACT, SUCH AS, PREMIUM PAY AND PAYROLL TAXES THEREON.

2. ELIMINATE ALL ITEMS OF AN ADMINISTRATIVE OVERHEAD NATURE.

PAYROLL TAXES AND INSURANCE

1. OBTAIN COPIES OF ALL SOCIAL SECURITY TAX AND STATE UNEMPLOYMENT INSURANCE RETURNS FILED DURING THE YEAR ENDED DECEMBER 31, 1947, AND RECORD IN WORK PAPERS THE GROSS, EXEMPT AND TAXABLE WAGES, AND TAXES PAID AND PAYABLE.

2. CHECK THE DATA SHOWN ON THE FEDERAL UNEMPLOYMENT RETURN WITH THAT SHOWN ON THE VARIOUS QUARTERLY RETURNS.

3. ELIMINATE THE ADMINISTRATIVE PAYROLLS FROM THE AGGREGATE OF ALL WAGES, AND IF THE CONTRACTOR S CHARGES ARE ON THE BASIS OF ESTIMATED YEARLY RATES DEVELOP THE AVERAGE RATES PAID BY DIVIDING THE GROSS WAGES INTO THE ACTUAL TAXES PAID AND PAYABLE.

4. COMPARE THE AVERAGE RATES DEVELOPED WITH THE ESTIMATED YEARLY RATES BILLED BY THE CONTRACTOR.

5. TEST THE AMOUNTS PAID TO INDIVIDUALS BY REFERENCE TO SOCIAL SECURITY CARDS

6. EXAMINE INSURANCE POLICIES AND STATE RETURNS FOR WORKMEN'S COMPENSATION, AND PUBLIC LIABILITY AND PROPERTY DAMAGE INSURANCE. DEVELOP AVERAGE RATES BY DIVIDING GROSS WAGES INTO WORKMEN'S COMPENSATION INSURANCE PAID OR PAYABLE, AND DIVIDING STRAIGHT TIME EARNINGS INTO PUBLIC LIABILITY AND PROPERTY DAMAGE INSURANCE PREMIUMS. COMPARE AVERAGE RATES DEVELOPED WITH RATES CHARGED BY THE CONTRACTOR

CASE PROBLEM IN CONSTRUCTION AUDITING

AUDIT WORK PAPER

THE ERECTO CONSTRUCTION COMPANY

CALCULATION OF OLD AGE BENEFIT TAX AND UNEMPLOYMENT INSURANCE

	FEDERAL OLD AGE BENEFIT TAX	STATE UNEMPLOYMENT COMPENSATION INSURANCE	FEDERAL UNEMPLOYMENT COMPENSATION INSURANCE	TOTAL
1. Total Gross Wages per Schedule B	$302,126.18	$302,126.18	$302,126.18	$302,126.18
2. Deduct Exemptions for Incomes over $3,000.00	42,343.64	42,343.64	42,343.64	42,343.64
3. Net Wages Taxable	$259,782.54	$259,782.54	$259,782.54	$259,782.54
* 4. Tax Rates	.01	.018	.003	.031
5. Taxes Paid	$ 2,597.83	$ 4,676.09	$ 779.35	$ 8,053.27
Average Rates Paid (5 ÷ 1)	.0086	.015476	.002578	.026654

* Rates secured from office copies of tax
  returns.

CASE PROBLEM IN CONSTRUCTION AUDITING
AUDIT WORK PAPER

THE ERECTO CONSTRUCTION COMPANY

CALCULATION AND COMPARISON OF PAYROLL TAX AND INSURANCE RATES

	STRAIGHT TIME EARNINGS	PREMIUM PAY	TOTAL EARNINGS	EXEMPT EARNINGS	NET TAXABLE EARNINGS	PAID BY CONTRACTOR RATES	AMOUNT	BILLED BY CONTRACTOR(c) (b) RATES	AMOUNT	ACTUAL RATES	AMOUNT
Federal Old Age Benefit Tax	$261,697.28	$40,428.90	$302,126.18	$42,343.64	$259,782.54	1.00	$ 2,597.83	1.00	$ 3,021.26	.8600	$ 2,597.83
Federal Unemployment Comp. Insurance	261,697.28	40,428.90	302,126.18	42,343.64	259,782.54	.30	779.35	.30	906.38	.2578	779.35
State Unemployment Compensation Insurance	261,697.28	40,428.90	302,126.18	42,343.64	259,782.54	1.80	4,676.09	2.70	8,157.41	1.5476	4,676.09
						3.10	$ 8,053.27	4.00	$12,085.05	2.6654	$ 8,053.27
Workmen's Compensation Insurance	261,697.28	40,428.90	302,126.18	—	—	1.65	4,984.92	3.10	9,365.91	1.6500	4,984.92
Public Liability & Property Damage Ins. (a)	261,697.28	—	—	—	—	2.96	7,746.00	3.70	11,178.67	2.9600	7,746.00
						7.71	$20,784.19	10.80	$32,629.63	7.2754	$20,784.19

(a) Contractor billed Public Liability and Property Damage on Total Earnings whereas he had paid premiums on the basis of Straight Time Earnings.

(b) All rates had been applied to Total Earnings by Contractor in charging the X-Y-Z Corporation.

(c) After auditor's labor adjustments.

CASE PROBLEM IN CONSTRUCTION AUDITING
AUDIT WORK PAPER

THE ERECTO CONSTRUCTION COMPANY

RECONCILIATION OF CONTRACTOR'S ORIGINAL CHARGES TO AUDITOR'S ADJUSTMENTS

	ORIGINAL CHARGES BILLED BY CONTRACTOR	LABOR AND MATERIAL ADJUSTMENTS	NET	ADJUSTMENT OF PAYROLL TAXES & INS. TO ACTUAL	NET TOTAL	LESS OVERHEAD AND PROFIT ON PREM. PAY COSTS	FINAL ADJUSTED CHARGES	TOTAL ADJUSTMENTS
Labor at Straight Time	$ 262,326.23	$ 628.95	$ 261,697.28	$ ---	$ 261,697.28	$ ---	$ 261,697.28	$ 628.95
Payroll Taxes and Insurance	28,331.23	67.93	28,263.30	9,223.78	19,039.52	---	19,039.52	9,291.71
Premium Pay	40,616.30	187.40	40,428.90	---	40,428.90	---	40,428.90	187.40
Payroll Taxes and Insurance	4,386.56	20.23	4,366.33	2,621.66	1,744.67	---	1,744.67	2,641.89
Material Purchases	329,842.73	4,836.16	325,006.57	---	325,006.57	---	325,006.57	4,836.16
Lumber	83,964.00	3,683.00	80,281.00	---	80,281.00	---	80,281.00	3,683.00
Mat'l Furnished By X-Y-Z Corp.	183,810.00	---	183,810.00	---	183,810.00	---	183,810.00	---
Painting Roof	15,360.00	4,300.80	11,059.20	---	11,059.20	---	11,059.20	4,300.80
	$ 948,637.05	$13,724.47	$ 934,912.58	$11,845.44	$ 923,067.14	$ ---	$ 923,067.14	$25,569.91
Overhead @ 10%	94,863.71	1,372.45	93,491.26	1,184.54	92,306.72	4,217.36	88,089.36	6,774.35
	$1,043,500.76	$15,096.92	$1,028,403.84	$13,029.98	$1,015,373.86	$4,217.36	$1,011,156.50	$32,344.26
Fee @ 10%	104,350.08	1,509.69	102,840.39	1,303.00	101,537.39	4,639.09	96,898.30	7,451.78
Total	$1,147,850.84	$16,606.61	$1,131,244.23	$14,332.98	$1,116,911.25	$8,856.45	$1,108,054.80	$39,796.04
Less Value of Material Furnished By X-Y-Z Corp.	183,810.00		183,810.00		183,810.00	---	183,810.00	
Total	$ 964,040.84	$16,606.61	$ 947,434.23	$14,332.98	$ 933,101.25	$8,856.45	$ 924,244.80	$39,796.04
Less 20% Holdback	192,808.17	3,321.32	189,486.85	2,866.60	186,620.25	1,771.29	184,848.96	7,959.21
Net Totals	$ 771,232.67	$13,285.29	$ 757,947.38	$11,466.38	$ 746,481.00	$7,085.16	$ 739,395.84	$31,836.83

CASE PROBLEM IN CONSTRUCTION AUDITING

AUDIT WORK PAPER

THE ERECTO CONSTRUCTION COMPANY

VERIFICATION OF AUGUST MATERIAL CHARGES TO CONTRACTOR'S JOB COST LEDGER
AND TO CONTRACTOR'S INVOICE NO. 81 OF SEPTEMBER 10, 1947

INVOICE DATE	INVOICE NO.	VENDORS	AMOUNT ENTERED IN JOB LEDGER	ADJUSTMENTS	ADJUSTED TOTALS	ADJUSTED CASH DISCOUNT (f)	NET	CHARGED TO X-Y-Z CORPORATION	TOTAL OVERCHARGE	RECEIVING REPORTS (g)	CANCELLED CHECKS DATE	CANCELLED CHECKS NO.
8- 5-47	A-56742	The Electrical Supply Co.	$ 816.68	$2,058.07	$ 2,874.75	$ 57.49	$ 2,817.26	$ 816.68	$2,000.58(a)*	None	9-10-47	5160
8- 3-47	S-4263	Iron and Steel Supply, Inc.	656.53	2.69*	653.84	13.08	640.76	3,005.98	2,365.22(b)	None	8-13-47	4168
8-22-47	A-5610	The Hardware Supply Co.	583.35	275.00	858.35	8.58	849.77	583.35	266.42(c)*	None	9- 1-47	4324
8-19-47	201	The Blank Stationery Co.	270.00	270.00*	—	—	—	270.00	270.00(d)	None	8-29-47	4376
8- 7-47	8-3213	Penn Builders Supply Co.	1,024.00	—	1,024.00	20.48	1,003.52	4,246.50	3,242.98	None	8-17-47	4259
8-21-47	CM-1893	The Electrical Supply Co.	431.25*	—	431.25*	8.63*	422.62*	—	422.62(e)	None	9-10-47	5160
8-16-47	CM-2147	The Electrical Supply Co.	272.93*	33.07*	306.00*	6.12*	299.88*	—	299.88(e)	None	9-10-47	5160
		Material Furnished By X-Y-Z Corp.	11,542.73		11,542.73		11,542.73	11,542.73	—	—	—	—
			$14,189.11	$2,027.31	$16,216.42	$ 84.88	$16,131.54	$20,465.24	$4,333.70			
		Overhead @ 10%	1,418.91	202.73	1,621.64	8.49	1,613.15	2,046.52	433.37			
			$15,608.02	$2,230.04	$17,838.06	$ 93.37	$17,744.69	$22,511.76	$4,767.07			
		Fee @ 10%	1,560.80	223.01	1,783.81	9.34	1,774.47	2,251.18	476.71			
			$17,168.82	$2,453.05	$19,621.87	$102.71	$19,519.16	$24,762.94	$5,243.78			
		Less Material Furnished By X-Y-Z Corp.	11,542.73		11,542.73		11,542.73	11,542.73	—			
			$ 5,626.09	$2,453.05	$ 8,079.14	$102.71	$ 7,976.43	$13,220.21	$5,243.78			

*Denotes red figures.
(a) Error in extension on vendor's invoice not caught by contractor.
(b) Error in extension on vendor's invoice not caught by contractor.
(c) Error in extension on vendor's invoice not caught by contractor.
(d) This represents an overhead charge.
(e) Credit memos not allowed to x-y-z corporation. Contractor also erroneously billed X-Y-Z Corporation.
(f) Contractor failed to allow cash discount.
(g) Vendors' invoices were matched to copies of packing slips and delivery tickets.

CASE PROBLEM IN CONSTRUCTION AUDITING

AUDIT WORK PAPER

THE ERECTO CONSTRUCTION COMPANY

RECONSTRUCTION OF PAYROLL FOR WEEK ENDED JUNE 14, 1947

BADGE NO.	OCCUPATION	M	T	W	T	F	S	TOTAL HOURS	RATES (A)	STRAIGHT TIME PAY	PREMIUM PAY HOURS	PREMIUM PAY AMOUNT (b)	GROSS WAGES	CHECKED TO EARNINGS CARDS	AS BILLED — STRAIGHT TIME HOURS	AMOUNT	AS BILLED — PREMIUM PAY HOURS	AMOUNT
1	Ironworker	8	8	8	8	8	8	48	2.75	$ 132.00	8	$ 22.00	$ 154.00	√	48	$ 132.00	8	$ 22.00
2	"	8	8	8	8	8	8	48	2.75	132.00	8	22.00	154.00	√	48	132.00	8	22.00
3	"	8	8	8	8	8		40	2.75	110.00	8	22.00	132.00	√	48	132.00	8	22.00
4	"	8	8	8	8	8		40	2.75	110.00		–	110.00	√	48	132.00	8	22.00
5	"	8	8	8	8	8	8	48	2.75	132.00	8	22.00	154.00	√	48	132.00	8	22.00
6	"	8	8	8	8	8	8	48	2.75	132.00	8	22.00	154.00	√	48	132.00	8	22.00
7	"	8	8	8	8			32	2.75	88.00	8	22.00	110.00	√	48	132.00	8	22.00
8	Bricklayer	8	8	8	8	8	8	48	2.25	108.00	8	18.00	126.00	√	48	108.00	8	18.00
9	"	8	8	8	8	8	8	48	2.25	108.00	8	18.00	126.00	√	48	108.00	8	18.00
10	"	8	8	8	8	8	8	48	2.25	108.00	8	18.00	126.00	√	48	108.00	8	18.00
11	"	8	8	8	8			32	2.25	72.00		–	72.00	√	48	108.00	8	18.00
12	"	8	8	8	8	8		40	2.25	90.00		–	90.00	√	48	108.00	8	18.00
13	Carpenter	8	8	8	8	8	4	44	2.75	121.00	4	11.00	132.00	√	48	132.00	8	22.00
14	"	8	8	8	8	8	4	44	2.75	121.00	4	11.00	132.00	√	48	132.00	8	22.00
15	"	8	8	8	8	8	4	44	2.75	121.00	4	11.00	132.00	√	48	132.00	8	22.00
16	"	8	8	8	8	8	4	44	2.75	121.00	4	11.00	132.00	√	48	132.00	8	22.00
17	"	8	8	8	8	8	4	44	2.75	121.00	4	11.00	132.00	√	48	132.00	8	22.00
18	"	8	8	8	8			32	2.75	88.00	8	22.00	110.00	√	48	132.00	8	22.00
19	"	8	8	8	8			32	2.75	88.00	8	22.00	110.00	√	48	132.00	8	22.00
20	Laborers	8	8	6	8	8		38	1.35	51.30	8	10.80	62.10	√	48	64.80	8	10.80
21	"	8	8	8	8	8		40	1.35	54.00		–	54.00	√	48	64.80	8	10.80
22	"	8	8	8	8	8		40	1.35	54.00	8	10.80	64.80	√	48	64.80	8	10.80
23	"	8	4	8	8	8		36	1.35	48.60		–	48.60	√	48	64.80	8	10.80
24	"	8	8	8	8	8		40	1.35	54.00	8	10.80	64.80	√	48	64.80	8	10.80
25	"	8	8	8	8	8	8	48	1.35	64.80	8	10.80	75.60	√	48	64.80	8	10.80
26	"	8	8	8	8	8		40	1.35	54.00	8	10.80	64.80	√	48	64.80	8	10.80
27	"	8	8	8	8	8	4	44	1.35	59.40	4	5.40	64.80	√	48	64.80	8	10.80
28	"	8	8	8	6	8	4	42	1.35	56.70	4	5.40	62.10	√	48	64.80	8	10.80
29	"	8	8	8	6	8	4	42	1.35	56.70	4	5.40	62.10	√	48	64.80	8	10.80
		216	204	214	212	208	160	1,214	–	$2,656.50	160	$355.20	$3,011.70		1,392	$3,036.00	232	$506.00

(A) Rates priced from Payroll Rate Schedules
(B) Saturday time and overtime paid at double time rates.

Above compared to payroll.

	STRAIGHT TIME	PREMIUM PAY	TOTAL
Labor billed per Invoice No. 62 of June 21, 1947	$3,036.00	$506.00	$3,542.00
Actual labor per reconstructed payroll	2,656.50	355.20	3,011.70
Overbilling	$ 379.50	$150.80	$ 530.30

January 31, 1948

Mr. H. J. Jones, Controller
X–Y–Z Corporation
11 Grant Street
Pittsburgh, Pennsylvania

Dear Sir:

Audit of Construction Contract with
The Erecto Construction Company

In accordance with your request, we have audited the field and
home office records of the Erecto Construction Company supporting
charges made on a cost-plus basis for the erection of a power plant
building at our Cincinnati, Ohio, Works. We have reviewed the
system of internal control of construction activities used by local
management. We have examined or tested accounting records of
the contractor by methods and to the extent we deemed appropriate.

1. *Appropriated Funds*

Funds, in the amount of $1,150,000, were appropriated by the
Directors to cover this project.

From a report submitted by the contractor, dated January 10,
1948, and approved by our Chief Engineer, construction was estimated to be 80% complete as of December 31, 1947. This included
all material purchased by the contractor and delivered to the job
site as of that date.

Charges made to the construction accounts as of December 31,
1947, are as follows:

Contractor's charges	$ 964,040.84
Material furnished by the X–Y–Z Corporation ..	183,810.00
	$1,147,850.84

A need for additional funds is indicated, as follows:

Funds required ($1,147,850.84 ÷ .80)	$1,434,813.55
Funds appropriated	1,150,000.00
Anticipated Overrun	$ 284,813.55

No request for additional funds has been submitted to the Directors as of the date of this audit, although it is evident that costs will be in excess of the appropriated amount.

Recommendation

A new estimate of the cost of the building should be made by the Engineering Department, and a request should be made for additional funds.

Comments of the Chief Engineer

The Engineering Department is preparing new estimates of construction costs, and a request will be made for additional funds required.

2. *Review of Local Internal Control*

Weekly payrolls are prepared by the contractor's field clerk from daily labor reports submitted by the foreman of each craft. There has been no field checking of construction workers by the Corporation's timekeepers. The auditor observed that the contractor's employes were permitted to enter or leave the Corporation's premises at any time by merely displaying their identification badges. Necessary overtime is determined by each craft foreman, and the approval of only the contractor's superintendent is required. Labor billings of the contractor exhibit only the straight and overtime hours in total for each craft and are passed for payment without any other detail or approval.

Material is purchased by the contractor without approval by the Corporation's Engineering Department. Purchases made by the contractor and delivered to the construction site are received by the contractor's field clerk, who initials accompanying packing slips or delivery tickets to show receipt of the shipment only. These forms are forwarded to the contractor's general office for matching with vendors' invoices. No representative of the Corporation is present when material is received to verify the quantity and acceptability of quality.

Furnished material is disbursed from the Corporation's stores on the basis of requisitions, without prior or subsequent approval by a representative of the X–Y–Z Corporation.

Material invoices are submitted by the contractor for payment once each month and are in summary form only. It is not possible to verify the charges at time of payment as no supporting detail is furnished by the contractor.

Construction accounting details are handled by the Accounts Payable Department, and it is evident that considerable confusion exists owing to insufficient knowledge of construction matters and the lack of authority to investigate construction charges.

Recommendations

Immediate steps should be taken to install the following internal controls of construction activities:

1. A member of the local Accounting Department should be delegated to supervise all construction accounting activities. All matters affecting the disbursement of allotted funds should be directed to his attention.

2. Periodic field checks should be made daily by timekeepers reporting directly to the Construction Accounting Supervisor.

3. The time of construction workers entering or leaving the premises between the beginning and end of daily construction activities should be recorded at the Corporation's gates and forwarded to the Construction Timekeepers for accounting.

4. The contractor's daily labor reports should be compared with the timekeepers daily field check reports.

5. The contractor should pre-schedule his overtime requirements, submitting lists of the workers, by crafts, and secure approval of our Chief Engineer. Lists should also be prepared of the employes who actually worked overtime and approval secured for any change in requirements.

6. Certified copies of the contractor's payroll should be checked to records of the Construction Timekeepers and be attached to the weekly labor billings.

7. The contractor should be required to submit his purchase requisitions to the Engineering Department for approval after checking to specifications and bills of material.

8. The contractor should record material receipts on a formal receiving report, and the material should be approved for quantity, specifications, and quality by the Engineering Department.

9. The contractor should be required to support his monthly material billings with copies of his vendors' invoices, matched

to approved copies of receiving reports, and such charges should be audited by the Construction Accounting Department.

10. Requisitions for materials disbursed from Corporation stores should be approved by the Engineering Department.

11. Approval should be secured by the contractor for material or equipment removed from the premises, and a record should be made and followed up by the Construction Accounting Department to see that credit is secured.

Comments of the Chief Accountant

A member of the Accounting Department has been appointed to supervise and coordinate all construction accounting activities.

The other recommendations of the auditors have been adopted.

Comments of the Chief Engineer

Overtime requirements are being approved by the Engineering Department before and after the hours are worked.

3. *Labor Charges*

The auditors reconstructed 20% of each payroll for the year, verifying the hours, rates, and extensions. The total of each payroll was checked to the weekly labor billings and the total of the annual construction payroll.

The auditors reconstructed the entire payroll for the week ended June 14, 1947, because of a difference between the total gross earnings and the amount invoiced by the contractor, as follows:

	Invoiced	*Per Payroll*	*Overcharge*
Straight time earnings	$3,036.00	$2,656.50	$379.50
Premium pay	506.00	355.20	150.80
Total earnings	$3,542.00	$3,011.70	$530.30
Payroll Taxes and Insurance @ 10.8%	382.53	325.26	57.27
	$3,924.53	$3,336.96	$587.57
Overhead @ 10%	392.45	333.70	58.75
	$4,316.98	$3,670.66	$646.32
Fee @ 10%	431.70	367.07	64.63
	$4,748.68	$4,037.73	$710.95

The overbilling was due to the contractor's bookkeeper estimating the invoice by multiplying a standard work week by 48 hours times the number of workers in each craft.

A general increase of $.15 an hour was granted to all construction employes as of Sunday, July 17, 1947, in accordance with an agreement dated Sunday, July 10, 1947, between the Union and the Erecto Construction Company.

In verifying the contractor's Invoice No. 72 of July 31, 1947, for a retroactive wage adjustment, it was found that the date of the agreement, July 10, 1947, had been confused with the date of the increase. As a result of this misinterpretation, the contractor has erroneously billed the X–Y–Z Corporation a wage adjustment for the week ended July 16, 1947, as follows:

Straight time earnings	1,663 hrs. @ $.15	$249.45
Premium pay	244 hrs. @ $.15	36.60
		$286.05
Payroll Taxes and Insurance @ 10.8%		30.89
		$316.94
Overhead @ 10%		31.69
		$348.63
Fee @ 10%		34.86
		$383.49

Recommendation

A credit should be secured from the contractor for $1,094.44.

Comments of the Chief Accountant

The contractor has been requested to issue credit for $1,094.44.

4. *Material Charges*

Charges for material purchased and billed by the contractor for the year amounted to $329,842.73. The auditors selected the August Invoice No. 81, dated September 10, 1947, for a complete verification and examined the other eleven monthly invoices on a test check basis. The audit of detail supporting Invoice No. 81 revealed the following:

a. The Electrical Supply Company charged the contractor for $816.68 per their Invoice A–56742 of August 5. A check of extensions indicated the correct amount to be $2,874.75 and resulted in an undercharge of $2,058.07.

b. The contractor purchased 6,908 pounds of angle iron from Iron and Steel Supply Company at $3.74 per cwt, for which he was billed $261.05. A check of the extensions on the vendor's invoice revealed the correct amount to be $258.36. In addition, the contractor erroneously charged the X–Y–Z Corporation for $2,610.50. These two errors resulted in an overcharge of $2,352.14.

c. The contractor charged $583.35 for wheelbarrows, shovels, picks, and handles. A check of the Hardware Supply Company's invoice revealed an error in extension for shovels, resulting in an undercharge of $275 to the X–Y–Z Corporation.

d. An invoice from the Blank Stationery Company, dated August 18, 1947, for $270, was found to represent charges for stationery used by the contractor's general office. The auditors consider this to be an overhead item and that the contractor had secured reimbursement through his overhead rate.

e. The contractor purchased fifty 300-foot rolls of tar paper from the Penn Builders Supply at $12.72 per roll, a total of $636, but billed the Corporation for 300 rolls at $12.72 each, a total of $3,816. This represented an overcharge of $3,180.

f. The Corporation was charged for 450 bags of cement at $.85 a bag, whereas 400 bags had been delivered and billed by the vendor. This represents an overcharge of $42.50.

g. The contractor had returned 3,750 feet of 1-inch BX cable to the Electrical Supply Company and received their credit of August 21, 1947, for $431.25. No allowance had been made to the Corporation.

h. The Electrical Supply Company issued a credit dated August 16, 1947, for $272.93 to correct their Invoice A–56742 of August 5. A check of extensions revealed the correct amount to be $306. No allowance had been made to the Corporation.

The above adjustments net $5,141.07, after including overhead and fee of $892.25.

Cash Discounts

The contractor failed to allow cash discounts from his August purchases. After adjusting the vendors' invoices for errors in extension, the discount including overhead and fee amounted to $102.71.

Recommendation

A refund should be secured for $5,243.78.

Comments of the Chief Accountant

The contractor has been requested to refund the above amount.

5. *Salvage Credits for Drums, Tools, and Lumber*

In reconciling an inventory of supplies taken at the request of the auditors, it was noted that the following items had been removed from the Corporation's premises, without notification or approval, because they were no longer needed for the construction work.

25 Returnable Drums @ $5.00 ...	$125.00
Overhead @ 10%	12.50
	$137.50
Fee @ 10%	13.75
	$151.25

	Quantity	Purchase Cost Unit Price	Total
Wheelbarrows	17	$14.75	$250.75
Shovels	73	2.75	200.75
Picks	18	1.65	29.70
Various Other Small Tools	—	—	273.71
			$754.91

An agreement was reached by the contractor and our Chief Engineer that, because of the used condition of this material, it should be valued at 50% of its purchase cost, as follows:

50% of $754.91	$377.46
Overhead @ 10%	37.75
	$415.21
Fee @ 10%	41.52
	$456.73

Two grades of lumber were used for the job, as follows:

1. First grade used solely for construction.
2. Second grade for use in making concrete forms.

Lumber was not charged to the job as purchased, but on a requisition basis as used. All lumber in the contractor's inventory account had been purchased specifically for this job.

The auditors arranged for and observed a physical inventory. In reconciling the inventory it was discovered that the contractor had made overcharges, as follows (see Exhibit 1–I) :

	Bd. Ft.	Price per M. Bd. Ft.	Amount
First-grade lumber	8,671	$150.00	$1,301.00
Second-grade lumber	21,657	110.00	2,382.00
			$3,683.00
Overhead @ 10%			368.30
			$4,051.30
Fee @ 10%			405.13
Total Overcharge			$4,456.43

The overbilling of first-grade lumber was apparently due to errors in measuring and calculating the number of board feet as charges were made to the job. The overcharge of second-grade lumber is attributed to the use of salvaged lumber from dismantled forms.

Recommendations

1. Inventories of salvable and returnable material should be taken at the end of the job and no materials should be taken from the property without approval.
2. The contractor should stop charging for the use of salvaged second-grade lumber.
3. Refunds should be secured from the contractor as follows:

Drums	$ 151.25
Tools	456.73
Lumber	4,456.43
	$5,064.41

Comments of the Chief Accountant

1. Inventories of salvable and returnable material, lumber, and other supplies will be taken at the end of the job.
2. The contractor has been instructed to charge only for new lumber used in making concrete forms.
3. A refund of $5,064.41 has been requested from the contractor.

6. *Payroll Taxes and Insurance*

A comparison of rates paid by the contractor for Federal Old Age Benefit Tax, State and Federal Unemployment Insurance, Workmen's Compensation Insurance, and Public Liability and Property Damage Insurance disclosed that:

    a. Federal Old Age Benefit Taxes had not been adjusted for non-taxable earnings in excess of $3,000 per annum.

b. Effect had not been given to merit rating and earnings in excess of $3,000 per annum in billing State and Federal Unemployment Compensation Insurance.

c. Workmen's Compensation Insurance rates had been reduced because of merit rating, by the State, but the contractor had not adjusted his rate accordingly.

d. The rates for Public Liability and Property Damage Insurance had been reduced without adjustment by the contractor. Although this type of insurance is not applicable to premium pay, the contractor had invoiced the Corporation on the total earnings of his employes.

The following comparative summary shows the actual rates paid by the contractor and the rates billed to the X–Y–Z Corporation.

	(1) Gross Payrolls	(2) Taxable Earnings	(3) Taxes and Prem. Paid	(4) Actual Rates (3 ÷ 1)	(5) Rates Used by Contractor
F.O.A.B.	$302,126	$259,783	$ 2,598	.8600	1.00
Fed. U.C.I.	302,126	259,783	779	.2578	.30
State U.C.I.	302,126	259,783	4,676	1.5476	2.70
			$ 8,053	2.6654	4.00
Work. Comp. Ins.	302,126	—	4,985	1.6500	3.10
P.L. & P.D. Ins.	261,697*	—	7,746	2.9600	3.70
Totals			$20,784	7.2754	10.80

* Based on straight time earnings only.

Recommendation

It is recommended that a credit be obtained from the contractor in the amount of $14,332.98, as summarized in Exhibit 1–II.

Comments of the Chief Accountant

Since this is a cost-plus contract, we should pay no more than the actual cost to the contractor for the subject taxes and insurance. A refund will be secured from the Erecto Construction Company.

7. Material Supplied by the X–Y–Z Corporation

An examination was made of the charges for material supplied by the Corporation to the contractor on a "no-charge" basis. No exceptions were found. Charges billed from the beginning of the construction through December 31, 1947, amounted to $183,810. These charges included a mark-up of 15% by the X–Y–Z Corporation to cover overhead costs for purchasing, accounting, warehousing, and disbursing materials as required by the contractor, as follows:

Purchase value of material	$159,834.78
X–Y–Z Corporation's overhead cost @ 15%	23,975.22
Total	$183,810.00

The contractor has recovered 10% overhead and 10% profit on the above value, amounting to $38,600.10, as follows:

Overhead	10% of $183,810.00	$18,381.00
Profit	10% of $202,191.00	20,219.10
		$38,600.10

The contractor explained these charges as being necessary in order for him to recover the overhead and profit he had planned and submitted in his proposal. The auditors contend, however, that as the cost of purchasing, accounting, warehousing, and disbursing this material to the contractor was paid for by the X–Y–Z Corporation, the contractor has recovered overhead for costs which he did not incur.

Recommendations

1. The auditors believe that the 10% profit is reasonable and fair as the contractor had figured the fee on the basis of the full value of all materials necessary for the job. However, it is the opinion of the auditors that the 10% overhead fee should be allowed only on items for which the contractor has actually incurred costs.
2. In view of the plans of the Corporation to erect a similar building at our Oil City Works, the Purchasing Department should clearly define the base for the application of overhead when placing future contracts.

Comments of the Purchasing Department

The auditor's recommendation number 2 will be followed in the placing of future contracts.

8. *Efficiency of the Contractor*

During the course of the examination, the auditor learned that the Corporation had made several complaints to the contractor about the progress of work and the disorganized way in which construction was conducted. Repeated requests that the contractor replace his superintendent with an efficient manager were finally heeded, and a new superintendent was appointed on November 1, 1947. These conditions have resulted in higher construction costs and increased profit for the contractor in undetermined amounts.

Recommendations

Subsequent construction contracts should provide for:

1. The payment of a bonus on a percentage basis, if the actual cost of the project is less than the estimated cost mutually agreed upon, exclusive of costs due to rising prices and premium pay.
2. The assessment of a penalty on a percentage basis, if the cost of the project is greater than the estimated cost mutually agreed upon, exclusive of costs due to rising prices and premium pay.

The inclusion of such provisions in a contract should act as an incentive to the contractor to control his costs rigidly, thus resulting in savings to the Corporation.

Comments of the Purchasing Department

Bonus and penalty provisions will be made in future construction contracts.

9. *Painting*

The roof has been painted by a subcontractor on a unit-price basis of $3.20 per square. The exact area of the roof surface was 4,800 squares, as reinvoiced by the contractor.

The auditor checked the painting specifications to blueprints for the roof and discovered that no allowance had been made in area measurements for glass skylights which were not painted.

An overbilling had therefore been made as follows:

Billed as being painted	4,800 squares @ $3.20	$15,360.00
Actually painted	3,456 squares @ $3.20	11,059.20
Area of skylights not painted	1,344 squares @ $3.20	$ 4,300.80
Overhead @ 10%		430.08
		$ 4,730.88
Fee @ 10%		473.09
Overcharge		$ 5,203.97

Recommendations

1. Charges of this nature should be approved by the Chief Engineer as the overcharge could have been easily detected had the specification and charges been checked to the blueprints.
2. A refund for $5,203.97 should be secured from the contractor.

Comments of the Chief Engineer

This was an oversight on our part. All similar charges will be checked to blueprints as suggested.

Comments of the Chief Accountant

A request for refund has been made to the contractor.

10. Application of Overhead to Premium Pay

The contractor has applied overhead and profit to premium pay and the payroll taxes and insurance paid thereon. As this is not permitted by the contract, a refund of the overhead and profit applied should be made.

Actual premium pay for year	$40,428.90
Plus payroll taxes and insurance at the actual rate of 4.3154%	1,744.67
	$42,173.57
Overhead @ 10% of $42,173.57	$ 4,217.36
Fee @ 10% of $46,390.93	4,639.09
Refund due	$ 8,856.45

Recommendation

A credit of $8,856.45 should be secured from the contractor, and he should be instructed to exclude the application of overhead and profit from future premium pay costs.

Comments of the Chief Accountant

The contractor has been advised to eliminate the overhead and profit application to premium pay costs and to make refund for $8,856.45.

11. Work Performed without Approval of the Purchasing Department

The Erecto Construction Company has billed the Corporation, per its Invoice No. 462, dated October 15, 1947, for $884.74 for a change in electrical specifications. This work was done on the basis of a verbal authorization of the Chief Engineer. The additional cost has not been approved by the Purchasing Department as it had not been advised of the change.

Recommendation

A request for a change order should be made to the Purchasing Department to cover the additional costs involved, and that in the future no additional work should be authorized without prior approval of the Purchasing Department.

Comments of the Chief Engineer

Additional work will not be authorized until written approval has been issued by the Purchasing Department.

12. *Contractor's Purchasing Procedure*

A review of the contractor's purchasing procedure revealed that no effort had been made to place large orders on a competitive basis.

This has resulted in the payment of higher costs for materials and added overhead and profit fees to the contractor.

Example 1

Purchased from Steel Sash Company,
F.O.B. Detroit, Freight Collect:

400 Steel Windows @ $27.00	$10,800.00
Freight Charges	378.00
	$11,178.00

Competitor's price, F.O.B. Cincinnati,
Freight Allowed:

400 Steel Windows @ $27.00	10,800.00
	$ 378.00
Plus overhead @ 10%	37.80
	$ 415.80
Fee @ 10%	41.58
Excess cost	$ 457.38

Example 2

The subcontract for painting the roof had been placed at a unit price rate of $3.20 a square. A bid secured from a competitor by our Purchasing Department indicated that the work could have been done for $2.80 a square, or a savings as follows:

Actual squares painted	3,456 @ $3.20	$11,059.20
Competitor's bid	3,456 @ $2.80	9,676.80
		$ 1,382.40
Overhead @ 10%		138.24
		$ 1,520.64
Fee @ 10%		152.06
Excess cost		$ 1,672.70

Recommendation

Before approving future purchase requisitions of the contractor, as recommended in Section 2 of this report, the Engineering Department should check with the contractor to see that he has placed his orders for large purchases on a competitive basis.

Comments of the Chief Engineer

The recommendation of the auditors will be followed in the future.

13. *Interpretations of Percentage Applications for Overhead, Fee, and Payroll Taxes and Insurance*

The contract is not clear as to the manner in which the various percentages should be applied by the contractor to recover his overhead costs, fee, and payroll taxes and insurance.

For example, the contractor had billed on the following basis:

Cost	$1,000.00
Plus 10.8% insurance and payroll taxes	108.00
	$1,108.00
Plus 10% overhead	110.80
	$1,218.80
Plus 10% fee	121.88
	$1,340.68

The contract could be interpreted as follows:

Cost	$1,000.00
Plus 10.8% insurance and payroll tax	108.00
Plus 10% overhead	100.00
Plus 10% fee	100.00
	$1,308.00

It is evident from the above that if the second interpretation is used there would be a reduction of costs to the *X–Y–Z* Corporation of $32.68 per thousand dollars of direct cost.

Recommendation

It is recommended that the Purchasing Department clarify the terms of the contract as to the application of percentages.

Comments of Purchasing Department

The first interpretation illustrated by the auditors is correct as it was the intent to reimburse the contractor on this basis.

The method of applying percentages for overhead, fee, and payroll taxes and insurance will be precisely described in future contracts.

CLASSIFIED SUMMARY OF ADJUSTMENTS

Labor at straight time	$ 628.95
Payroll taxes and insurance	9,291.71
Premium pay	187.40
Payroll taxes and insurance on premium pay	2,641.89
Material purchased by contractor	4,836.16
Lumber	3,683.00
Painting roof	4,300.80
Overhead	6,774.35
Profit fee	7,451.78
Total Savings	$39,796.04
Less 20% Holdback	7,959.21
	$31,836.83

CASE PROBLEM IN CONSTRUCTION AUDITING

EXHIBIT 1–I

THE ERECTO CONSTRUCTION COMPANY

ANALYSIS OF LUMBER USED IN CONSTRUCTION OF BUILDING FOR THE X-Y-Z CORPORATION
FROM BEGINNING OF JOB TO JANUARY 31, 1948

	Board Feet	
	First Grade	Second Grade
Opening Inventory	None	None
Purchases	555,500	57,142
Total Available	555,500	57,142
Inventory January 31, 1948	60,000	3,000
Actual Lumber Used	495,500	54,142
Charges to X-Y-Z Corporation	504,171	75,799
Overcharge	8,671	21,657

SUMMARY

Charged to X-Y-Z Corporation:

First Grade Lumber	504,171 Bd. Ft. @ $150.00 M	$75,626.00
Second Grade Lumber	75,799 Bd. Ft. @ $110.00 M	8,338.00
		$83,964.00

Actual Lumber Used:

First Grade Lumber	495,500 Bd. Ft. @ $150.00 M	$74,325.00
Second Grade Lumber	54,142 Bd. Ft. @ $110.00 M	5,956.00
		$80,281.00

Total Overcharge for Lumber	$ 3,683.00
Overhead @ 10%	368.30
Fee @ 10%	405.13
Total Overcharge	$ 4,456.43

CASE PROBLEM IN CONSTRUCTION AUDITING

EXHIBIT 1–II

<u>THE ERECTO CONSTRUCTION COMPANY</u>

<u>SUMMARY</u> OF REFUND DUE TO USE OF EXCESSIVE PAYROLL TAX AND INSURANCE RATES

	Earnings	
	Straight Time	Premium
Billed by Contractor	$262,326.23	$40,616.30
Less Adjustments:		
Payroll - June 14, 1947	379.50	150.80
Retroactive Wages.	249.45	36.60
Per Summary Contractor's Payrolls	$261,697.28	$40,428.90

Payroll Taxes and Insurance Billed After Adjustments:

Straight Time Earnings	$261,697.28 @ 10.8%	$28,263.30
Premium Pay	$ 40,428.90 @ 10.8%	4,366.33
		$32,629.63

Should Have Been:

Straight Time Earnings	$261,697.28 @ 7.2754%	$19,039.52
Premium Pay	$ 40,428.90 @ 4.3154%	1,744.67
		$20,784.19

Excess Payroll Tax and Insurance Billed	$11,845.44
Overhead @ 10%	1,184.54
Fee @ 10%	1,303.00
Total Refund Due	$14,332.98

CASE PROBLEM 2

PAYROLL CONTROL AUDITS

The Jones Machine Company, Pittsburgh, Pennsylvania, is engaged in die sinking, machining small castings, and repairing all small equipment. The company operates under a union agreement dated April 22, 1947. Several important union requirements which were agreed to by the company are as follows:

Checkoff. For employes who are members of the union, the company shall deduct from the first pay of each month the union dues of $1.50 for the preceding month.

Hourly wage rates in effect as of the date of this agreement shall remain in effect for the duration of this agreement. (See Wage Scale.)

Overtime payment at time and one-half will be allowed for all hours (with the exception of allowed hours) in excess of 8 hours per day or in excess of 40 hours per week.

Allowed Time (4-hour minimum provision). An employe who is notified to report and who does report for work and who works less than 4 hours shall be paid for a minimum of 4 hours at the rate in effect for the occupation at which he began to work.

You are assigned to review the degree of internal controls exercised within the payroll system now in use, which is a manual weekly payroll and is disbursed through the medium of bearer checks.

The procedural instructions and required preparation of forms to be used for the review are as follows:

1. *Wage Scale (See Exhibit 2A)*

It was determined that all wage scale changes must be approved by the President of the company and the Secretary-Treasurer.

The pay period ending May 22, 1948, was selected as a representative pay period for the purpose of this audit.

2. *Reporting of Time—Preparation of Weekly Clock Card and Summary of Cards [See Exhibits 2B and 2C(1) through 2C(6)]*

The employe will ring "in" and "out" on this card for the entire week. At the end of the week the total regular hours worked, allowed hours, and premium hours will be calculated and written on the cards.

Overtime, as well as all other time, is controlled by the use of these cards.

You will note that the approved preliminary payroll (Exhibit 2C) is a summary of all clock cards. This payroll, approved by the foreman, serves the purpose of computing the employes' earnings and making the labor distribution thereof.

All time reported must be properly approved.

3. *Payroll Journal* (*See Exhibit 2D*)

This conforms to the standard force for each position.

4. *Federal Old Age Benefit Tax*

Employes are exempted from paying tax when their earnings have reached $3,000.

5. *Employes' Withholding Tax*

The company requires each employe to complete and sign an Employe's Withholding Exemption Certificate, form W–4. (See Exhibit 2E.)

Method of withholding used—official Weekly Wage Bracket Table. (See Exhibit 2G.)

6. *Group Insurance*

The cost of insurance to employes is $.55 per month per $1,000 of insurance. To determine the proper insurance coverage for an employe, see Exhibit 2A.

Insurance deductions are authorized by the employe.

It is the general rule to make deductions from the first pay of each month; however, if earnings are insufficient at this time, deductions will be made at a subsequent pay period during the month.

7. *Union Dues*

In deductions for union dues, the same rule applies as in Item 6 above.

8. *Disbursement of Wages*

After the payroll checks are prepared and signed, they are delivered to the Machine Shop for disbursement on pay day.

The attached exhibits include a complete working payroll. You will find discrepancies within this payroll, pertaining to the general description of the various payroll phases outlined above.

As the audit progresses, you will prepare necessary working papers which will include your work program and related analyses in support of your findings.

From your working papers, prepare an audit report addressed to Mr. A. M. Smith, Controller of the Jones Machine Company, in which you will report your findings and make recommendations for the correction of internal control weaknesses, etc.

CASE PROBLEM IN PAYROLL CONTROL AUDITS
EXHIBIT 2A

JONES MACHINE COMPANY

WAGE SCALE

EFFECTIVE DATE July 1, 1947

POSITION TITLE	POSITION CODE	RESPONSIBILITY NAME	RESPONSIBILITY NO.	COST CODE	STANDARD FORCE	HOURLY WAGE RATE	EARNINGS PER MAN TURN (8 HRS.)	EXPECTED NORMAL ANNUAL EARNINGS	INSURANCE COST PER MONTH TO EMPLOYE
Foreman	3	Supervisory and Clerical	100	50	1	$2.75	$22.00 x 300 =	$6,600.00	$3.85
Clerk	6		100	60	2	1.25	10.00 x 300 =	3,000.00	1.65
Machinist – A –	10	Machine Shops	200	70	10	2.40	19.20 x 300 =	5,760.00	3.30
Machinist – B –	11	Machine Shops	200	72	15	2.20	17.60 x 300 =	5,280.00	3.30
Machinist – C –	12	Machine Shops	200	74	15	2.00	16.00 x 300 =	4,800.00	2.75
Tool Repairman	104	Machine Shops	200	76	1	1.75	14.00 x 300 =	4,200.00	2.20
Crane Man	107	Machine Shops	200	78	1	1.50	12.00 x 300 =	3,600.00	1.93
Tractor Operator	113	Machine Shops	200	80	1	1.50	12.00 x 300 =	3,600.00	1.93
Oiler	115	Machine Shops	200	82	2	1.25	10.00 x 300 =	3,000.00	1.65
Laborer	120	Machine Shops	200	84	5	1.20	9.60 x 300 =	2,880.00	1.65
Shipper	205	Warehouse	300	90	1	1.85	14.80 x 300 =	4,440.00	2.48
Laborer	210	Warehouse	300	92	1	1.20	9.60 x 300 =	2,880.00	1.65

Last three columns are used to establish the proper insurance coverage for employes.

T. V. Rose II, President
Approved

B. N. Jones, Secretary-Treasurer
Approved

JONES MACHINE COMPANY

WEEKLY CLOCK CARD

210

J. H. REYNOLDS

PAY PERIOD ENDING   MAY 22, 1948

DAY	IN	OUT	IN	OUT		OVERTIME IN	OVERTIME OUT	TOTAL HOURS
S								
M	17 8:00	12:01	12:31	4:32				8
T	18 8:00	12:01	12:32	4:31				8
W	19 8:00	12:01	12:31	4:30				8
T	20 7:55	12:02	12:32	4:32				8
F	21 8:00	12:04	12:32	4:35				8
S	22 8:00	12:01	12:32	4:30				8 4*

Regular ....48.........Hrs.

Allowed ....-.........Hrs.

Premium ....4.........Hrs.

Total ....52.........Hrs.

* Record Premium Hours in Red

CASE PROBLEM IN PAYROLL CONTROL AUDITS

EXHIBIT 2C(1)

JONES MACHINE COMPANY

SUMMARY OF WEEKLY CLOCK CARDS AND APPROVED PRELIMINARY PAYROLL

PAY PERIOD ENDING 5-22-48

EMPLOYE NUMBER		16 S	17 M	18 T	19 W	20 T	21 F	22 S	TOTAL HOURS	HOURLY RATE	GROSS EARNINGS	POS. CODE	COST CODE
100	R		8	8	8	8	8	8	48	$2.75	$132.00		
	A												
	P							4	4	2.75	11.00		
									52	2.75	$143.00	3	50
110	R		8	8	8	8	8	8	48	$1.25	$ 60.00		
	A												
	P							4	4	1.25	. 5.00		
									52	1.25	$ 65.00	6	60
112	R		8	8	8	8	8	8	48	$1.25	$ 60.00		
	A												
	P							4	4	1.25	5.00		
									52	1.25	$ 65.00	6	60
203	R		8	8	8	8	8	8	48	$2.40	$115.20		
	A												
	P							4	4	2.40	9.60		
									52	2.40	$124.80	10	70
204	R		8	8	8	8	8	8	48	$2.40	$115.20		
	A												
	P							4	4	2.40	9.60		
									52	2.40	$124.80	10	70
205	R		8	8	8	8	8	8	48	$2.40	$115.20		
	A												
	P							4	4	2.40	9.60		
									52	2.40	$124.80	10	70
206	R		8	8	8	2XX	8		34	$2.40	$ 81.60		
	A												
	P												
									34	2.40	$ 81.60	10	70
207	R		8	8	8	8	8		40	$2.40	$ 96.00		
	A												
	P												
									40	2.40	$ 96.00	10	70
208	R		8*	8	8	8	8	8	48	$2.40	$115.20		
	A												
	P							4	4	2.40	9.60		
									52	2.40	$124.80	10	70
209	R		8	8	8	8	8	8	48	$2.40	$115.20		
	A												
	P							4	4	2.40	9.60		
									52	2.40	$124.80	10	70

SIGNED *J. J. Curley* # 100
Foreman

CASE PROBLEM IN PAYROLL CONTROL AUDITS

EXHIBIT 2C(2)

		16 S	17 M	18 T	19 W	20 T	21 F	22 S	TOTAL HOURS	HOURLY RATE	GROSS EARNINGS	POS. CODE	COST CODE
JONES MACHINE COMPANY													
SUMMARY OF WEEKLY CLOCK CARDS AND APPROVED PRELIMINARY PAYROLL													
PAY PERIOD ENDING 5-22-48													
EMPLOYE NUMBER													
210	R		8*	8	8	8	8	8	48	$2.40	$115.20		
	A												
	P							4	4	2.40	9.60		
									52	2.40	$124.80	10	70
211	R		8	8	8	8	8	8	48	$2.40	$115.20		
	A												
	P							4	4	2.40	9.60		
									52	2.40	$124.80	10	70
212	R		8*	8	8	8	8	8	48	$2.40	$115.20		
	A												
	P							4	4	2.40	9.60		
									52	2.40	$124.80	10	70
213	R		8	8	8	8	8		40	$2.20	$ 88.00		
	A												
	P								40	2.20	$ 88.00	11	72
214	R		8*	8	8	8	8		40	$2.20	$ 88.00		
	A												
	P								40	2.20	$ 88.00	11	72
215	R		8	8	4	8	8		36	$2.20	$ 79.20		
	A												
	P								36	2.20	$ 79.20	11	72
216	R		8	8	8	8	8	8	48	$2.20	$105.60		
	A												
	P								48	2.20	$105.60	11	72
217	R		8	8	8	8	8		40	$2.20	$ 88.00		
	A												
	P								40	2.20	$ 88.00	11	72
218	R		8*	8	8	8	8	8	48	$2.20	$105.60		
	A												
	P							4	4	2.20	8.80		
									52	2.20	$114.40	11	72
219	R		8	8	8	8	8	8	48	$2.20	$105.60		
	A												
	P							4	4	2.20	8.80		
									52	2.20	$114.40	11	72

SIGNED *J. Z. Curley* #100.
Foreman

CASE PROBLEM IN PAYROLL CONTROL AUDITS

EXHIBIT 2C(3)

		JONES MACHINE COMPANY				
		SUMMARY OF WEEKLY CLOCK CARDS AND APPROVED PRELIMINARY PAYROLL				
		PAY PERIOD ENDING 5-22-48				

EMPLOYE NUMBER		16 17 18 19 20 21 22 S M T W T F S	TOTAL HOURS	HOURLY RATE	GROSS EARNINGS	POS. CODE	COST CODE
220	R	8* 8 8 8 8 8	48	$2.20	$105.60		
	A						
	P	4	4	2.20	8.80		
			52	2.20	$114.40	11	72
221	R	8 8 8 8 8	40	$2.20	$ 88.00		
	A						
	P						
			40	2.20	$ 88.00	11	72
222	R	8 8 8 8 8	40	$2.20	$ 88.00		
	A						
	P						
			40	2.20	$ 88.00	11	72
223	R	8 8 8 8 8 8	48	$2.20	$105.60		
	A						
	P	4	4	2.20	8.80		
			52	2.20	$114.40	11	72
224	R	8 2XX8 8 8 8	42	$2.20	$ 92.40		
	A						
	P	1	1	2.20	2.20		
			43	2.20	$ 94.60	11	72
225	R	8 8 8 8 8	40	$2.20	$ 88.00		
	A						
	P						
			40	2.20	$ 88.00	11	72
226	R	8 8 8 8 8 8	48	$2.20	$105.60		
	A						
	P	4	4	2.20	8.80		
			52	2.20	$114.40	11	72
227	R	8 8 8 8 8 8	48	$2.20	$105.60		
	A						
	P	4	4	2.20	8.80		
			52	2.20	$114.40	11	72
XXX 228	R	8 8 8 8 8	40	$2.20	$ 88.00		
	A						
	P						
			40	2.20	$ 88.00	12	72
XXX 229	R	2 8 8 8 8	34	$2.20	$ 74.80		
	A	2	2	2.20	4.40		
	P		36	2.20	$ 79.20	12	72

SIGNED *J. Z. Curley* #100
Foreman

CASE PROBLEM IN PAYROLL CONTROL AUDITS

EXHIBIT 2C(4)

JONES MACHINE COMPANY

SUMMARY OF WEEKLY CLOCK CARDS AND APPROVED PRELIMINARY PAYROLL

PAY PERIOD ENDING 5-22-48

EMPLOYE NUMBER		16 S	17 M	18 T	19 W	20 T	21 F	22 S	TOTAL HOURS	HOURLY RATE	GROSS EARNINGS	POS. CODE	COST CODE
230	R A P		8	8	8	8	8		40	$2.00	$ 80.00		
									40	2.00	$ 80.00	12	74
231	R A P		8	8	8	8	8	8	48	$2.00	$ 96.00		
									48	2.00	$ 96.00	12	74
232	R A P		8	8	8	8	8		40	$2.00	$ 80.00		
									40	2.00	$ 80.00	12	74
233	R A P		8	8	8	8	8		40	$2.00	$ 80.00		
									40	2.00	$ 80.00	12	74
234	R A P		8	8	8	8	8	8 4	48 4	$2.00 2.00	$ 96.00 8.00		
									52	2.00	$104.00	12	74
235	R A P		8	8	8	8	8	8 4	48 4	$2.00 2.00	$ 96.00 8.00		
									52	2.00	$104.00	12	74
236	R A P		8	8	8	2 2	8	8 1	42 2 1	$2.00 2.00 2.00	$ 84.00 4.00 2.00		
									45	2.00	$ 90.00	12	74
237	R A P		8	8	8	8	8	8 4	48 4	$2.00 2.00	$ 96.00 8.00		
									52	2.00	$104.00	12	74
238	R A P		8	8	8	8	8	8 4	48 4	$2.00 2.00	$ 96.00 8.00		
									52	2.00	$104.00	12	74
240	R A P		8	8	8	8			32	$2.00	$ 64.00		
									32	2.00	$ 64.00	12	74

SIGNED *J. Z. Curley* #100
Foreman

CASE PROBLEM IN PAYROLL CONTROL AUDITS

EXHIBIT 2C(5)

		16 17 18 19 20 21 22	TOTAL	HOURLY	GROSS	POS.	COST
EMPLOYE NUMBER		S M T W T F S	HOURS	RATE	EARNINGS	CODE	CODE
241	R	8 8 8 8 8 8	48	$2.00	$ 96.00		
	A						
	P	4	4	2.00	8.00		
			52	2.00	$104.00	12	74
242	R	8 8 8 8 8	40	$2.00	$ 80.00		
	A						
	P						
			40	2.00	$ 80.00	12	74
243	R	8 8 8 8 8	40	$2.00	$ 80.00		
	A						
	P						
			40	2.00	$ 80.00	12	74
244	R	8 2XX8 8 8 8	42	$1.75	$ 73.50		
	A						
	P	1	1	1.75	1.75		
			43	1.75	$ 75.25	104	76
245	R	8 8 8 8 8 8	48	$1.50	$ 72.00		
	A						
	P	4	4	1.50	6.00		
			52	1.50	$ 78.00	107	78
247	R	8 8 8 8 8 8	48	$1.50	$ 72.00		
	A						
	P	4	4	1.50	6.00		
			52	1.50	$ 78.00	113	80
249	R	8 8 8 8 8 8	48	$1.25	$ 60.00		
	A						
	P	4	4	1.25	5.00		
			52	1.25	$ 65.00	115	82
250	R	8 8 8 8 8 8	48	$1.25	$ 60.00		
	A						
	P	4	4	1.25	5.00		
			52	1.25	$ 65.00	115	82
252	R	8 8 8 8 8 8	48	$1.20	$ 57.60		
	A						
	P	4	4	1.20	4.80		
			52	1.20	$ 62.40	120	84
254	R	8 8 8 8 8 8	48	$1.20	$ 57.60		
	A						
	P	4	4	1.20	4.80		
			52	1.20	$ 62.40	120	84

JONES MACHINE COMPANY

SUMMARY OF WEEKLY CLOCK CARDS AND APPROVED PRELIMINARY PAYROLL

PAY PERIOD ENDING 5-22-48

SIGNED *J. J. Curley* #100
Foreman

CASE PROBLEM IN PAYROLL CONTROL AUDITS

EXHIBIT 2C(6)

JONES MACHINE COMPANY
SUMMARY OF WEEKLY CLOCK CARDS AND APPROVED PRELIMINARY PAYROLL

PAY PERIOD ENDING 5-22-48

EMPLOYE NUMBER		16 S	17 M	18 T	19 W	20 T	21 F	22 S	TOTAL HOURS	HOURLY RATE	GROSS EARNINGS	POS. CODE	COST CODE
256	R		8	8	8	8	8	8	48	$1.20	$ 57.60		
	A												
	P							4	4	1.20	4.80		
									52	1.20	$ 62.40	120	84 .
258	R		8	8	8	8	8	8	48	$1.20	$ 57.60		
	A												
	P							4	4	1.20	4.80		
									52	1.20	$ 62.40	120	84
260	R		8	8	8	8	2ˣˣ	8	42	$1.20	$ 50.40		
	A												
	P							1	1	1.20	1.20		
									43	1.20	$ 51.60	120	84
302	R		8	8	2	8	8	8	42	$1.85	$ 77.70		
	A				2				2	1.85	3.70		
	P							1	1	1.85	1.85		
									45	1.85	$ 83.25	205	90
307	R		8	8	8	8	8	8	48	$1.20	$ 57.60		
	A												
	P							4	4	1.20	4.80		
									52	1.20	$ 62.40	210	92

SUMMARY TOTALS		16 S	17 M	18 T	19 W	20 T	21 F	22 S	TOTAL HOURS			
	R		434	428	424	434	426	304	2,450	$4,830.40		
	A		2		2	2			6	12.10		
	P						129	129	245.60		
	T		436	428	426	436	426	433	2,585	$5,088.10		

Signed *J. Z. Curley #100*
Foreman

* Hours entered manually in ink and were not approved by foreman.

XX Minimum allowed time - 4 hours.

XXX Correct position is Machinist-C.

CASE PROBLEM IN PAYROLL CONTROL AUDITS

EXHIBIT 2D(1)

JONES MACHINE COMPANY
PAYROLL JOURNAL
PAY PERIOD ENDING DATE MAY 22, 1948

Position Title	No.	Name	Soc. Sec. No.	Total Hours	Rate Per Hour	Gross Earnings	F.O.A.B. Tax	No. Ex.	Withholding Tax	Ins. Prem.	Union Dues	Net Pay	Previous Year To Date Withholding	Year To Date Withholding	Previous Year To Date Earnings	Year To Date Earnings	Check Number
FOREMAN	100	J.Z. Curley	196 072 102	52	$2.75	$143.00	$1.43	4	$13.60	$	$	$127.97	$272.00	$285.60	$2,860.00	$3,003.00	1200
CLERKS	110	S.E. Bowman	195 201 972	52	1.25	65.00	.65	3	4.00			60.35	80.00	84.00	1,300.00	1,365.00	1201
	112	J.O. Bailey	196 051 870	52	1.25	65.00	.65	4	2.00			62.35	112.40	114.40	1,300.00	1,365.00	1202
MACHINIST-A	203	C.K. Mitchell	192 191 650	52	2.40	124.80	1.25	3	12.60			110.95	252.00	264.60	2,496.00	2,620.80	1203
	204	O.S. Tucker	191 022 090	52	2.40	124.80	1.25	2	14.50			109.05	290.00	304.50	2,496.00	2,620.80	1204
	205	J.A. Doby	196 071 840	34	2.40	81.60	.82	1	10.20	3.30	1.50	65.78	290.00	304.50	2,496.00	2,620.80	1205
	206	K.L. Keltner	196 074 602	52	2.40	124.80	1.25	2	14.50			109.05	204.00	214.20	1,632.00	1,713.60	1206
	207	R.S. Gordon	196 071 450	40	2.40	96.00	.96	5	4.60			90.44	92.00	96.60	1,920.00	2,016.00	1207
	208	A.B. Robinson	197 021 480	52	2.40	124.80	1.25	2	12.60			110.95	252.00	264.60	2,496.00	2,620.80	1208
	209	E.L. Mathias	196 052 572	52	2.40	124.80	1.25	2	14.50			109.05	290.00	304.50	2,496.00	2,620.80	1209
	210	R.R. Lemon	197 051 922	52	2.40	124.80	1.25	1	16.40			107.15	328.00	344.40	2,496.00	2,620.80	1210
	211	A.R. Keller	195 211 470	52	2.40	124.80	1.25	1	18.70			104.85	174.00	182.70	2,496.00	2,620.80	1211
	212	J.E. McQuinn	197 051 924	52	2.40	124.80	1.25	4	10.60			112.95	212.00	222.60	2,496.00	2,620.80	1212
MACHINIST-B	213	H.A. Yost	197 021 975	40	2.20	88.00	.88	2	7.30	3.30	1.50	75.02	146.00	153.30	1,760.00	1,848.00	1213
	214	R.A. Vernon	195 071 850	40	2.20	88.00	.88	2	9.20			77.92	184.00	193.20	1,760.00	1,848.00	1214
	215	J.H. Reynolds	195 051 924	36	2.20	79.20	.79	1	4.10			74.31	82.00	86.10	1,584.00	1,663.20	1215
	216	J.C. Evans	197 071 942	48	2.20	105.60	1.06	1	14.10			90.44	282.00	296.10	2,112.00	2,217.60	1216
	217	J.F. Page	195 071 272	40	2.20	88.00	.88	2	9.20	3.30	1.50	73.12	184.00	193.20	1,760.00	1,848.00	1217
	218	B.A. Lake	192 074 770	52	2.20	114.40	1.14	2	13.00			100.26	260.00	273.00	2,288.00	2,402.40	1218
	219	H.W. Williams	195 059 020	52	2.20	114.40	1.14	2	11.10			100.16	222.00	233.10	2,288.00	2,402.40	1219
	220	H.W. Johnson	195 077 219	40	2.20	88.00	.88	2	9.20			77.92	260.00	273.00	1,760.00	1,848.00	1220
	221	H.J. Wild	197 052 210	40	2.20	88.00	.88	2	7.30			79.82	184.00	193.20	1,760.00	1,848.00	1221
	222	G.J. McKinley	197 052 221	52	2.20	114.40	1.14	2	13.00			100.26	146.00	153.30	2,288.00	2,402.40	1222
	223	J.G. Baker	197 051 440	52	2.20	114.40	1.14	3	13.00			79.82	260.00	273.00	2,288.00	2,402.40	1223
	224	E.H. Whitefield	194 211 762	40	2.20	88.00	.88	2	10.40			83.25	208.00	218.40	1,892.00	1,986.60	1224
	225	V.J. Wright	195 051 472	52	2.20	114.40	1.14	3	7.60			79.52	182.00	191.10	1,760.00	1,848.00	1225
	226	W.W. Hammer	195 051 820	52	2.20	114.40	1.14	4	9.10			104.16	144.00	159.60	2,288.00	2,402.40	1226
	227	A.A. Rush	195 061 992	40	2.20	88.00	.88	5	7.20			106.06	182.00	151.10	1,760.00	1,848.00	1227
	228	K.E. Edwards	197 055 170	52	2.20	114.40	1.14	4	3.70			83.42	144.00	151.70	2,288.00	2,402.40	1228
	229	J.M. Brown	197 052 540	36	2.20	79.20	.79	4	4.10	3.30	1.50	69.51	82.00	86.10	1,760.00	1,663.20	1229
MACHINIST-C	230	R.A. Roberts	196 051 452	40	2.00	80.00	.80	3	6.40			72.80	128.00	134.40	1,600.00	1,680.00	1230
	231	J.M. Robertson	196 052 104	48	2.00	96.00	.96	2	10.70			84.34	214.00	224.70	1,920.00	2,016.00	1231
		PAGE TOTALS		1,489		$3,286.00	$32.86		$308.50	$13.20	$6.00	$2,925.44	$6,242.40	$6,550.90	$65,720.00	$69,006.00	

240

CASE PROBLEM IN PAYROLL CONTROL AUDITS

EXHIBIT 2D(2)

JONES MACHINE COMPANY

PAYROLL JOURNAL

PAY PERIOD ENDING DATE MAY 22, 1948

POSITION TITLE	NO.	NAME	SOC. SEC. NO.	TOTAL HOURS	RATE PER HOUR	GROSS EARNINGS	F.O.A.B. TAX	NO. EX.	WITH-HOLDING TAX	INS. PREM.	UNION DUES	NET PAY	PREVIOUS YEAR TO DATE WITH-HOLDING	YEAR TO DATE WITH-HOLDING	PREVIOUS YEAR TO DATE EARNINGS	YEAR TO DATE EARNINGS	CHECK NUMBER
MACHINIST-C (cont'd)	232	E. A. Smith	196 052 262	40	$2.00	$80.00	$ .80	6	$ .60			$78.60	$ 12.00	$ 12.60	$ 1,600.00	$ 1,680.00	1232
	233	H. H. Dobson	196 072 980	40	2.00	80.00	.80	5	2.50			76.70	50.00	52.50	1,600.00	1,680.00	1233
	234	R. J. Platt	196 051 070	52	2.00	104.00	1.04	4	7.70			95.26	154.00	161.70	2,080.00	2,184.00	1234
	235	W. A. Moss	196 051 880	52	2.00	104.00	1.04	3	9.60			93.36	192.00	201.60	2,080.00	2,184.00	1235
	236	R. H. Ross	196 072 740	45	2.00	90.00	.90	2	9.80			79.30	196.00	205.80	1,800.00	1,890.00	1236
	237	J. A. Stevens	192 041 909	52	2.00	104.00	1.04	1	13.40			89.56	268.00	281.40	2,080.00	2,184.00	1237
	238	J. A. Dark	195 073 220	52	2.00	104.00	1.04	1	7.70			95.26	154.00	161.70	2,080.00	2,184.00	1238
	240	W. W. Hetman	195 072 911	32	2.00	64.00	.64	2	5.90			57.46	118.00	123.90	1,280.00	1,344.00	1239
	241	J. W. Riley	195 051 674	40	2.00	80.00	1.04	3	9.60			69.60	192.00	201.60	1,600.00	1,680.00	1240
	242	G. E. Madden	195 074 291	40	2.00	80.00	.80	5	2.50			76.70	50.00	52.50	1,600.00	1,680.00	1241
	243	W. A. Meyer	195 072 104	40	2.00	80.00	.80	4	4.40			74.80	88.00	92.40	1,600.00	1,680.00	1242
TOOL REPAIRMAN	244	A. J. Power	195 073,717	43	1.75	75.25	.75	3	5.50			69.00	110.00	115.50	1,505.00	1,560.25	1243
CRANEMAN	245	P. J. Murray	197 056 270	52	1.50	78.00	.78	2	8.00	2.75	1.50	69.22	160.00	168.00	1,560.00	1,638.00	1244
TRACTOR OPERATOR	247	H. M. Brown	197 056 120	52	1.50	78.00	.78	1	9.90			67.32	198.00	207.90	1,560.00	1,638.00	1245
OILER	249	W. W. White	196 053 100	52	1.25	65.00	.65	4	2.00			62.35	40.00	42.00	1,300.00	1,365.00	1246
	250	B. C. Heller	196 072 149	52	1.25	65.00	.65	2	5.90			58.45	118.00	123.90	1,300.00	1,365.00	1247
LABORER (SHOPS)	252	J. A. Fair	195 051 944	52	1.20	62.40	.62	3	7.50			54.28	150.00	157.50	1,248.00	1,310.40	1248
	254	M. J. Michaels	196 072 927	52	1.20	62.40	.62	1	3.70			58.08	74.00	77.70	1,248.00	1,310.40	1249
	256	A. J. Wagner	196 072 940	52	1.20	62.40	.62	5	–			61.78	–	–	1,248.00	1,310.40	1250
	258	W. A. Mack	196 054 824	52	1.20	62.40	.62	4	1.80			59.98	36.00	37.80	1,248.00	1,310.40	1251
	260	A. A. McAfee	196 074 440	43	1.20	51.60	.52	3	1.90			49.18	38.00	39.90	1,032.00	1,083.60	1252
SHIPPER	302	B. W. Worth	197 078 220	45	1.85	83.25	.83	2	8.60			73.82	172.00	180.60	1,665.00	1,748.25	1253
LABORER (WHSE.)	307	J. E. Emmet	196 078 219	52	1.20	62.40	.62	4	1.80			59.98	36.00	37.80	1,248.00	1,310.40	1254
EXHIBIT D-2 TOTALS				1,096		$1,802.10	$18.00		$130.30	$2.75	$1.50	$1,649.55	$2,606.00	$2,736.30	$36,042.00	$37,844.10	
EXHIBIT D-1 TOTALS				1,489		3,286.00	32.86		308.50	13.20	6.00	2,925.44	6,242.40	6,550.90	65,720.00	69,006.00	
GRAND TOTALS				2,585		$5,088.10	$50.86		$438.80	$15.95	$7.50	$4,574.99	$8,848.40	$9,287.20	$101,762.00	$106,850.10	

241

CASE PROBLEM IN PAYROLL CONTROL AUDITS

EXHIBIT 2E

PRINT FULL NAME & HOME ADDRESS	J. H. REYNOLDS 145 PEARL AVENUE SWISSVALE, PA.
SOCIAL SECURITY NUMBER	195-05-1924
PLANT OFFICE DEPT.	JONES MACHINE COMPANY — Emp. No. 215

READ INSTRUCTIONS CAREFULLY

FORM W-4
(Revised April 1948)   FILE THIS FORM
U.S. Treasury Dept.   WITH YOUR
Internal Revenue Service   EMPLOYER

Otherwise he is required by law to withhold tax from your wages without exemption.

I certify that the number of withholding exemptions claimed on this certificate does not exceed the number to which I am entitled.

DATED __May 1,__ 1948 _____   (Signature) *J. H. Reynolds*

EMPLOYEE'S WITHHOLDING EXEMPTION CERTIFICATE
(Collection of Income Tax at Source on Wages)

HOW TO CLAIM YOUR WITHHOLDING EXEMPTIONS

I. If you are Single, write the figure "1" . . . . ___

II. If you are Married, one exemption is allowed for the husband and one exemption for the wife.
  (a) If you claim both of these exemptions, write the figure "2". __2__
  (b) If you claim one of these exemptions, write the figure "1". ___
  (c) If you claim neither of these exemptions, write "0" ___

III. Additional exemptions for age and blindness:
  (a) If you or your wife will be 65 years of age or older at the end of the year, and you claim this exemption, write the figure "1"; if both will be 65 or older, and you claim both of these exemptions, write the figure "2" . . . . ___
  (b) If you or your wife are blind, and you claim this exemption, write the figure "1"; if both are blind, and you claim both of these exemptions, write the figure "2". . . . . ___

IV. If during the year you will provide more than one-half of the support of persons closely related to you, write the number of such dependents. (See instruction 3 on other side.). . . . . __2__

V. Add the number of exemptions which you have claimed above and write the total. . . . . |_4_|

FRONT

1. NEW EMPLOYEES.—To receive the benefit of your withholding exemptions, file a withholding exemption certificate with your employer on or before beginning work.

2. CHANGES IN EXEMPTIONS.—You may file a new certificate at any time if the number of your exemptions INCREASES.

You must file a new certificate within 10 days if the number of your exemptions DECREASES for any of the following reasons:

(a) Your wife (or husband) for whom you have been claiming exemption is divorced or legally separated, or claims her (or his) own exemption on a separate certificate.

(b) The support of a dependent for whom you claimed exemption is taken over by someone else, so that you no longer expect to furnish more than half the support for the year.

(c) You find that a dependent for whom you claimed exemption will receive $500 or more of income of his own during the year.

OTHER DECREASES in exemption, such as the death of a wife or a dependent, do not affect your withholding until the next year, but require the filing of new certificates by December 1 of the year in which they occur.

For further information about changes in exemption status resulting from marriage, divorce, legal separa-

ration, birth, death, new dependents, old age, blindness, etc., consult your local collector of internal revenue or your employer.

3. DEPENDENTS.—To qualify as your dependent (line IV on other side), a person must (1) receive more than one-half of his or her support from you for the year, (2) have less than $500 of income of his or her own during the year, and (3) be closely related to you. "Closely related" means that the person is —

Your son, daughter, or their descendents; stepson, stepdaughter, son-in-law, or daughter-in-law;

Your father, mother, or ancestor of either; stepfather, stepmother, father-in-law, or mother-in-law;

Your brother, sister, stepbrother, stepsister, half brother, half sister, brother-in-law, or sister-in-law;

Your uncle, aunt, nephew, or niece (but not if related only by marriage).

The above relationships apply to a legally adopted child as if he or she were a child by blood. Do not claim a citizen of a foreign country as a dependent unless he or she is a resident of the United States, Canada, or Mexico.

4. PENALTIES.—Penalties are imposed for willfully supplying false information or willful failure to supply information which would reduce the withholding exemption.

BACK

CASE PROBLEM IN PAYROLL CONTROL AUDITS

EXHIBIT 2F(1)

EMPLOYE		SOC. SEC. NO.	TOTAL EX.	EFFECTIVE DATE	CERTIFIED BY EMPLOYE SIGNATURE CHECK (X)
JONES MACHINE COMPANY					
SUMMARY - EMPLOYE'S WITHHOLDING EXEMPTION CERTIFICATES					
NO.	NAME				
100	J. Z. Curley	196 072 102	4	May 1, 1948	X
110	S. E. Bowman	195 201 972	3	"	X
112	J. O. Bailey	196 051 870	4	"	X
203	C. K. Mitchell	192 191 650	3	"	X
204	O. S. Tucker	191 022 090	2	"	X
205	J. A. Doby	196 071 840	2	"	X
206	K. L. Keltner	196 074 602	1	"	X
207	R. S. Gordon	196 071 450	5	"	X
208	A. B. Robinson	197 021 480	3	"	X
209	E. L. Mathias	196 052 572	2	"	X
210	R. R. Lemon	197 051 922	1	"	X
211	A. R. Keller	195 211 470	5	"	X
212	J. E. McQuinn	197 051 924	4	"	X
213	H. A. Yost	197 021 975	3	"	X
214	R. A. Vernon	195 071 850	2	"	X
215	J. H. Reynolds	195 051 924	4	"	X
216	J. C. Evans	197 071 942	1	"	X
217	J. F. Page	195 071 272	2	"	X
218	B. A. Lake	192 074 770	2	"	X
219	H. W. Williams	195 059 020	3	"	X

CASE PROBLEM IN PAYROLL CONTROL AUDITS

EXHIBIT 2F(2)

JONES MACHINE COMPANY

SUMMARY – EMPLOYE'S WITHHOLDING EXEMPTION CERTIFICATES

EMPLOYE NO.	NAME	SOC. SEC. NO.	TOTAL EX.	EFFECTIVE DATE	CERTIFIED BY EMPLOYE SIGNATURE CHECK (X)
220	C. A. Johnson	195 077 219	2	May 1, 1948	X
221	H. J. Wild	197 072 140	2	"	X
222	G. J. McKinley	197 052 221	3	"	X
223	J. G. Baker	197 051 440	2	"	X
224	E. H. Whitefield	194 211 762	2	"	X
225	V. J. Wright	195 051 472	3	"	X
226	W. W. Hammer	195 021 820	4	"	X
227	A. A. Rush	195 061 992	5	"	X
228	K. E. Edwards	197 055 170	5	"	X
229	J. M. Brown	197 052 540	4	"	X
230	R. A. Roberts	196 051 452	3	"	X
231	J. M. Robertson	196 052 104	2	"	X
232	E. A. Smith	196 052 262	6	"	X
233	H. H. Dobson	196 072 980	5	"	X
234	R. J. Platt	196 057 070	4	"	X
235	W. A. Moss	196 051 880	3	"	X
236	R. H. Ross	196 072 740	2	"	X
237	E. J. Stevens	192 041 909	1	"	X
238	J. A. Dark	195 073 220	4	"	X
240	W. W. Herman	195 072 911	2	"	X

CASE PROBLEM IN PAYROLL CONTROL AUDITS

EXHIBIT 2F(3)

JONES MACHINE COMPANY					
SUMMARY - EMPLOYE'S WITHHOLDING EXEMPTION CERTIFICATES					

EMPLOYE		SOC. SEC. NO.	TOTAL EX.	EFFECTIVE DATE	CERTIFIED BY EMPLOYE SIGNATURE CHECK (X)
NO.	NAME				
241	J. M. Riley	195 051 674	3	May 1, 1948	X
242	G. E. Madden	195 074 291	5	"	X
243	W. A. Meyer	195 072 104	4	"	X
244	A. J. Power	195 073 717	3	"	X
245	P. J. Murray	197 056 270	2	"	X
247	H. M. Brown	197 056 120	1	"	X
249	W. W. White	196 053 100	4	"	X
250	B. C. Heller	196 072 149	2	"	X
252	J. A. Fair	195 051 944	1	"	X
254	M. J. Michaels	196 072 927	3	"	X
256	A. J. Wagner	196 072 940	5	"	X
258	J. M. Mack	196 054 824	4	"	X
260	A. A. McAfee	196 074 440	3	"	X
302	B. W. Worth	197 078 220	2	"	X
307	J. E. Emmel	196 078 219	4	"	X

CASE PROBLEM IN PAYROLL CONTROL AUDITS

EXHIBIT 2G

At least	But less than	Weekly pay-roll period - Continued										
		And the number of withholding exemptions claimed is -										
		0	1	2	3	4	5	6	7	8	9	10 or more
		The amount of tax to be withheld shall be -										
$ 50	$ 51	$ 7.50	$ 5.60	$ 3.70	$ 1.80	$ 0	$ 0	$ 0	$ 0	$ 0	$ 0	$ 0
51	52	7.70	5.80	3.90	1.90	0	0	0	0	0	0	0
52	53	7.80	5.90	4.00	2.10	.20	0	0	0	0	0	0
53	54	8.00	6.10	4.20	2.20	.30	0	0	0	0	0	0
54	55	8.10	6.20	4.30	2.40	.50	0	0	0	0	0	0
55	56	8.30	6.40	4.50	2.50	.60	0	0	0	0	0	0
56	57	8.40	6.50	4.60	2.70	.80	0	0	0	0	0	0
57	58	8.60	6.70	4.80	2.80	.90	0	0	0	0	0	0
58	59	8.70	6.80	4.90	3.00	1.10	0	0	0	0	0	0
59	60	8.90	7.00	5.10	3.10	1.20	0	0	0	0	0	0
60	62	9.10	7.20	5.30	3.40	1.50	0	0	0	0	0	0
62	64	9.40	7.50	5.60	3.70	1.80	0	0	0	0	0	0
64	66	9.70	7.80	5.90	4.00	2.00	.10	0	0	0	0	0
66	68	10.00	8.10	6.20	4.30	2.30	.40	0	0	0	0	0
68	70	10.30	8.40	6.50	4.60	2.60	.70	0	0	0	0	0
70	72	10.60	8.70	6.80	4.90	2.90	1.00	0	0	0	0	0
72	74	10.90	9.00	7.10	5.20	3.20	1.30	0	0	0	0	0
74	76	11.20	9.30	7.40	5.50	3.50	1.60	0	0	0	0	0
76	78	11.50	9.60	7.70	5.80	3.80	1.90	0	0	0	0	0
78	80	11.80	9.90	8.00	6.10	4.10	2.20	.30	0	0	0	0
80	82	12.10	10.20	8.30	6.40	4.40	2.50	.60	0	0	0	0
82	84	12.40	10.50	8.60	6.70	4.70	2.80	.90	0	0	0	0
84	86	12.70	10.80	8.90	7.00	5.00	3.10	1.20	0	0	0	0
86	88	13.00	11.10	9.20	7.30	5.30	3.40	1.50	0	0	0	0
88	90	13.30	11.40	9.50	7.60	5.60	3.70	1.80	0	0	0	0
90	92	13.60	11.70	9.80	7.80	5.90	4.00	2.10	.20	0	0	0
92	94	13.90	12.00	10.10	8.10	6.20	4.30	2.40	.50	0	0	0
94	96	14.20	12.30	10.40	8.40	6.50	4.60	2.70	.80	0	0	0
96	98	14.50	12.60	10.70	8.70	6.80	4.90	3.00	1.10	0	0	0
98	100	14.80	12.90	11.00	9.00	7.10	5.20	3.30	1.40	0	0	0
100	105	15.30	13.40	11.50	9.60	7.70	5.70	3.80	1.90	0	0	0
105	110	16.10	14.10	12.20	10.30	8.40	6.50	4.60	2.70	.70	0	0
110	115	16.80	14.90	13.00	11.10	9.10	7.20	5.30	3.40	1.50	0	0
115	120	17.60	15.60	13.70	11.80	9.90	8.00	6.10	4.10	2.20	.30	0
120	125	18.30	16.40	14.50	12.60	10.60	8.70	6.80	4.90	3.00	1.10	0
125	130	19.00	17.10	15.20	13.30	11.40	9.50	7.60	5.60	3.70	1.80	0
130	135	19.80	17.90	16.00	14.00	12.10	10.20	8.30	6.40	4.50	2.60	.60
135	140	20.50	18.60	16.70	14.80	12.90	11.00	9.10	7.10	5.20	3.30	1.40
140	145	21.30	19.40	17.50	15.50	13.60	11.70	9.80	7.90	6.00	4.10	2.10
145	150	22.00	20.10	18.20	16.30	14.40	12.50	10.50	8.60	6.70	4.80	2.90
150	160	23.20	21.20	19.30	17.40	15.50	13.60	11.70	9.70	7.80	5.90	4.00
160	170	24.70	22.70	20.80	18.90	17.00	15.10	13.20	11.20	9.30	7.40	5.50
170	180	26.10	24.20	22.30	20.40	18.50	16.60	14.70	12.70	10.80	8.90	7.00
180	190	27.60	25.70	23.80	21.90	20.00	18.10	16.10	14.20	12.30	10.40	8.50
190	200	29.10	27.20	25.30	23.40	21.50	19.60	17.60	15.70	13.80	11.90	10.00
$200 and over		15 percent of the excess over $200 plus -										
		29.90	28.00	26.00	24.10	22.20	20.30	18.40	16.50	14.60	12.60	10.70

CASE PROBLEM IN PAYROLL CONTROL AUDITS

EXHIBIT 2H

JONES MACHINE COMPANY
Pittsburgh, Pa.

PAY STATEMENT — DETACH AND RETAIN

EMPLOYE NAME   EMPLOYE NO.
J. H. Reynolds   215

PAY PERIOD ENDING

MO. | DAY | YR.
5 | 22 | 48

GROSS PAY	—	$ 79.20
FOAB TAX	—	.79
WITHHOLDING TAX	—	4.10
OTHER	—	
NET PAY	—	$ 74.31

HOURS
PREM. | ACTUAL
      | 36.00

YR. TO DATE EARNINGS $1,663.20

JONES MACHINE COMPANY
Pittsburgh, Pa.

MO. | DAY | YR.
5 | 22 | 48

EMPLOYE NO.
215

PAY TO
J. H. Reynolds
OR BEARER NO PROTEST

NOT GOOD FOR AMOUNT EXCEEDING 200 DOLLARS

Exactly $74.31

For Wages Due

Payable if presented within
30 days from date at
Mellon National Bank
Pittsburgh, Pa.

A. M. Smith
Authorized Signature

SAMPLE PAY CHECK

CASE PROBLEM 3

TRAFFIC AND TRANSPORTATION AUDITS

The Whitaker Steel Company has an integrated steel mill located in Pittsburgh, Pennsylvania. Switching service for this mill is performed by the Penobscott Connecting Railroad and generally includes all movements of cars and/or material within the plant.

Mr. G. G. Grant, Controller of the Whitaker Steel Company, has requested his Internal Audit Supervisor to review the degree of control exercised over plant transportation activities as performed by the carrier, and the system of internal check, and to make an examination of the tariffs on file to determine the legality of the charges assessed.

You are assigned to comply with the Controller's request, and upon arrival at the plant, you find the following routines have been established:

1. Responsibility for the issuance and control of switching orders has been delegated to Operating personnel at various locations.

2. Clerical distribution of charges is divided between Operating and Accounting personnel at various locations.

3. Daily invoices by the Railroad are supplemented at month-end by monthly invoices which are paid by the Accounting Department, based on approvals by the Operating Department. Such approvals are meaningless (except in demurrage cases) inasmuch as pertinent records necessary for verification are either nonexistent or scattered throughout the plant.

4. Monthly invoices for track repairs are not submitted in detail.

5. Claims against the Railroad are being presented, and settlement is being accepted by the Operating Department.

You prepare a summary of charges billed for the month of August 19 (Exhibit 3A).

In the conduct of the audit you find it impossible to verify switching and respot charges because:

1. The daily invoices do not reflect car numbers.
2. Charges are rendered by "total number of cars" from "specific track" to "specific track."
3. Several types of switching orders, including verbal, are being used.
4. The filing of these orders is not formalized; some are being destroyed immediately after the switch; and in some instances, no copies are retained of the original order being sent to the Railroad.

As noted by the Tariff, provisions for demurrage under the average agreement in effect are, briefly, as follows:

1. Free time, consisting of 48 hours, shall begin at 7:00 A.M., following placement of the car. Sundays and holidays do not enter into the computation of free time.
2. Subsequent days are known as "debit" days, and charges are assessed for each day or portion thereof. The first two of these days are charged at $3.30 each. These may be offset by earned "credit" days. (Examination of plant records reveals that each month more than enough "credits" are earned to offset the "debits.")

Arbitrary demurrage then begins to run as follows:

First day	$ 5.50
Second day	11.00
Each succeeding day	16.50

With respect to proper tender or delivery, the Tariff provides that in the case of constructively placed cars being "run-around" by actually placing recent arrivals ahead of previous arrivals, demurrage will be charged on the basis of the amount that would have been accrued except for such run-arounds. The first two debit days are not to be considered in figuring run-arounds.

A comparison of dates of placement with the dates of actual switching revealed that run-around provisions were not being observed by the Railroad (Exhibits 3B and 3C).

It was determined that reasonable control of assessed charges for demurrage was being exercised through car control records which accounted for each move. A 20% check revealed no discrepancies other than the above.

Company-owned tracks are being maintained by the Railroad
under Order No. 472 (Exhibit 3D). Monthly invoice (Exhibit 3E)
is the only repair notification that the Company receives. The
Company has no established inspection service relative to either
contemplated or completed repairs.

Existing controls are not being utilized to verify assessed weighing charges. On inter-departmental transfers, weights are obtained
from the Railroad for inventory control purposes. A comparison of
the daily invoices against No. 1 and No. 2 Track Scale Record cards
revealed no discrepancies.

Railroad weights obtained from No. 3 and No. 4 Track Scale
Record cards on outbound shipments are being used for billing
purposes. In accordance with the Tariff provisions, no charge will
be made for the above service. The Tariff further provides that
"when a shipper or consignee requests that a car containing a commodity which is not subject to shrinkage from its inherent nature
be reweighed, this service, whenever practicable, will be performed
without charge providing such reweighing discloses error in the
billed weight of more than one per cent on a minimum of 500
pounds." This provision is not being followed (Exhibit 3F).

Tariff provisions for Hot Metal Movements are as follows:

Hot metal transported in molten condition in special ladles
from the Blast Furnaces to the Steel Works Mixer—$.18 per
gross ton (subject to a minimum of 50 gross tons).

No control is being exercised. A comparison of tonnage produced at the Blast Furnaces to the monthly invoice for hot metal
revealed differences which were localized to the following:

1. Blast Furnace Production of August 10, 19 (Exhibit 3G).
2. Penobscott Connecting Railroad's Invoice No. 810 for $554.14
   (Exhibit 3H).
3. Blast Furnace Production of August 13, 19 (Exhibit 3I).
4. Penobscott Connecting Railroad's Invoice No. 813 for $567.84
   (Exhibit 3J).

Ore Spotting contemplated the placing of the ore cars at the Car
Dumper. No verification of assessed charges was made. A comparison of tonnage reported on the freight statements of incoming
ore with the monthly invoice revealed differences which were
localized to the following:

1. Penobscott Connecting Railroad's Invoice No. 804 for $1,074.23 (Exhibit 3K).
2. Penobscott Connecting Railroad's Invoice No. 809 for $674.69 (Exhibit 3L).
3. Penobscott Connecting Railroad's Invoice No. 818 for $749.73 (Exhibit 3M).
4. Pittsburgh & Lake Erie Railroad's Invoice No. 35 (Exhibit 3N).

According to Tariff provisions on No Trunk Line Allowance where a freight haul of less than one hundred miles is involved, main line carriers do not absorb switching charges. In which event, switching charges are assessed the Company by the Penobscott Connecting Railroad.

No verification of assessed charges is being made. A review of shipping points and destinations upon which charges were assessed revealed that the town of Amelia was 105 miles distant from the plant (Exhibit 3O).

A comparison of tonnage reported on the daily invoices with that shown on freight statements revealed no discrepancies.

Sometimes empty cars or ladles are placed by the carrier at spots designated by the customer and then not loaded. Owing to some operating difficulty on the part of the customer, it becomes necessary for the railroad to move the unloaded car without it producing the customary tariff revenue. Similarly, an empty car or ladle may be moved at the request of the customer without it carrying any pay load. These empty cars or ladles so moved are known as Revenue Empties, for which the carrier assesses a minimum charge.

It has not been the practice to verify the Railroad's charges for Revenue Empties. A comparison of car receiving records at the various locations with the monthly invoice revealed a difference which was traced to the following:

1. Blast Furnace Ladle Report of August 12, 19 (Exhibit 3P).
2. Penobscott Connecting Railroad's Invoice No. 812 for $112.50 (Exhibit 3Q).

The Tariff provides for a Special Movement of a car. This necessitates an engine being taken from previously assigned work to perform a special move—the charge for such service to be in addition to the regular switching rate.

Reasonable control over such charges is obtained through use of a Special Movement Record Book which shows the time ordered, time arrived, and time completed. Comparison of the daily billing with this record revealed one apparent discrepancy (Exhibit 3R).

Reasonable control was exercised over Terminal Service Delays, and no exceptions were noted in your test check.

On Outbound and Inbound Freight, switching charges are absorbed by the main line carriers. Controls over material shipped, or received, are well established, and freight statements are forwarded to the Home Office Traffic Department for rate verification. No rate verification was therefore attempted at the plant.

As the audit progresses, you will prepare necessary working papers which will include your work program and related analyses in support of your findings.

From your working papers you will prepare an audit report, addressed to Mr. G. G. Grant, Controller of the Whitaker Steel Company, in which you will report your findings and make recommendations for the correction of internal control weaknesses.

CASE PROBLEM IN TRAFFIC AND TRANSPORTATION AUDITS

EXHIBIT 3A

<table>
<tr><td colspan="5">THE PENOBSCOTT CONNECTING RAILROAD

SUMMARY OF CHARGES BILLED THE WHITAKER STEEL COMPANY

For The Month of August 19--</td></tr>
<tr><td></td><td>No.Cars</td><td>Weight</td><td>Rate</td><td>Amount</td></tr>
<tr><td>Switching</td><td>5,136</td><td>-</td><td>$ 5.48 Per Car</td><td>$28,145.28</td></tr>
<tr><td>Re-spots</td><td>1,798</td><td>-</td><td>4.40 Per Car</td><td>7,911.20</td></tr>
<tr><td>Demurrage</td><td>-</td><td>-</td><td>-</td><td>10,450.00</td></tr>
<tr><td>Repairs To Tracks</td><td>-</td><td>-</td><td>-</td><td>8,714.03</td></tr>
<tr><td>Weighing</td><td>1,617</td><td>-</td><td>4.80 Per Car</td><td>7,761.60</td></tr>
<tr><td>Special Movements</td><td>-</td><td>-</td><td>18.00 Per Hr.</td><td>756.00</td></tr>
<tr><td>Revenue Empties</td><td>879</td><td>-</td><td>3.75 Per Car</td><td>3,296.25</td></tr>
<tr><td>No Trunk Line Allowance</td><td>143</td><td>5,228.15 N.T.</td><td>.20 Per N.T.</td><td>1,045.63</td></tr>
<tr><td>Ore Spotting</td><td>3,518</td><td>228,076.00 G.T.</td><td>.03 Per G.T.</td><td>6,842.28</td></tr>
<tr><td>Hot Metal Movements</td><td>1,427</td><td>99,767.00 G.T.</td><td>.18 Per G.T.</td><td>17,958.06</td></tr>
<tr><td>Terminal Service Delays</td><td>-</td><td>-</td><td>1.40 Per 5 Min.</td><td>51.10</td></tr>
<tr><td></td><td></td><td></td><td></td><td>$92,931.43</td></tr>
</table>

CASE PROBLEM IN TRAFFIC AND TRANSPORTATION AUDITS

EXHIBIT 3B

CODE	CAR		CONSTRUCTIVE PLACEMENT		SPOTTED.	RELEASED TO CARRIER		DETENTION DAYS	ARBITRARY DEMURRAGE
	INIT.	NO.	DATE	HOUR		DATE	HOUR		
#1	P.R.R.	154965	8/15	6 A.M.	8/20	8/23	10 A.M.	4	$ 49.50
"	"	702147	"	"	"	8/24	11 A.M.	5	66.00
"	"	701863	"	"	"	"	"	5	66.00
"	"	747635	"	"	"	"	"	5	66.00
"	"	747823	"	"	"	"	"	5	66.00
"	"	194553	"	"	"	"	"	5	66.00
"	"	866951	"	"	"	"	"	5	66.00
"	"	183210	"	"	"	"	"	5	66.00
"	"	164091	"	"	"	"	"	5	66.00
#2	"	193465	8/17	5 A.M.	8/17	8/20	10 A.M.	—	—
"	"	178240	"	"	"	"	"	—	—
"	"	220942	"	"	"	"	"	—	—
"	"	178390	"	"	"	"	"	—	—
"	"	169326	"	"	"	"	"	—	—
"	"	177579	"	"	"	"	"	—	—
"	"	263676	"	"	"	"	"	—	—
"	"	761328	"	"	"	"	"	—	—
"	"	538083	"	"	"	"	"	—	—
#1	"	438229	8/25	4 A.M.	8/29	8/30	9 A.M.	2	16.50
"	"	191966	"	"	"	"	"	2	16.50
"	"	175233	"	"	"	"	"	2	16.50
"	"	167205	"	"	"	"	"	2	16.50
"	"	140541	"	"	"	"	"	2	16.50
"	"	144874	"	"	"	"	"	2	16.50
"	"	892704	"	"	"	"	"	2	16.50
"	"	677148	"	"	"	"	"	2	16.50
"	"	210912	"	"	"	"	"	2	16.50
"	"	263226	"	"	"	"	"	2	16.50
#2	"	187575	8/28	7 A.M.	8/28	8/29	10 P.M.	—	—
"	"	195103	"	"	"	"	"	—	—
"	"	155376	"	"	"	"	"	—	—
"	"	149975	"	"	"	"	"	—	—
"	"	155270	"	"	"	b	"	—	—
"	"	676035	"	"	"	"	"	—	—
"	"	673597	"	"	"	"	"	—	—
"	"	164675	"	"	"	"	"	—	—
"	"	164468	"	"	"	"	"	—	—
"	"	156537	"	"	"	"	"	—	—
									742.50

THE WHITAKER STEEL COMPANY

RUN-AROUNDS - NOT ALLOWED BY RAILROAD

CASE PROBLEM IN TRAFFIC AND TRANSPORTATION AUDITS

EXHIBIT 3C

THE WHITAKER STEEL COMPANY
CALENDAR
August 19--
FOR DEMURRAGE CALCULATIONS

S	M	T	W	T	F	S
						1
2	3	4	5	6	7	8
9	10	11	12	13	14	15
16	17	18	19	20	21	22
23 / 30	24 / 31	25	26	27	28	29

CASE PROBLEM IN TRAFFIC AND TRANSPORTATION AUDITS

EXHIBIT 3D

PURCHASE ORDER

THE WHITAKER STEEL COMPANY
70 Ellis Avenue
Pittsburgh, Pennsylvania

To: The Penobscott Connecting Railroad   Date: May 3, 1938
1017 Wilson Street   Order #472
Pittsburgh, Pennsylvania

To provide necessary labor, material, track walker service,

etc., necessary for the maintenance and upkeep of tracks

and roadbeds now belonging to the Whitaker Steel Company.

Signed: *Ralph McGill*
Plant Superintendent

CASE PROBLEM IN TRAFFIC AND TRANSPORTATION AUDITS

EXHIBIT 3E

THE PENOBSCOTT CONNECTING RAILROAD
1017 Wilson Street
Pittsburgh, Pennsylvania

To: The Whitaker Steel Company   August 19--
      70 Ellis Avenue
      Pittsburgh, Pennsylvania

Your Order #472

To Cover Material, Labor, and Expense, Inspecting and Repairing
Tracks, for Period 8/1/19-- to 8/31/19--.

Labor and Expense

Order No.	Track No.	Amount
O - 39170	G - Tracks	$ 911.92
"	X - Tracks	463.74
"	T-1	711.37
"	412-414	413.77
"	419	286.74
"	719	138.88
O - 39079	751	281.78
"	811	431.62
"	851	281.79
"	861	471.43
"	602-606	366.49
O - 39077	611	550.32
O - 39081	623-624	415.39
O - 39100	631-632-633	65.96
O - 39166	643-644	1,420.81
O - 39171	821	846.42
		$8,058.43
3.0 % Unemployment Tax		224.77
5.75% R.R. Retirement Tax Act Tax		430.83
Total Labor and Expense		$8,714.03

CASE PROBLEM IN TRAFFIC AND TRANSPORTATION AUDITS

EXHIBIT 3F

ORDERED REWEIGHING IN EXCESS OF TOLERANCE WEIGHTS USED FOR BILLING PURPOSES MATERIAL - PIPE			
Car No.	Date	Initial R.R. Weight	Ordered . Reweigh (Billed Wt.)
C. G. 27715	8- 4	94,300	88,700
B & O 354906	8-11	75,900	79,500
" 351607	"	46,600	48,500
" 359412	8-18	122,200	118,200
PRR 444457	8-19	108,700	105,700
" 445216	8-23	128,000	130,000
B & O 353472	"	47,700	49,700
" 352665	8-25	138,900	130,900
" 353543	8-28	58,400	65,400
" 352954	8-29	77,500	74,500

CASE PROBLEM IN TRAFFIC AND TRANSPORTATION AUDITS

EXHIBIT 3G

<table>
<tr><td colspan="3">THE WHITAKER STEEL COMPANY

BLAST FURNACE PRODUCTION REPORT

Blast Furnace #1   Date: August 10, 19--</td></tr>
<tr><td>Cast No.</td><td>Ladle No.</td><td>Weight (Lbs.)</td></tr>
<tr><td>7744</td><td>43</td><td>172,000</td></tr>
<tr><td></td><td>46</td><td>169,200</td></tr>
<tr><td></td><td>49</td><td>87,300</td></tr>
<tr><td>7745</td><td>41</td><td>159,800</td></tr>
<tr><td></td><td>45</td><td>81,500</td></tr>
<tr><td></td><td>49</td><td>121,300</td></tr>
<tr><td>7746</td><td>43</td><td>175,200</td></tr>
<tr><td></td><td>47</td><td>24,600</td></tr>
<tr><td>7747</td><td>42</td><td>173,900</td></tr>
<tr><td></td><td>49</td><td>159,600</td></tr>
<tr><td>7748</td><td>43</td><td>108,500</td></tr>
<tr><td></td><td>47</td><td>167,100</td></tr>
<tr><td></td><td>12</td><td>1,600,000</td></tr>
</table>

Gross Ton = 2,240 lbs.

CASE PROBLEM IN TRAFFIC AND TRANSPORTATION AUDITS

EXHIBIT 3H

THE PENOBSCOTT CONNECTING RAILROAD
1017 Wilson Street
Pittsburgh, Pennsylvania

To: The Whitaker Steel Company   Invoice No. 810
     70 Ellis Street   Date: August 10, 19--
     Pittsburgh, Pennsylvania

Hot Metal Movements

Blast Furnace	Ladles	Actual Tonnage	Billed Tonnage	Rate Gr. Ton	Amount
#1	13	764.29	829.51	$ .18	$ 149.31
#2	13	791.34	857.86	"	154.42
#3	11	582.59	671.43	"	120.86
#4	10	717.81	719.73	"	129.55
Total	47	2,856.03	3,078.53		$ 554.14

CASE PROBLEM IN TRAFFIC AND TRANSPORTATION AUDITS

EXHIBIT 31

THE WHITAKER STEEL COMPANY

BLAST FURNACE PRODUCTION REPORT

Blast Furnace #2   Date: August 13, 19--

Cast No.	Ladle No.	Weight (Lbs.)
9185	46	154,000
	48	185,400
	49	120,800
9186	41	168,200
	43	88,200
9187	45	178,300
	47	168,100
	48	50,900
9188	41	156,300
	48	128,400
9189	42	105,800
	48	189,100
	12	1,693,500

CASE PROBLEM IN TRAFFIC AND TRANSPORTATION AUDITS

EXHIBIT 3J

THE PENOBSCOTT CONNECTING RAILROAD
1017 Wilson Street
Pittsburgh, Pennsylvania

To: The Whitaker Steel Company   Invoice No. 813
      70 Ellis Street   Date: August 13, 19--
      Pittsburgh, Pennsylvania

Hot Metal Movements

Blast Furnace	Ladles	Actual Tonnage	Billed Tonnage	Rate Gr. Ton	Amount
#1	12	749.60	771.25	$ .18	$ 138.82
#2	12	833.26	873.93	"	157.31
#3	10	683.43	693.31	"	124.80
#4	12	790.09	816.16	"	146.91
Total	46	3,056.38	3,154.65		$ 567.84

CASE PROBLEM IN TRAFFIC AND TRANSPORTATION AUDITS

EXHIBIT 3K

THE PENOBSCOTT CONNECTING RAILROAD
1017 Wilson Street
Pittsburgh, Pennsylvania

To: The Whitaker Steel Company
      70 Ellis Street
      Pittsburgh, Pennsylvania

Invoice No. 804
Date: August 4, 19--

Spotting Iron Ore

Date	Bill No.	Sheet No.	Railroad	No. Cars	Weight
8/2	8	11	P&LE	84	13,166,200
8/4		10	B&O	122	14,853,200
8/3		8	PRR	76	11,877,200
8/4		19	P&LE	38	5,837,000
8/5		26	"	103	15,974,800
		6	PRR	137	18,501,000
				560	80,209,400
	35,807.77	Gross Tons @ .03 G.T.			$1,074.23
		Gross Ton = 2,240 lbs.			

CASE PROBLEM IN TRAFFIC AND TRANSPORTATION AUDITS

EXHIBIT 3L

THE PENOBSCOTT CONNECTING RAILROAD
1017 Wilson Street
Pittsburgh, Pennsylvania

To: The Whitaker Steel Company   Invoice No. 809
70 Ellis Street   Date: August 4, 19--
Pittsburgh, Pennsylvania

Spotting Iron Ore

Date	Bill No.	Sheet No.	Railroad	No. Cars	Weight
8/5	8	7	PRR	1	56,000
		13	B&O	77	9,796,100
		21	P&LE	48	7,346,500
		26	"	103	15,974,800
8/8		18	"	5	593,200
8/9		21	B&O	21	2,925,200
8/8		17	"	1	121,200
8/9		36	PRR	86	13,563,500
				342	50,376,500
	22,489.51	Gross Tons @ .03 N.T.			$674.69

CASE PROBLEM IN TRAFFIC AND TRANSPORTATION AUDITS

EXHIBIT 3M

THE PENOBSCOTT CONNECTING RAILROAD
1017 Wilson Street
Pittsburgh, Pennsylvania

To: The Whitaker Steel Company
70 Ellis Street
Pittsburgh, Pennsylvania

Invoice No. 818
Date: August 18, 19--

Spotting Iron Ore

Date	Bill No.	Sheet No.	Railroad	No. Cars	Weight
8/15	8	35	P&LE	28	5,344,200
8/16		56	P&LE	26	4,050,800
8/17		42	B&O	24	3,067,600
8/16		40	PRR	72	10,632,200
8/18		46	B&O	107	13,279,100
8/17		43	PRR	139	19,606,300
				396	55,980,200
	24,991.16	Gross Tons @ .03 G.T.			$749.73
		Gross Ton = 2,240 lbs.			

CASE PROBLEM IN TRAFFIC AND TRANSPORTATION AUDITS

EXHIBIT 3N

PITTSBURGH & LAKE ERIE RAILROAD
900 Tenth Street
Pittsburgh, Pennsylvania

To: The Whitaker Steel Company   Bill No. 8
      70 Ellis Street   Sheet No. 35
      Pittsburgh, Pennsylvania   Date: August 15, 19--

Car Identification		Grade Ore	Weight	Amount
P&LE	65382	Vermillion	162,400	
"	50679	"	166,500	
"	66762	"	160,400	
"	75683	"	162,400	
"	68787	"	160,000	
"	41309	"	129,300	
"	69299	"	158,500	
"	65916	"	159,300	
"	42596	"	130,500	
"	65071	"	163,400	
"	41949	"	129,000	
"	76175	"	162,000	
"	68310	"	159,200	
"	50299	#12	165,700	
"	75708	"	163,400	
"	76435	"	161,000	
"	69464	"	156,000	
"	66929	"	159,400	
"	65403	"	158,500	
"	65104	"	158,400	
"	67190	#3	158,000	
"	67757	"	159,800	
"	41891	"	129,400	
"	68581	"	159,200	
"	60358	"	152,400	
"	66008	"	160,100	
"	69010	"	140,000	
"	68351	"	160,000	
			4,344,200	

CASE PROBLEM IN TRAFFIC AND TRANSPORTATION AUDITS

EXHIBIT 3O

THE PENOBSCOTT CONNECTING RAILROAD
1017 Wilson Street
Pittsburgh, Pennsylvania

To: The Whitaker Steel Company·   Invoice No. 815
     70 Ellis Street   Date: ·August 15, 19--
     Pittsburgh, Pennsylvania

<u>No Trunk Line Allowance</u>

Outbound

Date	Car Initial and No.		From	To	Commodity	Weight
8/14	B&O	250845	Ship. Dept.	Lewiston	Pipe	86,900
	"	251076	"	"	"	85,500
	"	257733	"	"	"	87,200
8/15	"	250646	"	"	"	85,900
	"	251024	"	"	"	85,500
	"	256287	"	Amelia	"	87,600
	"	256321	"	"	"	87,300
	"	255750	"	"	"	87,100
	"	257087	"	Felixtown	"	87,400
	"	260246	"	"	"	84,600
8/16	"	258303	"	Lewiston	"	83,700
	"	259655	"	"	"	85,300
	"	257412	"	Amelia	"	85,300
	"	258347	"	"	"	85,100
	C.N.J.	88580	"	Canton	"	85,700
	B&O	257378	"	Lewiston	"	85,100
	"	250657	"	"	"	88,200
	"	258453	"	"	"	88,000
					18 Cars	1,551,400

775.7 Net Tons @ .20¢ Ton = $155.14

CASE PROBLEM IN TRAFFIC AND TRANSPORTATION AUDITS

EXHIBIT 3P

THE WHITAKER STEEL COMPANY

BLAST FURNACE LADLE REPORT

Date: August 12, 19--

Fce. No.	Cast	Ladles Spotted	Ladles Loaded	Ladles Not Loaded	Remarks
3	11.36	45-42-43	45-42	43	
2	12.48	47-43-48	47-43	48	
1	2.00	49-46-41	49-46	41	
4	3.12	42-48-45	42-48	45	
3	4.24	43-41-47	43-41	47	
2	5.36	46-45-49	46-45	49	
1	6.48	48-47-42	48-47	42	
4	8.00	41-49-43	41-49	43	
3	9.12	45-42-46	45-42	46	
2	10.24	47-43-48	43-47	48	
1	11.36	49-46-41	49-46	41	
4	12.48	42-48-45	42-48-45		
3	2.00	43-41-47	43-41	47	
2	3.12	46-48-49	46-48	49	
1	4.24	42-47-45	42-47-45		
4	5.36	41-49-43	41-49	43	
3	6.48	48-43-46	48-43	46	
2	8.00	47-45-42	47-45	42	
1	9.12	49-46-41	49-46	41	
4	10.24	43-42-48	43-42	48	
Total		60	42	18	

CASE PROBLEM IN TRAFFIC AND TRANSPORTATION AUDITS

EXHIBIT 3Q

THE PENOBSCOTT CONNECTING RAILROAD
1017 Wilson Street
Pittsburgh, Pennsylvania

To: The Whitaker Steel Company
      70 Ellis Street
      Pittsburgh, Pennsylvania

Invoice No. 812
Date: August 12, 19--

Revenue Empties

Dept.	Track No.	Dept.	Track No.	No. Cars
Steel Works	621	Blast Furnace	413	3
"	"	"	432	4
"	"	"	423	3
"	"	"	443	4
"	"	"	433	1
"	"	"	424	1
"	"	Ladle House	406	4
Bar Mill	87	Billet Yard	74	8
"	83	Car Repair	517	1
Car Shop	631	Car Shop	41	1
				30
		30 Cars @ $3.75	$ 112.50	

EXHIBIT 3R

THE PENOBSCOTT CONNECTING RAILROAD
1017 Wilson Street
Pittsburgh, Pennsylvania

To: The Whitaker Steel Company   Invoice No. 817
      70 Ellis Street   Date: August 17, 19--
      Pittsburgh, Pennsylvania

Special Movements

Date	Conductor	Time Consumed			Track Nos.		Remarks
		From	To	Total	From	To	
8-16	Koin	4:00P	5:15P	2H .15M	641	S-1	NTX 326, 124, 323, 303, 350, 351 Rounds

Service
Requested By: Merrill

Reported By: Lynch

Charge:
2¼ Hrs. @ $18.00 = $40.50

CASE PROBLEM 4

INCENTIVE AUDITING

American Steel Products, Inc., whose General Office is in Pittsburgh, Pennsylvania, manufactures steel products of various types. Plants of the Corporation are located in Wilmerding, Pennsylvania; Cleveland, Ohio; and Chicago, Illinois.

In 1947, the officers of this company decided to install a wage incentive system and chose the Cleveland Works Skelp Mills for pilot installation of incentive plans. Three plans were developed by the Works Industrial Engineers for installation on February 1, 1948: #1-10″ Skelp Mill Crew, #2-10″ Skelp Mill Crew, and #3-12″ Skelp Mill Crew. A fourth plan, Mill Foremen—Skelp Mills, was installed March 28, 1948.

On August 16, 1948, Mr. R. G. Evans, Vice President, Finance, requested an audit of the plans installed at the Cleveland Works.

In the conduct of this audit, you determine from examination of the company's policy manual relative to incentives that the following approval procedure is prescribed for incentive plans:

1. Any new installation must be approved by the Works Manager, Works Chief Industrial Engineer, and Works Chief Clerk, and by the Vice President, Finance, and the Vice President, Operations.

2. Revisions or addenda to existing plans require similar approval when:
   a. The standard force of any incentive position is increased or decreased.
   b. Additional positions are added to a plan.
   c. The revision or addendum changes the earnings level of any inventive position.

3. Revisions or addenda to existing plans require only the approval of Works Management when:
   a. The revision or addendum merely clarifies the provisions of a plan.

  b. Incentive coverage is extended to include additional products, product sizes, or operations, without comprehending any of the changes listed in 2*b*.

At the Works, examinations of plan brochures, source data furnished for incentive performance application, and application practices satisfy you that a detailed audit of the #1–10″ Skelp Mill Crew Plan (Exhibit 4A) and the Mill Foremen-Skelp Mills Plan (Exhibit 4B) will be sufficient coverage to test existing control and application practices. You select the pay period ending August 14, 1948, for audit and check three turns on the #1–10″ Skelp Mill in detail.

Your study of reporting and control practices establishes that the Skelp Mill Production Report (Exhibit 4C) is prepared by the Mill Recorder on each mill, which employe is not a participant in any incentive plan. Information required in the calculation of the plan is obtained by the Recorder as follows:

1. Heat number, order number, section, section size, and sheared length of finished product are transcribed from the Roller's copy of the Production Order which originates in the Production Scheduling Division.
2. The size, number of pieces, and piece weights of billets charged are furnished by the Heater.

The Product Clerk in the Standard Cost Bureau calculates Total Charged Weight from the Recorder's entries and then calculates Total Sheared Weight by multiplying Total Charged Weight for each order by the predetermined Standard Yield for the section rolled. Posting these figures to the Production Report completes the report which is forwarded to the Payroll Bureau for calculation of earnings.

All Skelp Mill sheared product is bundled in the Warehouse. The bundles are weighed on an automatic recording scale, at which point tags showing complete production information are prepared and attached to the bundles. Information on the bundle tags is used by the Shipper to prepare loading reports, etc. Carbon copies of the bundle tags, with the corresponding scale tickets attached, are forwarded each turn to the Production Scheduling Division which maintains complete Order Item records in actual weights. Weight entries on bundle tag carbons are verified by comparison with the scale tickets.

Roller's Reports (Exhibit 4D) are prepared by the Rollers on the respective mills and are forwarded to the Payroll Bureau after each turn. This report contains a chronological record of mill activity.

The information contained in the Production Reports and Roller's Reports is used by the Payroll Bureau to prepare the Performance Calculation Sheets for the Mill Crew Plans (Exhibit 4E) and the Production Recap and Bonus Calculation Sheet for the Mill Foreman Plan (Exhibit 4F).

Performance charts are maintained by the Industrial Engineering Division and are analyzed regularly to detect and investigate unusual trends.

Your study of the methods used to report total time worked by each employe establishes that this function is adequately controlled. The allocation of this time to measured work, unmeasured work, delays, etc., as required for calculating Performance, is performed in the Payroll Bureau from the Roller's Reports.

After ascertaining that adequate control is maintained over the accuracy of the Production Scheduling Division's Order Item records, you reconstruct the record of production for #1–10″ Skelp Mill on an actual scale weight basis, the period covered being the three turns subjected to detailed audit, and compare the resulting weights with those used for calculating incentive earnings (Exhibit 4G).

Industrial Engineering files are examined for information concerning the development of performance standards for the Mill Crew Plans. You determine that:

1. Production standards were developed by correlation of time studies during September, October, and November, 1947, with the sections rolled and the Warehouse scale weights of production during that period.
2. Production standards include allowances for the first 30 minutes of mechanical, electrical, and service delays, and the first 15 minutes of incidental mill delays.
3. Mill change standards were engineered to comprehend the period of time from the shut-down of the unit until the first good product is rolled after the change and include allowances for the first 30 minutes of mechanical, electrical, and service delays.

4. Time worked by a partial crew on nonproductive work is not included in any performance standard development.
5. All standards contain allowances for rest and personal needs. These and such process and delay allowances as are required were incorporated in the standards in accordance with established policies and procedures.

Your analysis of operating practices and their related payroll calculations reveals that, when a mill has been shut down for one or more turns, the Heater and Heater Helper report for work to light-up the reheat furnace 2 hours before the balance of the Mill Crew reports to start the cold mill. The Heater and Heater Helper are paid incentive earnings for this light-up time on the basis of the percentage performance attained by their Mill Crew on the rolling turn immediately following the light-up period.

Examination of the Payroll Ledgers for the pay period audited establishes that the calculations therein are mathematically correct for the hours worked by all employes covered by the plans.

As previously indicated, your examination of the conditions surrounding the application of the plans for the #2 and #3 Mill Crews reveals conditions identical with those set forth above for the #1 Mill Crew Plan.

Your responsibilities relative to planning and making the audit include the preparation of a work program and the necessary working papers and analyses describing and supporting your findings; the preparation of a report to Mr. R. G. Evans, Vice President, Finance, of such findings, regardless of their effect on earnings; your recommendations for the strengthening of any internal control weaknesses; and the correction of any exceptions taken regarding the application and administration of the plans.

EXHIBIT 4A

Incentive Plan No. 101—#1–10″ Skelp Mill Crew

American Steel Products, Inc., Cleveland Works, Cleveland, Ohio

(Installation Date: February 1, 1948)

CASE PROBLEM IN INCENTIVE AUDITING

EXHIBIT 4A (Continued)

			Plan No. 101 Page 1

SECTION I.   THE POSITIONS AND THEIR RESPECTIVE STANDARD HOURLY RATES

The positions covered by this plan and their respective standard hourly rates are as follows:

Position No.	Position Title	Standard Crew Per Turn	Standard Hourly Rate
501	Charger	1	1.050
503	Heater	1	1.635
504	Heater Helper	1	1.160
510	Roller	1	1.950
511	Assistant Roller	1	1.400
515	Rougher	1	1.315
516	Strander	2	1.205
517	Finisher	1	1.315
540	Hot Bedman	1	1.130
572	Hot Billet Shearman	1	1.100
580	Shear Leader	1	1.155
585	Shearman	2	1.130
586	Shearman Helper	2	1.050

CASE PROBLEM IN INCENTIVE AUDITING

EXHIBIT 4A (Continued)

Plan No. 101
Page   2

SECTION II. PERFORMANCE STANDARDS

The following performance standards cover the production of plain and
bevel edge skelp within the sizes stated, include allowances for delays
ordinarily occurring during such production, and are applicable only to
the standard crew as listed in section I:

A. HOT ROLLED SKELP - SHEARED   STANDARD MINUTES PER 1,000 LBS.
        WIDTHS 2¼" TO 5"

SHEARED LENGTH	3'0" TO 3'8"	3'8 1/16" TO 4'7"	4'7 1/16" TO 5'10"	5'10 1/16" TO 7'7"	7'7 1/16" TO 9'9"	9'9 1/16" TO 12'9"	12'9 1/16" TO 45'0"
Gauge (inches)							
.060 to .067	4.37	3.75	3.21	2.72	2.33	2.04	1.99
.068 to .077	4.01	3.26	2.85	2.50	2.06	1.83	1.79
.078 to .090	3.47	2.93	2.46	2.22	1.83	1.58	1.52
.091 to .107	2.81	2.47	2.09	1.92	1.55	1.35	1.22
.108 to .128	2.30	2.12	1.79	1.65	1.31	1.14	1.06
.129 to .153	1.96	1.79	1.52	1.40	1.12	.97	.95
.154 to .182	1.63	1.53	1.30	1.19	.95	.95	.95
.183 to .215	1.38	1.34	1.15	1.02	.95	.95	.95
.216 to .255	1.16	1.16	1.00	.95	.95	.95	.95

CASE PROBLEM IN INCENTIVE AUDITING

EXHIBIT 4A (Continued)

				Plan No. 101 Page 3

SECTION II.   PERFORMANCE STANDARDS (Continued)

B. ROLL CHANGES (WITH OR WITHOUT SIMULTANEOUS MOVE-OVERS ON #7 STAND)
STANDARD MINUTES PER OCCURRENCE

FINISHING STANDS CHANGED	MOVE-OVER ON STAND	ROUGHING STANDS CHANGED				
		0		1		2
		WITHOUT SECTION CHANGE	WITH SECTION CHANGE	WITHOUT SECTION CHANGE	WITH SECTION CHANGE	WITH OR WITHOUT SECTION CHANGE
0	–	–	–	22.03	28.24	37.95
	#7	–	–	31.73	37.52	54.08
1	–	17.67	26.87	32.59	39.08	55.20
	#7	27.89	35.40	41.01	48.93	65.47
2	–	28.62	36.29	42.97	49.87	66.28
	#7	37.77	47.85	53.75	60.27	80.61
3	–	38.22	48.03	54.80	61.55	81.75
	#7	49.08	55.37	63.92	69.74	95.63

For purposes of this plan, Stands numbered 1 to 6, inclusive, are considered "roughing" stands, Stands numbered 7 to 10 are considered "finishing" stands.

A section change is considered to be any change of 1/8" or more in width or .015" or more in gauge. Successive sub-limit section changes can be added to equal one section change, as defined, unless such sub-limit changes occur simultaneously with roll changes and/or move-overs.

CASE PROBLEM IN INCENTIVE AUDITING

EXHIBIT 4A (Continued)

	Plan No. 101
	Page 4

SECTION II. PERFORMANCE STANDARDS (Continued)

C. MOVE-OVERS UNACCOMPANIED BY ROLL CHANGES
STANDARD MINUTES PER OCCURRENCE

MOVE-OVERS ON ROUGHING STANDS	MOVE-OVERS ON FINISHING STANDS	WITH SECTION CHANGE	WITHOUT SECTION CHANGE
	Any 1	8.04	7.50
0	Any 2	9.53	8.59
	Any 3	10.05	9.43
	0	8.04	7.50
Any 1	Any 1 or 2	10.05	9.43
	Any 3	12.41	11.67
	0	14.98	13.31
Any 2 or 3	Any 1 or 2	20.47	18.96
	Any 3	26.04	24.43

D. SECTION CHANGE UNACCOMPANIED BY ROLL CHANGES OR MOVE-OVERS
STANDARD MINUTES PER OCCURRENCE

SECTION CHANGE ONLY   10.45

All of the above performance standards were established to cover operating conditions and practices as of February 1, 1948, as specified in the Operating Department Standard Prac- tice Manual. Any change of the conditions under which these performance standards were established shall be sufficient reason to nullify these standards and to establish new standards reflecting the changed conditions or practices.

CASE PROBLEM IN INCENTIVE AUDITING

EXHIBIT 4A (Continued)

Plan No. 101
Page   5

SECTION III.   GENERAL INFORMATION

Production to be used in the calculation of Performance shall be the sheared weight of product hot-rolled on the #1-10" Skelp Mill. No standards shall be applied to work considered defective by the Inspection Department when such defective work is the responsibility of the #1-10" Skelp Mill Crew.

Mill change and delay occurrences shall be reported on the Roller's Report.

The performance standard for a mill change started on one rolling turn and finished on the next rolling turn shall be prorated to the two crews on the basis of the actual time spent by each crew making the change.

All time worked during a rolling turn on work not covered by performance standards and on mill changes extending into a non-rolling turn shall be classified as Unmeasured Work and shall be included as such in the calculation of Performance only when approved by the Mill Foreman.

Time in excess of the first 30 minutes of each occurrence of delays caused by mechanical, electrical or other service failure, and time in excess of the first 15 minutes of each occurrence of delays caused by hot bed blocks, furnace delays and minor mill adjustments during rolling shall be classified as Allowable Delays and shall be included as such in the calculation of Performance only when approved by the Mill Foreman.

All time worked during a non-rolling turn shall be classified as Special Work and shall be paid at Standard Hourly Rates when approved by the Mill Foreman.

CASE PROBLEM IN INCENTIVE AUDITING

EXHIBIT 4A (Continued)

	Plan No. 101
	Page 6

SECTION IV.   CALCULATION OF PERFORMANCE AND INCENTIVE EARNINGS

Performance and Incentive Earnings shall be calculated for each turn worked, and Standard Hourly Rates shall be guaranteed for the hours worked during each turn.

Performance and Incentive Earnings shall be calculated as follows:

a. Total Standard Minutes Earned = the units of production multiplied by the applicable performance standard per unit of production.

b. Total Minutes of Unmeasured Work and/or Allowable Delays = the actual minutes worked on work not covered by standards plus the excesses over the first 15 or 30 minutes of delay occurrences as specified in Section III.

c. Total Minutes Worked = the number of minutes worked on the job during the rolling turn.

d. Performance = (Total Standard Minutes Earned plus Total Minutes of Unmeasured Work and/or Allowable Delays, if any) divided by Total Minutes Worked.

e. Base Pay = total hours worked by each employe multiplied by the Standard Hourly Rate of the position occupied.

f. Incentive Earnings = (Performance in per cent minus 100) multiplied by Base Pay of the employe.

CASE PROBLEM IN INCENTIVE AUDITING

	Plan No. 101
	Page 7

SECTION V. APPROVAL

This plan is hereby approved for installation on

February 1, 1948.

Cleveland Works	General Office
/s/ T. L. Dilworth	/s/ R. G. Evans
Works Manager	Vice President - Finance
/s/ R. M. Hayes	/s/ A. M. Thorpe
Works Chief Industrial Engineer	Vice President - Operations
/s/ D. P. Hudson	
Works Chief Clerk	

Date: January 6, 1948   Date: January 12, 1948

EXHIBIT 4B

Incentive Plan No. 201—Mill Foremen-Skelp Mills

American Steel Products, Inc., Cleveland Works, Cleveland, Ohio

(Installation Date: March 28, 1948)

CASE PROBLEM IN INCENTIVE AUDITING

EXHIBIT 4B (Continued)

Plan No. 201
Page   1

SECTION I.   POSITION, RATES AND APPLICATION PROVISIONS

Position No.	Position Title	Standard Crew	Monthly Salary
105	Mill Foreman - Skelp Mills	1 per turn	$375

This is a combination salary and tonnage bonus plan.

In addition to monthly salary, this position shall be paid $ .75 per 100 net tons of sheared skelp produced by the Skelp Mill Crews on the turns which the respective Foremen supervise.

Incentive earnings shall be calculated and paid on a biweekly basis corresponding with the regular two-week pay period established for the Skelp Mill.

Incentive earnings shall be paid the regular incumbents of the position for absences as follows:

        A.   Vacations not exceeding 3 weeks per year.

        B.   Sick leave not exceeding 4 weeks at one time.

During the absence of a regular incumbent, compensable as above, a substituting employe shall be paid $2 per hour, but if the absence exceeds the stated limit, the substitute shall receive the regular salary and tonnage bonus for the position during such further time that the regular incumbent is absent.

CASE PROBLEM IN INCENTIVE AUDITING

	Plan No	201
	Page	2

SECTION II. APPROVALS

This plan is hereby approved for installation on March 28, 1948, to replace, for a trial period of 90 days, the straight monthly salaries paid these employes prior to that date.

/s/ T. L. Dilworth
Works Manager

/s/ R. M. Hayes
Works Chief Industrial Engineer

/s/ D. P. Hudson
Works Chief Clerk

Date: March 17, 1948

CASE PROBLEM IN INCENTIVE AUDITING

EXHIBIT 4C(1)

AMERICAN STEEL PRODUCTS, INC.
CLEVELAND WORKS

SKELP MILL PRODUCTION REPORT

MILL NO. **#1 - 10" Skelp Mill**   DATE **Aug. 3, 1948**   CREW **#1**   **12:00 To 8:00**

FOREMAN /s/ C. K. Woods

RECORDED BY /s/ R.J. Olson

HEAT NUMBER	ORDER NUMBER	NO. BILLETS CHARGED	SIZE	WT./PC.	TOTAL CHARGED WT.	NAME OF SECTION	SIZE	PRODUCTION				
								SHEARED LENGTH	WT./FT.	STD. YIELD	TOTAL SHEARED WT.	
7H7034	14602-1	76	2 x 2	420	31,920	Plain Skelp	2 5/8x.102	16' 9"	.91	92.6%	426,532	
9H8045		347		434	150,598							
9H6943		380		425	161,500							
		275		424	116,600							
		1,078			460,618							

286

CASE PROBLEM IN INCENTIVE AUDITING

EXHIBIT 4C(2)

AMERICAN STEEL PRODUCTS, INC.
CLEVELAND WORKS

FOREMAN /s/ J. F. Craig

SKELP MILL PRODUCTION REPORT

RECORDED BY /s/ C.E. Price

MILL NO. **#1 - 10" Skelp Mill**   DATE _Aug. 3, 1948_   CREW **#2**   _8:00 To 4:00_

HEAT NUMBER	ORDER NUMBER	NO. BILLETS CHARGED	SIZE	WT./PC.	TOTAL CHARGED WT.	NAME OF SECTION	SIZE	SHEARED LENGTH	WT./FT.	STD. YIELD	TOTAL SHEARED WT.
								PRODUCTION			
8H6920	15619-3	150	2½ X 2½	670	100,500	Plain Skelp	3 1/16 X.095	18' 0"	.990	94.7%	238,171
"	"	85	"	668	56,780	"					
"	"	140	"	673	94,220	"					
7H6982	14798-1	115	"	605	69,575	"	3.X.120	24' 0"	1.220	94.5%	163,424
"	"	170	"	608	103,360	"					
8H6727	14400-1	78	2 X 2	433	33,774	"	2 9/16 X.105	30' 8 3/4"	.914	92.5%	31,241
		738			458,209						432,836

287

CASE PROBLEM IN INCENTIVE AUDITING

EXHIBIT 4C(3)

AMERICAN STEEL PRODUCTS, INC.
CLEVELAND WORKS

SKELP MILL PRODUCTION REPORT

MILL NO. __#1 – 10" Skelp Mill__   DATE __Aug. 5, 1948__   CREW __#2__   __8:00 To 4:00__

FOREMAN __/s/ J. F. Craig__   RECORDED BY __/s/ C. E. Price__

HEAT NUMBER	ORDER NUMBER	NO. BILLETS CHARGED	SIZE	WT./PC.	TOTAL CHARGED WT.	NAME OF SECTION	PRODUCTION				
							SIZE	SHEARED LENGTH	WT./FT.	STD. YIELD	TOTAL SHEARED WT.
9H8122	16301-1	204	2½ x 2½	676	137,904	Bevel Edge Skelp	3 1/16x.148	31' 8 5/8"	1.540	95.0%	241,572
8H6445	"	110	"	677	74,470						
"	"	62	"	676	41,912						
7H5433	16453-1	50	"	663	33,150		3 1/16x.095	31' 8 5/8"	.990	94.7%	286,401
"	"	143	"	660	94,380						
7H6997	"	183	"	660	120,780						
"	"	82	"	660	54,120						
		834			556,716						527,973

288

CASE PROBLEM IN INCENTIVE AUDITING

EXHIBIT 4D(1)

AMERICAN STEEL PRODUCTS, INC.
CLEVELAND WORKS

ROLLER'S REPORT

MILL NO. #1 - 10" Skelp Mill   ROLLER /s/ G. C. Williams DATE Aug. 3, 1948   CREW #1 12 To 8

STARTING TIME	DESCRIPTION OF WORK OR DELAY	ELAPSED TIME					
		ROLLING		MILL CHANGES		DELAYS	
		HRS.	MIN.	HRS.	MIN.	HRS.	MIN.
12:00	Rolling Order #14602-1 2 5/8 X .102		45				
12:45	Change #8-9-10, Move Over #7				50		
1:35	Rolling #14602-1	2	5				
3:40	Hot Bed Blocked						10
3:50	Rolling #14602-1	2	20				
6:10	Hot Bed Blocked						5
6:15	Rolling #14602-1	1	15				
7:30	Order #14602-1 Completed. Change #8-9-10, Move Over #7 for New Order #15619-3, 3 1/16 X .095				30		
8:00	End of Turn						
		6	25	1	20		15

CASE PROBLEM IN INCENTIVE AUDITING

EXHIBIT 4D(2)

AMERICAN STEEL PRODUCTS, INC.
CLEVELAND WORKS

ROLLER'S REPORT

MILL NO. __#1 – 10" Skelp Mill__   ROLLER __/s/ J. T. Ryan__   DATE __Aug. 3, 1948__   CREW __#2 8 To 4__

STARTING TIME	DESCRIPTION OF WORK OR DELAY	ROLLING		MILL CHANGES		DELAYS	
		HRS.	MIN.	HRS.	MIN.	HRS.	MIN.
8:00	Continue change #8-9-10, Move-Over #7 for order #15619-3 3 1/16 x .095				40		
8:40	Rolling #15619-3	1	50				
10:30	Power Failure (Elec. Delay)						30
11:00	Rolling #15619-3	1	25				
12:25	Order #15619-3 completed; Move-Over #7 and 10 for new order #14798-1 3 x .120				20		
12:45	Rolling #14798-1	1	45				
2:30	Adjust guide, #3 Stand						5
2:35	Rolling #14798-1		15				
2:50	Order #14798-1 completed; Change #10, Move-Over #7, for new order #14400-1 2 9/16 x .105				35		
3:25	Rolling #14400-1		35				
4:00	End of Turn						
		5	50	1	35		35

CASE PROBLEM IN INCENTIVE AUDITING

EXHIBIT 4D(3)

AMERICAN STEEL PRODUCTS, INC.
    CLEVELAND WORKS

ROLLER'S REPORT

MILL NO. #1 - 10" Skelp Mill   ROLLER /s/ J. T. Ryan   DATE Aug. 5, 1948   CREW #2 8 To 4

STARTING TIME	DESCRIPTION OF WORK OR DELAY	ELAPSED TIME					
		ROLLING		MILL CHANGES		DELAYS	
		HRS.	MIN.	HRS.	MIN.	HRS.	MIN.
8:00	Rolling Order #16301-1, 3 1/16 x .148		50				
8:50	Change #3-4-8-9-10			1	15		
10:05	Started rolling, first bar cobbled in #3 stand						20
10:25	Restart order, mill rolling ok	1	50				
12:15	Adjust #6 delivery trough						6
12:21	Rolling #16301-1		9				
12:30	Order #16301-1 completed, adjust mill for new order $16453-1 3 1/16 x .095				5		
12:35	Rolling #16453-1	3	5				
3:40	Move-Over #5-6				10		
3:50	Rolling #16453-1		10				
4:00	End of Turn						
		6	04	1	30		26

CASE PROBLEM IN INCENTIVE AUDITING

EXHIBIT 4E(1)

AMERICAN STEEL PRODUCTS, INC.
       CLEVELAND WORKS

PERFORMANCE CALCULATION SHEET

MILL NO. - #1 - 10" Skelp Mill   DATE   - 8/3/48

ROLLER   -   G. C. Williams   CREW #1 - 12 to 8

HOT ROLLED PRODUCT - SHEARED

Size	Sheared Wt.	Std. Min. Per 1000#	Std. Min. Earned	Total
2-5/8 x .102 x 16'9"	426532	1.22	520.37	
				520.37

MILL CHANGES

Started	Std. Min. Per Occurrence	Std. Min. Earned	
12:45	49.08	49.08	
7:30	49.08	49.08	
			98.16

UNMEASURED WORK AND ALLOWABLE DELAYS

Started	Class	Duration	Exclude	Allowed

Total Std. Min. Earned + Unmeasured Work & Allowable Delays   618.53

Total Minutes Worked   480.

Performance $\frac{618.53}{480}$ = 128.86%

CASE PROBLEM IN INCENTIVE AUDITING

EXHIBIT 4E(2)

AMERICAN STEEL PRODUCTS, INC.
    CLEVELAND WORKS

PERFORMANCE CALCULATION SHEET

MILL NO. - #1-10" Skelp Mill   DATE   - 8/3/48

ROLLER   -   J. T. Ryan   CREW #2 - 8 to 4

HOT ROLLED PRODUCT - SHEARED

Size	Sheared Wt.	Std. Min. Per 1000#	Std. Min. Earned	Total
3-1/16 x .095 x 18'0"	238171	1.22	290.57	
3 x .120 x 24'0"	163424	1.06	173.23	
2-9/16 x .105 x 30'8-3/4"	31241	1.22	38.11	
				501.91

MILL CHANGES

Started	Std. Min. Per Occurrence	Std. Min. Earned
8:00	49.08	49.08
12:25	9.53	9.53
2:50	35.40	35.40
		94.01

UNMEASURED WORK AND ALLOWABLE DELAYS

Started	Class	Duration	Exclude	Allowed

Total Std. Min. Earned + Unmeasured Work & Allowable Delays   595.92

Total Minutes Worked   480.

Performance $\frac{595.92}{480}$ = 124.15%

CASE PROBLEM IN INCENTIVE AUDITING

EXHIBIT 4E(3)

AMERICAN STEEL PRODUCTS, INC.
CLEVELAND WORKS

PERFORMANCE CALCULATION SHEET

MILL NO. - #1-10" Skelp Mill   DATE   8/5/48

Roller   -   J. T. Ryan   CREW #2 - 8 to 4

HOT ROLLED PRODUCT - SHEARED

Size	Sheared Wt.	Std. Min. Per 1000#	Std. Min. Earned	Total
3-1/16 x .148 x 31'8-5/8"	241572	.95	229.49	
3-1/16 x .095 x 31'8-5/8"	286401	1.22	349.41	
				578.90

MILL CHANGES

Started	Std. Min. Per Occurrence	Std. Min. Earned	
8:50	81.75	81.75	
12:30	10.45	10.45	
3:40	13.31	13.31	
			105.51

UNMEASURED WORK AND ALLOWABLE DELAYS

Started	Class	Duration	Exclude	Allowed
10:05	Mill Delay	20	15	5.00
				5.00

Total Std. Min. Earned + Unmeasured Work & Allowable Delays	689.41
Total Minutes Worked	480
Performance	$\frac{689.41}{480}$ = 143.63%

CASE PROBLEM IN INCENTIVE AUDITING

EXHIBIT 4F

AMERICAN STEEL PRODUCTS, INC.
CLEVELAND WORKS

INCENTIVE PLAN NO. 201 - MILL FOREMEN - SKELP MILLS

BIWEEKLY   **PRODUCTION RECAP AND BONUS CALCULATION SHEET**
PAY PERIOD
ENDING   August 14, 1948

RECAP OF PRODUCTION

DATE	#1 -- 10" SKELP MILL			#2 -- 10" SKELP MILL			#3 12" SKELP MILL			DAILY & PAY PERIOD TOTALS
	#1 CREW	#2 CREW	#3 CREW	#1 CREW	#2 CREW	#3 CREW	#1 CREW	#2 CREW	#3 CREW	
8/1/48	–	–	–	–	–	–	–	–	–	
2	357,202	462,909	428,314	432,843	427,118	418.932	501,063	525,002	560,732	
3	426,532	432,836	440,760	409,107	420,794	440,136	498,647	560,136	573,375	
4	441,891	418,875	415,895	454,975	440,275	409,060	524,435	564,095	563,860	
5	416,017	527,973	473,049	398,052	416,192	440,507	550,089	572.352	558,075	
6	454,340	500,163	487,247	422,835	473,589	454,394	560.292	558,589	587,094	
7	–	–	–	–	–	–	–	–	–	
8	–	–	–	–	–	–	–	–	–	
9	409,118	418,694	340.175	435,118	462,194	451,036	572,589	570,186	492,960	
10	462,092	454,189	410,894	442,881	454,209	392,286	492,191	563,606	525,847	
11	420,775	443,335	451,891	432,049	451,006	430,901	550,852	581.791	563,136	
12	462,109	392,906	465,017	451,952	392,717	442.633	562,302	559,681	557,117	
13	440,786	430,672	429,740	443,621	429,352	440,402	498,796	562.294	582,063	
14	–	–	–	–	–	–	–	–	–	
Totals	4,290,862	4,482,552	4,342,982	4,323,433	4,367,446	4,320,287	5,311,256	5,617,732	5,564,259	42,720,809

CALCULATION OF BONUS

CREW MILL		FOREMAN	POUNDS	TONS	BONUS PER 100 TONS	TOTAL BONUS
#1	#1	C. K. Woods	4,390,862			
	2		4,323,433			
	3		5,311,256			
			14,025,551	7,012.78	$.75	$ 52.60
2	1	J. F. Craig	4,482,552			
	2		4,367,446			
	3		5,617,732			
			14,467,730	7,233.87	.75	54.25
3	1	O. R. Elliott	4,342,982			
	2		4,320,287			
	3		5,564,259			
			14,227,528	7,113.76	.75	53.35
			42,720,809	21,360.41		$160.20

EXHIBIT 4G

AMERICAN STEEL PRODUCTS, INC.
   CLEVELAND WORKS

INCENTIVE AUDIT

RECAP OF PRODUCTION ON SCALE WEIGHT BASIS

ABC - 8/23/48

DATE	TURN	ORDER NO.	SECTION	SIZE	SHEARED LENGTH	TOTAL SCALE WEIGHT	INCENTIVE PRODUCTION WEIGHT
8/3/48	12-8	14602-1	Pl. Skelp	2 5/8 x .102	16'9"	427,600	426,532
8/3/48	8-4	15619-3	" "	3 1/16 x .095	18'0"	227,900	238,171
		14798-1	" "	3. x .120	24'0"	162,800	163,424
		14400-1	" "	2 9/16 x .105	30'8 3/4"	29,300	31,241
8/5/48	8-4	16301-1	B.E. Skelp	3 1/16 x .148	31'8 5/8"	240,900	241,572
		16453-1	" "	3 1/16 x .095	31'8 5/8"	285,400	286,401
						1,373,900	1,387,341

CASE PROBLEM 5

SHIPPING AND INVOICING CONTROLS

The Armstrong Steel Car Company, Pittsburgh, Pennsylvania, is engaged in the manufacture of railroad equipment. The American Steel Corporation is its chief supplier of steel. Since railroad equipment is produced and purchased to the buyer's drawings and specifications, long-range buying of steel for the production of a specified or contracted number of railroad cars is necessary. For this reason, the American Steel Corporation has allocated sufficient quota, on a quarterly year basis, to the Armstrong Steel Car Company, which, in turn, is to be specified by authorized purchase orders at least three months in advance of the scheduled rolling dates for the producing mills.

The Armstrong Steel Car Company has accepted a contract to build 250 steel boxcars and 150 hopper cars for the Dayton and Southern Railroad. This equipment is to be produced in accordance with the railroad's specifications. The date of delivery is to be one year from the date the contract was accepted.

After a complete review of the railroad's drawings and specifications, the Armstrong Steel Car Company has placed purchase orders for steel to be produced and delivered by the American Steel Corporation. (See Exhibits 5A, 5B, 5C, 5D, and 5E.)

Upon receipt of these purchase orders by the American Steel Corporation, mill orders were prepared by the Sales Division and forwarded to the producing mills for scheduling. (See Exhibits 5F, 5G, 5H, 5I, and 5J.) A careful analysis and comparison of the products ordered, weights or quantities, sizes, processing extras, packaging, etc., should be made between the purchase orders and mill orders to determine that all requirements are reflected on the mill orders. This factor is of major importance for two reasons, namely, to produce the customer's desired product, and for accurate pricing at the time of invoicing.

After the steel has been produced and all processing and special instructions have been fulfilled, the material is delivered to the shipping docks for loading. The loader or shipping foreman prepares a Loading and Shipping Report from the lift tags or process identification cards that accompany the product from the time it leaves the Finishing Mills. (See Exhibits 5K, 5L, 5M, 5N, and 5O.) You are asked to determine that the information concerning customer name, order number, size, routing, etc., as reflected on the Loading and Shipping Report is correct.

The Billing Bureau then prepares and prices the invoice for each shipment. (See Exhibits 5P, 5Q, 5R, 5S, and 5T.) The invoice is prepared from the mill order and the Loading and Shipping Report. At this point a complete audit of the invoices should be made to determine that all pertinent information for pricing is reflected in either the Show on Invoice caption or the Differential column. This feature is extremely important since all extra charges, with the exception of size, have to be reflected under one or both of these captions in order to determine the correct unit price of the product. Also, a comparison should be made of all other information shown on the invoice, such as customer name, order number, routing, terms, quantity ordered, and special instructions, with that reflected on the mill order.

The List of Extras (see pages 299–303) (published individually by steel companies), for pricing purposes, will guide you in determining that all applicable charges are reflected on both the mill orders and the invoices. These lists are classified by products and apply to corresponding products as reflected on the purchase orders, mill orders, and invoices.

By careful comparison of Loading and Shipping Reports and invoices you will be able to detect any discrepancies or omissions. The List of Extras will guide you for invoicing discrepancies or omissions which would result in over- or underbillings to the customer.

You are requested to audit all records for shipping and invoicing discrepancies for the steel purchased by the Armstrong Steel Car Company. As the audit progresses, you will prepare necessary working papers which will include your work program and related analysis in support of your findings.

From your working papers you will prepare an audit report addressed to Mr. D. J. Tully, Controller of the American Steel Corporation, in which you will report the results of your audit and make recommendations for the correction of internal control weaknesses, etc.

Note: Differential symbols exhibited in the following Extra Lists are governed by maximum per cent range for chemistry, tonnage limits for quantity, and length by feet for cutting. The decimal expressed at the extreme right side of the schedule or list is expressed in cents per hundred pounds. *Example:* Plates ordered to a carbon range of .37/.45 would result in the assessment of carbon differential V–7, or $.10 per hundred pounds times the ordered item weight.

In comparing pieces and weights ordered and shipped, bear in mind that, in most cases, the customer has specified a shipping leeway, plus percentage over and minus percentage under of ordered weights.

CARBON STEEL PLATES

Chemical Requirement Extras

Physical tests will not be furnished for plates ordered to chemical requirements only.

Note: Carbon and Manganese: The maximum of the specified range shall determine the extra.

Carbon

Any maximum per cent (see the preceding Note):

Type of Steel	Carbon Ranges	Extra per Cwt	Symbol
Bessemer	.08 to .33 inclusive	None	Base
Open Hearth	.11 max.	$.10	V–6
	.12 to .33 inclusive	None	Base
	.34 to .45 inclusive	.10	V–7
	.46 to .60 inclusive	.20	V–8
	.61 to 1.10 inclusive	.30	V–9

Manganese

Any maximum per cent (see the preceding Note):

Manganese Ranges	Extra per Cwt
.40 to .60 inclusive	None (Base)
.61 to .90 inclusive	$.10
.91 to 1.15 inclusive	.20

Phosphorus

	Extra per Cwt
Minimum not specified or required	None (Base)
Any specified minimum .08% or under, open hearth only	$.05

Sulphur

Minimum not specified or required	None (Base)
Minimum specified per cent:	

Sulphur Ranges	Extra per Cwt
.10 or under	$.15
.11 to .20 inclusive	.25

HOT ROLLED CARBON STEEL BARS

Quantity Extras

The following quantity extras are to be added to the price of the material. These extras shall be determined by the total weight of the size ordered (each gauge or thickness of a section is a separate size) of one grade or analysis, released and accepted for shipment to one destination at one time.

Weights, Tons	Amount per Cwt	Symbol
20 and over	None	
Under 20 to 10, inclusive	$.05	E-1
Under 10 to 5, inclusive	.10	E-2
Under 5 to 3, inclusive	.15	E-3

Length and Cutting Extras

Length, Feet	Extra per Foot	Symbol
45 or over	$.75	L-1
40 to under 45	.60	L-2
35 to under 40	.50	L-3
30 to under 35	.20	L-4
20 to under 30	.15	L-5
10 to under 20	.10	L-6
5 to under 10	.05	L-7

Extras for Specified Length will not be charged, provided the buyer will accept (1) random lengths, or (2) multiples of any unit not over 5 feet, or (3) specified length with a maximum of 10% random shorts.

Chemical Requirements Extras

Copper

Extra per Cwt

Minimum per cent only to be specified
When copper-bearing steel is specified, or for any specified
    minimum up to and including 20% $.15

Carbon

The maximum of the range of carbon, manganese, phosphorus,
sulphur, and silicon shall determine the extra. Where minimum
limit only is specified, the maximum of the standard range applicable
shall determine the extra.

Maximum of range, per cent:

Type of Steel	Carbon Ranges	Extra per Cwt	Symbol
Bessemer only	.08 to .28 inclusive	None	Base
Open Hearth only	.09 to .28 inclusive	None	Base
Open Hearth or Bessemer	.28 to .65 inclusive	$.10	V–4
	.65 to 1.35 inclusive	.15	V–5

Manganese

Maximum of range, per cent:

Manganese Ranges	Extra per Cwt
.04 to .90 inclusive	None (Base)
Over .90 to 1.05 inclusive	$.05
Over 1.05 to 1.30 inclusive (Maximum Carbon 20% or over)	.10
Over 1.30 to 1.50 inclusive (Maximum Carbon 20% or over)	.20
Over 1.50 to 1.65 inclusive (Maximum Carbon 20% or over)	.25

HOT ROLLED CARBON STEEL SHEETS

Processing Extras

	Extra per Cwt
Stretcher Leveled Standard of Flatness	$.25
Pickled—oiled or dry	.20
Greased Edges—cut lengths or coils	.05
Limed	.10
Breaker Passed or Back Coiled (coils only)	.15

Specification Extras

	Extra per Cwt
Structural Quality:	
Commercial Grades	None (Base)
Grades A, B, or C	$.25
Ordinary Flange Steel, A.S.T.M. A–285 or equivalent	.30
Ordinary Firebox Steel, A.S.T.M. A–285 or equivalent	.40
Locomotive Flange Steel, A.S.T.M. A–30 or equivalent	.55

Packaging Extras

Multiple Lift Package

When a full-size package is divided into loose, unwrapped lifts of less than 10,000 pounds each, with metal or wood separators, the following extras will apply:

	Extra per Cwt	Symbol
Lift weights under 10,000 pounds to 5,000 pounds	$.015	P–109
Lift weights under 5,000 pounds to 2,000 pounds	.025	P–71
No lifts to be lighter than 2,000 pounds		

Item Extra for Exact Quantity

	Extra per Cwt	Symbol
When the exact quantity is ordered with no permissible variation	$.10	K

Chemical Requirement Extras

Carbon

The maximum of the specified range shall determine the extra. Maximum of range, per cent:

Carbon Ranges	Extra per Cwt	Symbol
.08 max.	$.15	V–4
Over .08 to .25 max.	None	(Base)
Over .25 to .40 max.	$.20	V–5
Over .40 to .70 max.	.25	V–6
Over .70 to 1.05 max.	.35	V–7
Over 1.05 on application		

Manganese

The maximum of the specified range shall determine the extra.
Maximum of range, per cent:

Manganese Ranges	Extra per Cwt
.40 to .60 inclusive	None (Base)
.61 to .90 inclusive	$.05
.91 to 1.15 inclusive	.10
1.16 to 1.35 inclusive	.15

Phosphorus

Minimum not specified or required — **None**

Sulphur

Minimum not specified or required — **None**

CASE PROBLEM ON SHIPPING AND INVOICING CONTROLS

EXHIBIT 5A

ARMSTRONG STEEL CAR COMPANY
211 Tenth Street
Pittsburgh 3, Pennsylvania

American Steel Corporation
1412 Liberty Bank Building
Pittsburgh 12, Pennsylvania

Order - 10015
Date   - May 19, 1948
Terms - 30-$\frac{1}{2}$-10
Ship Via - Union R. R.
F.O.B. - Shipping Point

Please enter our order for the following:

Item	Steel Bars - Spec. M-116-45 Grade "B" 0.20% Copper Bearing - Angles	Req. No.	Weight
1	100 pcs. - 2$\frac{1}{2}$" x 2$\frac{1}{2}$" x 3/8" - 14'5" Door Guide Support	40125	8,873#
2	250 pcs. - 2$\frac{1}{2}$" x 2$\frac{1}{2}$" x $\frac{1}{4}$" - 17'3" Side Ladder Stile	40126	17,773#
3	250 pcs. - 2$\frac{1}{2}$" x 2$\frac{1}{2}$" x $\frac{1}{4}$" - 16'8" End Ladder Stile	40127	17,708#
4	800 pcs. - 1-3/4" x 1-3/4" x 1/8" - 11'8" Hatch Door	40128	13,500#

Please Roll in October with Order 9030
Shipping Leeway - 5% over, 5% under the ordered weight
For 250 - New 70-ton Hopper Cars for Dayton and
Southern R. R.

J. T. Block
Purchasing Agent

CASE PROBLEM ON SHIPPING AND INVOICING CONTROLS

EXHIBIT 5B

```
                    ARMSTRONG STEEL CAR COMPANY
                          211 Tenth Street
                       Pittsburgh 3, Pennsylvania
```

American Steel Corporation   Order   - 10030
1412 Liberty Bank Building   Date   - May 21, 1945
Pittsburgh 12, Pennsylvania   Terms   - 30-½-10
                                    Ship Via - Union R. R.
                                    F.O.B.   - Shipping Point

Please enter our order for the following:

Item	Sheet Steel - Spec.- A.S.T.M.-A-285-Ordinary Flange Steel Pickled and Oiled	Req. No.	Weight
1	205 pcs. - 27-3/4" x 3/16" x 112-5/8" End Sheets	47211	38,850#
2	130 pcs. - 47-3/4" x 3/16" x 84" End Side Sheets	47212	29,200#

Shipping Leeway - 10% over, 10% under ordered weight

Please include 50% in September, 50% October Rolling

J. T. Block
Purchasing Agent

CASE PROBLEM ON SHIPPING AND INVOICING CONTROLS

EXHIBIT 5C

ARMSTRONG STEEL CAR COMPANY
211 Tenth Street
Pittsburgh 3, Pennsylvania

American Steel Corporation
1412 Liberty Bank Building
Pittsburgh 12, Pennsylvania

Order   - 10045
Date   - April 30, 1948
Terms   - 30-½-10
Ship Via - Union R. R.
F.O.B.   - Shipping Point

Please enter our order for the following:

Item	Open Hearth Steel Plates Carbon .25/.35, Manganese .50/.80, Phosphorus .04 Maximum, Sulphur .05 Maximum	Req. No.	Weight
1	2,000 pcs. - 21½" x ½" x 93½" Spring Planks	49050	596,000#
	Delivery - 1/3 August, 1/3 Sept., 1/3 October, 1948		
	Shipping Leeway - 10% over, 10% under the ordered weight		

J. T. Block
Purchasing Agent

CASE PROBLEM ON SHIPPING AND INVOICING CONTROLS

EXHIBIT 5D

ARMSTRONG STEEL CAR COMPANY
211 Tenth Street
Pittsburgh 3, Pennsylvania

American Steel Corporation
1412 Liberty Bank Building
Pittsburgh 12, Pennsylvania

Order   - 10060
Date   - April 15, 1948
Terms   - 30-$\frac{1}{2}$-10
Ship Via - Union R. R.
F.O.B.   - Shipping Point

Please enter our order for the following:

Item	Steel Bars - A.I.S.I. Grade C-1033 Carbon .30/.36, Manganese .70/1.00	Req. No.	Weight
1	200 pcs. - 2$\frac{1}{2}$" x 5/8" x 26'8" Ribs - Top	55125	24,500#
2	200 pcs. - 2" x 3/4" x 18'9" Ribs - Bottom	55126	19,500#
	Please include in September rolling		

J. T. Block
Purchasing Agent

CASE PROBLEM ON SHIPPING AND INVOICING CONTROLS

EXHIBIT 5E

ARMSTRONG STEEL CAR COMPANY
211 Tenth Street
Pittsburgh 3, Pennsylvania

American Steel Corporation
1412 Liberty Bank Building
Pittsburgh 12, Pennsylvania

Order   - 10075
Date   - April 6, 1948
Terms   - 30-$\frac{1}{2}$-10
Ship Via - Union R. R.
F.O.B.   - Shipping Point

Please enter our order for the following:

Item	Hot Rolled Sheets Carbon .28/.35, Manganese .50/.80, Phos. .04 Sulphur .05 4000# maximum lifts	Req. No.	Weight
1	1,050 pcs. - 1/8" x 33$\frac{1}{4}$" x 115" Roof End Sheet	58125	145,750#
2	1,050 pcs. - 1/8" x 33$\frac{1}{2}$" x 115" Roof End - Intermediate	58126	139,850#
3	1,000 pcs. - 1/8" x 59$\frac{1}{2}$" x 115" Roof Sheet - Between Hatchets	58127	248,400#

Shipping Leeway - 0% over, 0% under

Please ship as follows:
$\frac{1}{4}$ each item - Sept., Oct., Nov., Dec., 1948

J. T. Block
Purchasing Agent

CASE PROBLEM ON SHIPPING AND INVOICING CONTROLS

EXHIBIT 5F

```
Form - G-811
                              MILL ORDER

                      AMERICAN STEEL CORPORATION


Ship To:  Armstrong Steel Car Co.      Customer Order #  - 10015
          211 Tenth Street             Mill Order #      - J-2001
          Pittsburgh, Pa.              Date,             - May 21, 1948
                                       Product           - Carbon Bars
Specification and Tolerance:           Total Wt.-Pounds  - 57,854
   Spec. M-116-45 - Grade B            Routing           - Union R. R.
   20% Copper Bearing Angles           Credit            - Approved
                                       Shipping Tolerance - +5% -5%
Special Instructions:                  Sales Basis       - Carload
   Packing - Standard

Show on Invoice Instructions:
   Copper Steel - 20%
```

Item No.	Pieces	Description	Length	Diff.	Item Weight
1	100	2½" x 2½" x 3/8"	14'5"	E-3 L-6	8,873#
2	250	2½" x 2½" x ¼"	17'3"	E-1 L-6	17,773#
3	250	2½" x 2½" x ¼"	16'8"	E-1 L-6	17,708#
4	800	1-3/4" x 1-3/4" x 1/8"	11'8"	E-2 L-6	13,500#

CASE PROBLEM ON SHIPPING AND INVOICING CONTROLS

EXHIBIT 5G

```
Form - G-811
                                 MILL ORDER

                        AMERICAN STEEL CORPORATION


Ship To:  Armstrong Steel Car Co.      Customer Order #  ← 10030
          211 Tenth Street             Mill Order #      - J-2532
          Pittsburgh, Pa.              Date             - May 24, 1948
                                       Product          - H.R. Sheets
Specification and Tolerance:           Total Wt.-Pounds - 68,050
  ASTM-A-285 Ordinary Flange Steel     Routing          - Union R. R.
  Pickled and Oiled                    Credit           - Approved
                                       Shipping Tolerance - + 10% - 10%
Special Instructions:                  Sales Basis      - Carload
  Standard Packaging

Show on Invoice Instructions:
  Ordinary Flange Steel - Pickled and Oiled
```

Item No.	Pieces	Description	Length	Diff.	Item Weight
1	205	27-3/4" x 3/16" x	112-5/8"		38,850#
2	130	47-3/4" x 3/16" x	84"		29,200#

CASE PROBLEM ON SHIPPING AND INVOICING CONTROLS

EXHIBIT 5H

Form - G-811

MILL ORDER

AMERICAN STEEL CORPORATION

Ship To: Armstrong Steel Car Co.
          211 Tenth Street
          Pittsburgh, Pa.

Customer Order #	- 10045
Mill Order #	- J-2150
Date	- May 4, 1948
Product	- Plates
Total Wt.-Pounds	- 596,000
Routing	- Union R. R.
Credit	- Approved
Shipping Tolerance	- +10% -5%
Sales Basis	- Carload

Specification and Tolerance:
  Carbon .25/.35, Manganese .50/.80
  Phosphorus .04 Max., Sulphur .05 Max.

Special Instructions:
  Standard Loading

Show on Invoice Instructions:
  Manganese .50/.80

Item No.	Pieces	Description	Length	Diff.	Item Weight
1	2,000	$21\frac{1}{2}$" x $\frac{1}{2}$" x	$93\frac{1}{2}$"	V-7	596,000#
		Scheduled: 1/3 August 1/3 September 1/3 October			

CASE PROBLEM ON SHIPPING AND INVOICING CONTROLS

EXHIBIT 5I

Form - G-811

MILL ORDER

AMERICAN STEEL CORPORATION

Ship To: Armstrong Steel Car Co.
          211 Tenth Street
          Pittsburgh, Pa.

Customer Order #	- 10060
Mill Order #	- J-2230
Date	- Apr. 20, 1948
Product	- Carbon Bars
Total Wt.-Pounds	- 44,000
Routing	- Union R. R.
Credit	- Approved
Shipping Tolerance	- + 5% - 5%
Sales Basis	- Carload

Specification and Tolerance:
  Grade C-1033 - Carbon .30/.36,
  Mang. .70/1.00, Phos. .04 max.,
  Sulphur .05 max.

Special Instructions:
  5 Ton lifts

Show on Invoice Instructions:
  Manganese .70/1.00

Item No.	Pieces	Description	Length	Diff.	Item Weight
1	200	$2\frac{1}{2}$" x 5/8" x	26'8"	L-5 E-1 V-4	24,500#
2	200	2" x 3/4" x	18'9"	L-6 E-2 V-4	19,500#
	Promised	- October, 1948			

CASE PROBLEM ON SHIPPING AND INVOICING CONTROLS

EXHIBIT 5J

```
Form - G-811
                              MILL ORDER

                      AMERICAN STEEL CORPORATION


Ship To:  Armstrong Steel Car Co.    Customer Order #    - 10075
          211 Tenth Street           Mill Order #        - J-2378
          Pittsburgh, Pa.            Date                - Apr. 8, 1948
                                     Product             - H.R. Sheets
Specification & Tolerance:           Total Wt.-Pounds    - 534,000
  Carbon .28/.35, Manganese .50/.80  Routing             - Union R. R.
  Phos. .04, Sulphur .05             Credit              - Approved
                                     Shipping Tolerance - +0% -0%
Special Instructions:                Sales Basis         - Carload
  Packaging 4,000 maximum lifts

Show on Invoice Instructions:
  Manganese .50/.80
```

Item No.	Pieces	Description		Length	Diff.	Item Weight
	Hot Rolled Carbon Sheets					
1	1,050	1/8" x 33$\frac{1}{4}$"	x	115"	V-5 P-71	145,750#
2	1,050	1/8" x 33$\frac{1}{2}$"	x	115"	V-5 P-71	139,850#
3	1,000	1/8" x 59$\frac{1}{2}$"	x	115"	V-5 P-71	248,400#

CASE PROBLEM ON SHIPPING AND INVOICING CONTROLS

EXHIBIT 5K

```
Form - G-320
                        AMERICAN STEEL CORPORATION

                        LOADING AND SHIPPING REPORT


Sold To       - Armstrong Steel Car Company        Date   - 10-6-48
Ship To       - Same                               Car In. - B & O
Destination - Pittsburgh, Pennsylvania             Car No. - 11445
Routing       - Union R. R.                        Track  - #6
```

Cust. No.	Mill No.	Bdls.-Pcs.	Description and Size	Weight Shipped
			Bar Angles	
10015	J-2001	100	$2\frac{1}{2}$" x $2\frac{1}{2}$" x 3/8" - 14'5"	8,870#
10015	J-2001	255	$2\frac{1}{2}$" x $2\frac{1}{2}$" x $\frac{1}{4}$" - 17'3"	18,000#
10015	J-2001	249	$2\frac{1}{2}$" x $2\frac{1}{2}$" x $\frac{1}{4}$" - 16'8"	17,300#
10015	J-2001	808	1-3/4" x 1-3/4" - 11'8" x 1/8"	14,200#
Totals		1,412		58,370#

```
        Gross Wt.     169,470#
        Tare Wt.      110,250
        Net Wt.        59,220
        Dunnage           850
        Actual Wt.     58,370#

                              Prepared By
                              J. T. Jones
```

CASE PROBLEM ON SHIPPING AND INVOICING CONTROLS

EXHIBIT 5L

Form - G-320

AMERICAN STEEL CORPORATION

LOADING AND SHIPPING REPORT

Sold To   - Armstrong Steel Car Company   Date   - 9-25-48
Ship To   - Same   Car In.   - B & O
Destination   - Pittsburgh, Pennsylvania   Car No.   - 73420
Routing   - Union R. R.   Track   - #4

Cust. No.	Mill No.	Bdls.-Pcs.	Description and Size	Weight Shipped
10030	J-2532	195	27-3/4" x 3/16" x 112-5/8"	38,850#
10030	J-2532	130	47-3/4" x 3/16" x 84"	29,200#
Totals		325		68,050#

Gross Wt.	189,610#
Tare Wt.	120,200
Net Wt.	69,410
Dunnage	1,360
Actual Wt.	68,050#

Prepared By
N. E. Scott

CASE PROBLEM ON SHIPPING AND INVOICING CONTROLS

EXHIBIT 5M

Form - G-320

AMERICAN STEEL CORPORATION

LOADING AND SHIPPING REPORT

Sold To - Armstrong Steel Car Company	Date - 9-22-48
Ship To - Same	Car In. - N.Y.C.
Destination - Pittsburgh, Pennsylvania	Car No. - 150123
Routing - Union R. R.	Track - #4

Cust. No.	Mill No.	Bdls.-Pcs.	Description and Size	Weight Shipped
		Plates		
10045	J-2150	325	$21\frac{1}{2}$" x $\frac{1}{2}$" x $93\frac{1}{2}$"	103,625#
Totals		325		103,625#

Gross Wt.	203,976#
Tare Wt.	99,201
Net Wt.	104,775
Dunnage	1,150
Actual Wt.	103,625#

Prepared By
B. L. Smith

CASE PROBLEM ON SHIPPING AND INVOICING CONTROLS

EXHIBIT 5N

```
Form - G-320
                        AMERICAN STEEL CORPORATION

                        LOADING AND SHIPPING REPORT


Sold To       - Armstrong Steel Car Company      Date    - 10-15-48
Ship To       - Same                             Car In. - P.R.R.
Destination - Pittsburgh, Pennsylvania           Car No. - 188585
Routing       - Union R. R.                      Track   - #6
```

Cust. No.	Mill No.	Bdls.-Pcs.	Description and Size	Weight Shipped
10060	J-2230	200	$2\frac{1}{2}$" x 5/8" x 26'8"	24,500#
10060	J-2230	200·	2" x 3/4" x 18'9"	19,500#
Totals		400		44,000#

```
      Gross Wt.   140,110#
      Tare Wt.     95,260
      Net Wt.      44,850
      Dunnage         850
      Actual Wt.   44,000#

                              Prepared By
                              J. T. Jones
```

CASE PROBLEM ON SHIPPING AND INVOICING CONTROLS

EXHIBIT 50

Form - G-320

AMERICAN STEEL CORPORATION

LOADING AND SHIPPING REPORT

Sold To   - Armstrong Steel Car Company   Date   - 9-20-48
Ship To.   - Same   Car In. - L & N
Destination - Pittsburgh, Pennsylvania   Car No. - 70551
Routing   - Union R. R.   Track   - #5

Cust. No.	Mill No.	Bdls.-Pcs.	Description and Size	Weight Shipped
10075	J-2378	200	1/8" x 33¼" x 115"	27,400#
10075	J-2378	175	1/8" x 33½" x 115"	22,750#
10075	J-2378	105	1/8" x 59½" x 115"	26,040#
Totals		480		76,190#

Gross Wt.	153,630#
Tare Wt.	76,190
Net Wt.	77,440
Dunnage	1,250
Actual Wt.	76,190#

Prepared By
B. L. Smith

CASE PROBLEM ON SHIPPING AND INVOICING CONTROLS

EXHIBIT 5P

```
Form - G-922
```

AMERICAN STEEL CORPORATION
Liberty Bank Building
Pittsburgh 12, Pa.

Sold To - Armstrong Steel Car Co.
211 Tenth Street
Pittsburgh, Pa.

Cust. No. - 10015
Mill No. - J-2001

Terms - 30-½-10

Invoice Date 10-8-48	Invoice No. 91-1-14351
Date Shipped 10-6-48	From Etna, Pa.
Sales Basis C.L.	Routing U.R.R.

Item	Bdls.-Pcs.	Size	Length	Diff.	Pounds	Unit Price	Amount
		Open Hearth Steel Angles Copper Steel 20%					
1	100	2½" x 2½" x 3/8"	14'5"	E-3 L-6	8,870	$3.70	$ 328.19
2	255	2½" x 2½" x ¼"	17'3"	E-1 L-6	18,000	3.55	639.00
3	249	2½" x 2½" x ¼"	16'8"	E-1	17,300	3.45	596.85
4	808	1-3/4" x 1-3/4" x 1/8"	11'8"	E-2 L-6	14,200	3.40	482.80
Total	1,412				58,370		$2,046.84

How Shipped   - C.L.
Sales Basis   - CL-40M
Shipment F.O.B. - Shipping Point

CASE PROBLEM ON SHIPPING AND INVOICING CONTROLS

EXHIBIT 5Q

Form - G-922

AMERICAN STEEL CORPORATION
Liberty Bank Building
Pittsburgh 12, Pa.

Sold To - Armstrong Steel Car Co.
211 Tenth Street
Pittsburgh, Pa.

Invoice Date	Invoice No.
9-26-48	85-0-14260

Cust. No. - 10030
Mill No. - J-2532

Date Shipped	From
9-25-48	Etna, Pa.

Terms - 30-½-10

Sales Basis	Routing
C.L.	U.R.R.

Item	Bdls.-Pcs.	Size Length	Diff.	Pounds	Unit Price	Amount
		Hot Rolled Sheets - Pickled & Oiled				
1	195	27-3/4" x 3/16" x 112-5/8"		38,850	$3.23	$1,254.82
2	130	47-3/4" x 3/16" x 84"		29,200	3.42	998.64
Total	325			68,050		$2,253.46

How Shipped   - C.L.
Sales Basis   - CL-40M
Shipment F.O.B. - Shipping Point

CASE PROBLEM ON SHIPPING AND INVOICING CONTROLS

EXHIBIT 5R

```
Form - G-922
                        AMERICAN STEEL CORPORATION
                           Liberty Bank Building
                             Pittsburgh 12, Pa.
```

Sold To - Armstrong Steel Car Co.			**Invoice Date** 9-25-48			**Invoice No.** 92-1-12480	
	211 Tenth Street						
	Pittsburgh, Pa.		**Date Shipped** 9-22-48			**From** Mars, Pa.	
Cust. No. - 10045							
Mill No. - J-2150							
			Sales Basis C.L.			**Routing** U.R.R.	
Terms - 30-½-10							

Item	Bdls.-Pcs.	Size	Length	Diff.	Pounds	Unit Price	Amount
		Open Hearth Steel Plates					
1	325	21½" x ½"	93½"	V-7	100,625	$3.38	$3,401.13
		Partial Shipment					
Total	325				100,625		$3,401.13

```
    How Shipped      - C.L.
    Sales Basis      - CL-40M
    Shipment F.O.B. - Shipping Point
```

CASE PROBLEM ON SHIPPING AND INVOICING CONTROLS

EXHIBIT 5S

```
Form - G-922
                        AMERICAN STEEL CORPORATION
                          Liberty Bank Building
                          Pittsburgh 12, Pa.
```

Sold To - Armstrong Steel Car Co.
          211 Tenth Street
          Pittsburgh, Pa.

Cust. No. - 10060
Mill No. - J-2230

Terms - 30-½-10

Invoice Date 10-16-48	Invoice No. 91-1-15300
Date Shipped 10-15-48	From Etna, Pa.
Sales Basis C.L.	Routing U.R.R.

Item	Bdls.-Pcs.	Size		Length	Diff.	Pounds	Unit Price	Amount
		H. R. Carbon Bars - Grade C-1033 Manganese .70/1.00						
1	200	2½" x 5/8"	x	26'8"	E-1 L-5	24,500	$3.66	$ 896.70
2	200	2" x 3/4"	x	18'9"	E-2 L-6	19,500	3.46	674.70
Total	400					44,000		$1,571.40

```
How Shipped       - C.L.
Sales Basis       - CL-40M
Shipping F.O.B. - Shipping Point
```

CASE PROBLEM ON SHIPPING AND INVOICING CONTROLS

EXHIBIT 5T

```
Form - G-922
```

AMERICAN STEEL CORPORATION
Liberty Bank Building
Pittsburgh 12, Pa.

Sold To - Armstrong Steel Car Co.
    211 Tenth Street
    Pittsburgh, Pa.

Cust. No. - 10075
Mill No. - J-2378

Terms - 30-½-10

Invoice Date	Invoice No.
9-22-48	85-0-13230

Date Shipped	From
9-20-48	Etna, Pa.

Sales Basis	Routing
C.L.	U.R.R.

Item	Bdls.-Pcs.	Size	Length	Diff.	Pounds	Unit Price	Amount
	Hot Rolled Carbon Sheets Manganese .50/.80						
1	200	1/8" x 33¼"	x 115"	V-5	27,400	$3.71	$1,016.54
2	175	1/8" x 33½"	x 115"	V-5	22,750	3.71	844.03
3	105	1/8" x 58½"	x 115"	V-5	26,040	3.91	1,018.16
	Partial Shipment						
Total	480				76,190		$2,878.73

How Shipped   - C.L.
Sales Basis   - CL-40M
Shipment F.O.B. - Shipping Point